THE PRACTICE OF PRESENCE

FIVE PATHS FOR DAILY LIFE

T'ai Chi & Taoism ♦ *Jung & Individuation*
The Teaching of Gurdjieff ♦ *Prayer & Meditation*
F. M. Alexander's Mind / Body Integration

PATTY DE LLOSA

MORNING LIGHT
PRESS

Sandpoint, Idaho

Morning Light Press
323 North First, Suite 203
Sandpoint, ID   83864

morninglightpress.com

Published by Morning Light Press 2006
Copyright ©2006 by Patty de Llosa

Back Cover photo © John Hemminger

Library of Congress Cataloging-in-Publication Data

Llosa, Patty de.
  The practice of presence : five paths for daily life / by Patty de Llosa.
     p. cm.
  ISBN 1-59675-004-9 (alk. paper)
  1. Spiritual life. 2. Self-help techniques. I. Title.
  BL624.L62 2006
  204'.4--dc22
                         2005036204

Printed in Canada on Acid-free Recycled Paper

ISBN-13: 978-1-59675-004-3
ISBN-10: 1-59675-004-9

MORNING
   ◯ LIGHT
 P R E S S

For Louise Welch,
my mother and fellow seeker,
with profoundest gratitude.

❧

My search is your search. We each have a common wish to find out who we are and the direction in which we can grow.

— Louise Welch

TABLE OF CONTENTS

THE SEARCH FOR PRESENCE

In the middle of the journey of our life I found myself in a dark wood.

— Dante

Waking in the Wood

A time comes when we feel the urgent need to re-examine our lives. Yesterday's dream is not going to provide tomorrow's haven, so we wake up, as Dante did, in the middle of life and in the dark. Surprised by the uncertainty of the place where we suddenly discover ourselves, we wonder whether there is a path that will lead us out of it.

Perhaps our dissatisfaction was triggered by a feeling of uneasiness. We ask ourselves, "Where did I go wrong?" Some people can point to a clearly identified incident, or a decision made in the heat of the moment, which sent them in a long-term direction that somehow compromised their own best interests. Others realize that a gradual shift has taken place, perhaps through a generally passive attitude of "going with the flow" or, on the contrary, an overactive, narrow focus on "making it big," which pulled them off their original track. Maybe our dreams were impossibly grandiose and our standards unrealistically high. In any case, we're out of sync with the stars we wished to live by.

However, one thing is certain: rather than spend time regretting how things have turned out, it would be more useful to accept the facts of our already-lived life, and begin to look for a way out of our own dark wood.

Can we deepen our experience of being right here, right now, as we hold down our jobs, raise our families, and generally get on with the business of living? And not by withdrawing and dedicating ourselves exclusively to spiritual practices as monks and yogis do, but by engaging in a more authentic life in the world?

This book details five possible paths to another way of living. Any of them can lead you, no matter how busy you are, to an increased awareness of your own presence in the midst of an active life.

Who Are We Working For?

Throughout the centuries, people have asked: "Who am I?" "What am I here on earth for?" We want to know what life is about. Is everything relative or am I responsible in some way for the quality of my life today? Am I a victim of the push-me, pull-me forces of life—forces beyond my control—or is something expected of me that I haven't known how to give? Have I challenged my abilities to discover what I'm really made of or is there somewhere in me a strand of genius or pure grit that I haven't yet called on because I don't even know it's there?

A key question for me has always been, "Who am I working for?" The question bubbled up from somewhere deep inside me in the midst of struggles for material and psychological survival, while raising and supporting a family in Peru. I wanted to make sense of all the pressures life thrust on me as well as the ones I put on myself. When my children were small, we played a card game called *Nobody Knows Who They're Working For*. We'd each pile up and discard cards in what seemed a meaningless exchange of winning and losing. Was I, too, winning and losing in a vacuous passing of time?

How am I spending the time of my life? *Who* am I working for? These questions bring me back to myself, to my own reality. If I identify myself too much with what I'm doing or care too much what other people think, I may make decisions based on what others expect rather than my own priorities. You could even say that every time I put on a show for others or react with annoyance at their (perceived) lack of appreciation, I'm working for *them*. It's only when I can give up the pseudo self-image I often desperately thrust forward, that I can be myself, choose for myself, and work for my own authentic development.

Imagine a closet in which what you seek is buried under all the discarded garments and equipment of your past life since childhood. You feel it's urgent to get to what's important but you are distracted by everything that's in the way. That's our situation. We get so caught up in the immediate demands on our time that there's none left for feeling alive, for being present to ourselves. A daily commitment to intensify our sense of presence might help us respond to life more often from the depths of our being rather than the surface of ourselves. We were born with this possibility and it still vibrates in each of us today, though often buried under a huge pile of future urgencies and past psychic debris.

What's going on in me right now? Coming into awareness leads to a sense of presence. Although we typically rush through our day in little contact with the reality of our inner life, daily practice to connect to a deeper sense of Self could transform the outer tasks that press on us so urgently. Then the ordinary work we often consider a grind might take on the quality of ritual. There is, in fact, no ordinary life. There is only an *extraordinary* one—the one we were given. Daily practice, the practice of presence, can give us the help we need to remember that.

What Are We Waiting For?

Peru, one of the world's poorest nations, is often described as a beggar seated on a golden bench because its land is full of valuable minerals and natural resources that have never been tapped. Perhaps that's also true of each of us. We sit atop our unimaginable riches with no idea that they're there, let alone how to get access to them in our daily lives. Enormous possibilities are hidden in every human being, waiting to be developed if we can abandon our dream of success (or our conviction of failure) and move on to accept the reality that we are already rich inside. Yes, our gold is buried, let's admit, in attitudes of pretty solid rock. It needs to be mined and processed. But it awaits within us.

We can ask ourselves, "In what hidden lode are my riches embedded?" We were born with energy, talents, a craft with which to travel the river of life, and a good rudder to steer it by. What went wrong? Is it possible to begin again? Starting over is hard. It may seem easier to stay angry at not finding what one wanted from life, or feed on self-pity or despair. Those who have been tragically buffeted by life may feel all that's left is to eat, drink and be unhappy. But although we may be trapped in a dark mineshaft, we are surrounded by buried treasure. A little light on our situation might lead us to a richer and more authentic life.

Even if we feel it's too late, that we've already failed, the seed of a possible new life is present in us every day. All that we were born with and all that happened to us has led to this precious, uncomfortable moment of doubt and questioning. So to cling to a sense of failure is just one more way of putting off a face-to-face confrontation with one's own reality. The real defeat may be of quite another kind—a failure to develop the many possibilities waiting to be expressed.

It's not that despair should be ignored. On the contrary, coming to the end of one's rope and realizing that one is rudderless is the first step toward finding the courage to look for guidance. As psychologist Rollo May said: "Despair means I can leave the past behind."

Yes. You can begin life again, right where you are. The first step would be to take stock of your present situation with all the honesty you can muster. Clarify for yourself both your past trajectory and your present here-and-now. Then you may want to explore the five paths described in this book, which I've followed intensively for decades. Each of them offers a daily practice to deepen awareness and develop potentiality.

Any of these disciplines—the Gurdjieff teaching, the Chinese meditation-in-movement T'ai Chi Ch'uan, Jungian depth psychology and bodywork, the Alexander Technique and the path of daily prayer and meditation—could help you discover your own blueprint to self-renewal. Each of them represents a hands-on possibility to begin a new life. Every day.

My Journey

Let me share my search with you. All my life I've been a hunter. At every age there was something I wanted so much I was ready to give up almost everything else for it. When I was little, I pursued the "true truth," according to my mother. Naive and determined, I hunted it down wherever I thought it was hidden, often exposing myself to ridicule in the process. Truth had something to do with God, and as a small child I had a very close association with Him, or rather with his representative, Jesus, who was safer and more intimate. I could share my inmost thoughts with Jesus without fear of retribution. God, on the other hand, disapproved of an awful lot of me, I was sure.

As a teenager I began to think about the handsome (and wealthy) prince who would sweep me off to happily-ever-after land, though, as I matured, his coat of armor morphed into jeans or a business suit. But whatever he wore he was always Practically Perfect, and I was, of course, richly deserving of him. This led me down the garden path to a wedding, and children whom I worked very hard to raise through all kinds of difficulties. They meant the world to me and I lived a constant challenge, refusing to be the "Good-Enough Mother" I read about later in psychology books. I demanded of myself to be the very best—whatever the cost to them or to me. The price of perfection did not enter into my calculations.

As for the marketplace, though there was never a doubt in my mind that my priorities lay with family, the need for money drove me to several careers—teaching, management and journalism. In New York City I worked as a reporter for *Time* and *Fortune* magazines. In between, I lived in Peru as wife of the governor of Loreto, the country's vast jungle province, where I headed the Green Cross, which provided medicines and medical help to impoverished natives of the Amazon. Through the Peace Corps, I organized summer volunteers—a group of American doctors to care for the sick and young people to build roads and schools.

After a military coup we moved back to Lima with small children and no income. Teaching became my only immediate solution to hold the family together. I founded a preschool in association with the United Nations' International Playgroup and ran it for eight years. When the inflationary crisis forced me to close it, I taught fifth grade at the American School of Lima and organized a summer program for 400 students.

Other challenges and adventures punctuated my path, from roaring with laughter and oxygen deprivation while peeing at the peak of the highest road in the world to canoeing up treacherous jungle rivers against the current. Through it all, my ceaseless ambition remained *perfection*. And I was very ambitious. Essentially, I wanted to find inner truth, whatever that was, in order to perfect myself as a human being, whatever that meant.

Several great sources of hands-on knowledge informed my quest for practical, day-by-day understanding of who I am and why I'm here on earth. I was born into a small band of seekers who gathered around the enigmatic teacher, G. I. Gurdjieff, to engage in his path for the development of consciousness. The study of this oral teaching continues to enrich every aspect of my life and sheds light on all my other investigations. However, as I grew up I explored many other spiritual paths, including Christianity, Hinduism, Buddhism,

Confucianism, Judaism, Sufism and Zen. Soaking myself in the literature of many of the world's great religions, I thought of myself, in turn, as a faithful adept of each.

Early in my marriage I discovered T'ai Chi Ch'uan, a living heritage of Taoism, and took private lessons in New York for several months with Master T. T. Liang, recently arrived from Formosa. He told me, "Begin to teach as soon as you return to Peru, so that T'ai Chi will become an integral part of your life." Subsequently, I practiced daily and taught a weekly class for forty years.

Later, after my marriage fell apart and I returned to live in the United States, I explored psychiatrist Carl Jung's interpretation of the psyche in the second half of life. He postulated that the first half belongs to the development of the ego. In his view, whether or not we've succeeded or failed in our dream of life, as we enter midlife our enthusiasm for dancing to the drumbeat of success and power recedes. If we are mature men and women, we turn to the depths of our own nature to seek the meaning of our lives. His governing idea, filled with good common sense but sometimes hard to accept, is that most of what moves us *to do* and *to be* is, like an iceberg, nine-tenths hidden from view. We contain many things, including what he called the Transpersonal Self. This Self is not the small self we live from daily, which we may think of as the ego, but a connection with an inner guide from the larger psychic world of the Collective Unconscious.

At the same time, all my life I have been a student of movement and dance, exploring methods that relate body and mind. My first and longest association has been practicing and teaching the Gurdjieff sacred dances and movements. Next came T'ai Chi. Later, I underwent Jungian analysis and took part in the *BodySoul Rhythms* intensive weeks led by Jungian analyst Marion Woodman. In recent decades I embarked on a new voyage with classes in the Alexander Technique. A few years ago I retired from *Fortune*, where I had been Deputy Chief of Reporters, in order to take the three-year teacher-training course at the American Center for the Alexander Technique (ACAT) in New York City. For three hours every day I explored Alexander's key to human well-being: the quality of our own use of ourselves.

The Work for Presence

My life has been grounded in the practice of presence in these five traditions. For fifty-five years, I've been a student of the Gurdjieff teaching; for more than forty years I've studied and taught T'ai Chi; for thirty years both Jungian studies and the Alexander Technique nourished my practice. Prayer and meditation have also sustained me from an early age. From the monk's daily rituals to the Taoist's "circulation of the light," many paths include prayer, whether recognized or not by that name, as an intrinsic part of working for presence. Gathering one's attention, putting aside one's likes and dislikes, and seeking the truth of the inner moment as it is lived right now is a way of saying, as many times a day as one turns inward, "Lord, not *my* will, but *Thy* will be done."

Someone recently asked, "Why do you pursue so many different paths?" My answer: each provides a way for me to return to my authenticity. In Gurdjieffian terminology, each path leads to the development of *being* rather than merely affirming *personality*. Although different, the five paths have much in common. Their key concepts are recognizable and sometimes interchangeable. All are a means for centering, for developing conscious awareness, for living in the present, for making contact with what is truer in oneself. They offer practical ways of searching that can bring us to a sense of presence in our daily activities.

Why, you might ask, is daily work necessary? After all, for a lot of dedicated religious people it's enough to go to church or celebrate Sabbath once a week. That's fine if one spiritual encounter is enough to keep them connected to a larger reality the rest of the week, but for most people it isn't. Presence must be practiced. Returning repeatedly to contact with our innermost being renews our intention again and again and reminds us of aims we may have temporarily forgotten. It's how we can maintain ourselves within the bandwidth of a connection that fades when we become too preoccupied.

What exactly is this daily work and how do these paths envisage it?

• Gurdjieff would speak of the work of "remembering yourself," the practice of finding a harmonious relationship among your three parts—your head, your body and your feelings—and the study of your personality as differentiated from what is essential in you. The aim: to develop your real "I", the master within.

• The Chinese martial art T'ai Chi Ch'uan invites you to surrender unnecessary physical tension and mental "gaining" attitudes as you practice a series of flowing movements in an exact, gentle and steady way, as if you were pulling a delicate thread of silk slowly from a cocoon without breaking it. The aim: to develop your sense of balance, calmness of mind; rejuvenation.

• Jung would urge you to become aware of the dark side of your nature, the shadow side that you unconsciously refuse to contemplate, in order to find integration with the larger Self, and your place in the larger context of society. The aim: your individuation as a unique human being.

• F. M. Alexander would suggest that you study your reactions and your body in movement following his non-judgmental method, to learn how to stop interfering with the primary neuro-physical organization you were born with. The aim: to return to the natural poise and ease which were your rightful inheritance as a small child.

• And Thomas Merton, Adin Steinsaltz, Rumi, Sri Anirvan, Shunryu Suzuki and other dedicated spiritual leaders point the way to a harvest of joy by opening yourself to the daily availability of the divine through prayer and meditation.

Five Paths, One Encounter

These paths speak in different ways about the importance of the practice of presence. You could say they lead to a more authentic sense of Self and, using Gurdjieffian terminology, all of them foster the development of being, as opposed to most of the other influences in our lives, which feed personality.

Gurdjieffians, Jungians and Alexander teachers often refer to their method as "the Work." The first two have even called the efforts they make "inner work." Gurdjieffians speak about *relaxation* as a key to inner freedom, while T'ai Chi masters would agree with Alexander, who feared that the word relaxation might evoke collapse and advocated the term *release*.

Gurdjieffians affirm the need to increase our capacity for attention and find harmony among the energies of head, heart and body. As we attempt to do this we see that our lives and energy are eternally subject to the push-pull play of universal forces, which act on us entirely beyond our control. Taoism concurs with this view. T'ai Chi sinks the power of thought or attention into the abdomen where our intrinsic or vital energy rests, then invites us to follow it as it circulates through the slowly moving body. Taoists say that daily repetition of such an effort leads to true balance between the active masculine force, *yang*, and the passive feminine force, *yin*.

Jungians also celebrate the "marriage" of masculine and feminine. They speak of the fragmentation with which we live in spite of our need for wholeness, telling us that nothing should be rejected. Indeed, it is most important that we find a way to embrace the parts of ourselves we've hidden even from ourselves, through shame or disapproval, because it is there that our energy is imprisoned.

One might say that inner and outer poise best expresses the goal of the Alexander Technique, except that Alexander himself highly disapproved of words like *goal, aim* or *target*, preferring the term *direction*. He reasoned that work today will make yesterday's goal tomorrow's actuality, so a word suggesting movement was better than one that represents a static end result.

These five ways all advocate receptivity, acceptance, learning to listen to conscience, to the heart or one's true Self. Finally, each of them emphasizes the need for a new relationship between the mind and the body.

How, then, will you decide which path to choose? For those who wish to undertake a study of ideas and activities leading to a development of consciousness and will, Gurdjieff's teaching may be the appropriate path, with its primary emphasis on self-knowledge and self-remembering (another term for being in the present, connected with all that "I am"). Or, at a certain moment in life, some people may prefer to build a wordless new relationship between mind and body through the gentle movements of T'ai Chi.

And at another time, Jung's way of individuation may beckon them to discover the dark and bright sides of themselves as they explore the depths of the misunderstood psyche. Those who suffer from physical pain or serious handicap may first prefer the Alexander Technique for immediate relief and then to search for freedom from fixed attitudes and reactivity. They may then discover how the power of thought and awareness of their present reality can transform their lives.

This journey may be quite different for each of us. If you read about the possibilities described here, investigate the relevant books, and meet and talk to the people engaged in these five "ways," it may become clear which is right for you. Take introductory classes wherever possible to experience the practical work involved. You will find that one or several of these paths accords more truly with your nature and feels most authentic. Like coming home.

One

Remembering Oneself: G. I. Gurdjieff

Inquiring minds long for the truth of the heart, seek it, strive to solve the problems set by life, try to penetrate to the essence of things and phenomena, and into themselves. ... Socrates' words, 'know thyself' remain an imperative for all those who seek true knowledge and being.

— G. I. Gurdjieff, *Views from the Real World*

❖

Who was Gurdjieff? People called this enigmatic and powerfully influential 20th-century figure philosopher, psychologist, Tiger of Turkestan, Eastern master, even charlatan. He called himself "a teacher of dancing." By this he meant not only the sacred dances he brought to the west from hidden monasteries in Asia and the Middle East, but also the dance of life itself. Both had a profound effect on me as I grew up.

I learned from Gurdjieff that at any moment it's possible to be attentive to myself, to where I am and what's going on around me. He called this state of listening to myself, of connecting with all that I am in fact and in potentiality, "remembering oneself." For instance, certain memories of childhood, full of color and flavor, are moments of self-remembering—unforgettable because they connect our deepest inner world with what's happening to us and around us. Such impressions are as alive now as they were then, no matter how long ago they took place, quite different from other times we remember as the story of what happened to us.

From his early days of teaching amid the turmoil of pre-revolutionary Russia in 1912 to his death in Paris in 1949, Gurdjieff's voice resonated with this call for a more conscious participation in life. He urged his students to develop a deeper awareness of themselves and of the world around them in order to contact the whole of themselves rather than the more superficial persona who plays many parts on the stage of life.

To uncover these depths, he proffered a new method of practical work in the midst of an active life in the world, aimed at creating a balanced relationship between the three basic parts of ourselves—head, heart and body. At the same time, his message is as old as man's aspiration to become an adult in the true sense of the word. Challenging "the hypnotic sleep" in which he said we spend our life, he invited us to make a fresh start and to make it *now*. Why, he asked, did we always put off until tomorrow what needs to be done today? He called "the disease of 'tomorrow'" our worst affliction.

I don't know when I first realized my family was part of a study group delving into a system of ideas. Certainly as children, my brother and I wondered where our parents went several evenings a week, when they attended talks by Gurdjieff's major disciple, P. D. Ouspensky or met with his pupils. Their silence about it reflected the secrecy that surrounded the teaching at that time. Students were told not to discuss it, even among themselves, because their partial understanding might distort the ideas. What's more, they must have felt vulnerable to accusations of being "weird," as I did.

Few people, apart from avant-garde artists and intellectuals in Europe and New York's Greenwich Village, had heard of Gurdjieff. Words such as *consciousness, being* and *self-observation* were strangers to the mainstream of cultural thought and no books were yet available to expand upon and clarify what he taught.

✦

The Terror of the Situation

There's nobody home. — Gurdjieff

When I was a child, Gurdjieff's teaching was called the "System," then it later became the "Ideas" or the "Teaching," and is currently known as the "Work." Its central message is that human beings are born incomplete and can only develop our potential through study and practice. Most of us are totally unaware of our hidden possibilities. We will only commit to developing them if we face the fact that we lack qualities most people assume they already possess, such as will, consciousness and the ability to do what we intended. We are like people who don't know they are in prison, said Gurdjieff. Instead of putting all our energy into trying to escape, we just dream our lives away.

How do we get out of prison? He invited us to invest our energy and intelligence in learning how to bring the three major aspects or "centers" of our being—head, heart and body—into harmonious relationship with each other, rather than allowing ourselves to be isolated in only one at a time. Comparing our situation to that of someone who has been given a large house with many beautiful rooms, he asked why we chose to be holed up in a dark corner of the basement. The terror of the situation is that we could spend a lifetime down there in the dark, without developing our faculties or finding a harmonious relationship among these three aspects of our being.

To put his ideas into practice, Gurdjieff met with his students in Moscow and St. Petersburg. Then, to escape the vortex of the Russian Revolution, he moved with some of his followers to Essentuki. Later, when it became impossible to continue there, he and his followers made an incredibly dangerous and difficult journey by train and foot over the Caucasus Mountains to Tiflis, in Georgia, dodging both revolutionary and Czarist troops that crossed their path. There he opened his Institute for the Harmonious Development of Man but soon had to move on to Europe. Reopening his school near Paris, he set his students a fast pace of heavy physical work, special mental exercises and daily practice of the movements and sacred dances he had brought back from isolated monasteries in Asia.

No matter where Gurdjieff was or what he was doing, a state of emergency always seemed to exist around him. No one knew what would happen next, including where the money for tomorrow's food and shelter would be found. There was also little wasted time. His students were expected to do whatever they did, from ditch digging to cooking dinner, with total attention. Gurdjieff liked to say he could *talk* to someone who could make coffee well. Such a person already knew something. "There is a thousand times more value even in polishing the floor as it should be done than in writing twenty-five books," he would say to his followers.

A major premise of his teaching was that people attribute to themselves a single and permanent self whom we imagine is always in charge of our lives and directs us wherever we wish to go. But if we looked deeply into ourselves at frequent intervals during a single day, we would discover many little "i's" or personality fragments, completely unrelated to each other, each of which randomly and chaotically takes charge of our whole psycho-physical being. Temporary King of our Castle, each of these little "i's" has a viewpoint that may be totally at odds with whoever was in command a short time before.

Finally, after presenting the human predicament as almost hopeless, Gurdjieff affirmed that buried deep in our subconscious is a real conscience, not based on social morality or tribal custom, but objective and the same for everyone. Our life-long task is to uncover it so that we can act from the whole of ourselves, not just one of our many parts.

Simple as that may sound, it certainly isn't easy to achieve. He often said that he had come here to teach people that "when it rains, the streets get wet," and urged us to wake up and see "all our beauties" so we might become convinced that there's no easy way out. Making unpleasant realistic discoveries about ourselves would provide the energy and determination to begin real work on ourselves, he explained, for it is the suffering produced by seeing what we are and how we live that creates the possibility of change.

What are we supposed to struggle with? All of our likes and dislikes, little personas with different tastes, desires and beliefs, are separated from each other by what he called "buffers." Developed through habit, education and fear, the buffers prevent us from experiencing the pain of our divided state. Nevertheless, he insisted, through dedicated work on oneself, these buffers can be gradually eliminated so that objective conscience can emerge and assume its rightful function as guide to our decisions.

In my opinion, more and more people experience this pain of division as our protective coatings wear thin and our profound uncertainty about what will happen next is exposed. Day after day, we confront world events that bear witness to all the horror human beings are capable of, as well as the nobility and sacrifice of a few. As the buffers that protect us from reality wear thin, the suffering brought about by our insecurity and conflict often leads to depression and thoughts of suicide. However, it's devoutly to be wished that, on the contrary, it could bring us to a new threshold—the determination to find a way out of our prison of pain. And there is a way, promised Gurdjieff, if we are willing to work.

♦

Self-Observation and The Science of Being

He who has not a critical mind has no place here. — Gurdjieff

Gurdjieff called his system of ideas and exercises the Fourth Way, to differentiate it from the three central spiritual paths that demand total renunciation of ordinary life: the Way of the Fakir or of austere bodily discipline, the Way of the Monk or of religious devotion, and the Way of the Yogi or of development of mental powers. These disciplines focus their deep work on only one part of a human being, or as he liked to put it, on only one of our three "rooms," while his teaching aims to develop all three "rooms" simultaneously. The fourth "room," as yet undiscovered, is the dwelling place of the Master.

In a world desperate for sanity, the Fourth Way has special appeal because it is lived amidst the clamor of ordinary life rather than isolated in forest or monastery. "In your room you cannot develop the master," said Gurdjieff. "A man may be strong in a monastery, but weak in life, and we want strength for life. For instance, in a monastery, a man could be without food for a week, but in life he cannot be without food even for three hours. What then is the good of his exercises?"

The Gurdjieff Work also differs from many spiritual paths because it's not based on a belief system, and at no time is blind faith encouraged. "Trust no one; not even me," said Gurdjieff, suggesting that students invest ten percent of their faith in the accuracy of his ideas for a little while as they experimented with his teaching, and if that turned out to be worthwhile, add another ten percent. Scientist Robert DeRopp was skeptical when urged by his intellectual friends to come to a meeting with P. D. Ouspensky in the mid 1930s. Ouspensky, author of *In Search of the Miraculous*, a commentary on his years in Russia with Gurdjieff, had a journalist's healthy skepticism himself and met the challenge. DeRopp revised his opinion when Ouspensky told him to "'Believe nothing. Test everything.'" Added DeRopp: "It was an attitude that my (inner) Scientist accepted. … This system is not the way of faith but the way of understanding." (*Warrior's Way*)

From the beginning, students were expected to observe themselves for at least a few minutes several times every day as if they were scientists examining elements of an experiment. Only then could they learn what they were really like behind their often inaccurate idea of themselves. Self-observation is an effort to attend, moment by moment, to all that is going on in oneself and between oneself and the world, without judgment or opinion about it. Although we all house an inner judge ready to categorize and criticize everything and everyone we meet as well as our own thoughts and actions, as soon as that accusatory element enters, we are no longer engaged in a disinterested investigation.

Such efforts could bring a surprising number of different attitudes and desires into view. After attending his first Ouspensky lecture in 1923, Harley Street physician Kenneth Walker reported that "All that one saw when one watched one's inner psychic processes was an endless procession of thoughts, sensations, imaginings, and emotions, but nothing that could possibly be called a permanent and sovereign self … Man … has innumerable 'i's' that are always changing. One 'i' is there at one moment and at the next it is replaced by another." (*Venture With Ideas*)

My own experiments with self-observation involved taking "snapshots" of myself during the day by simultaneously recording thoughts, emotional state and physical position at any given moment of reaction. It provided unexpected and often unappealing glimpses of myself in action. Here's a recent example: while working at *Fortune* magazine, I was suddenly summoned to the managing editor's office to explain some complex details of a story I had been assigned. Totally immersed in gathering data for another story, I was challenged to provide an instant presentation that would make or break his decision to run it. I was also aware that it would expose me as one of his best or worst reporters! So, heart in mouth, I called on all my faculties while walking down the hall to his office. Gallons of adrenaline flowed through me as I stood in front of his desk, excruciatingly aware of my body's tension and position in space as well as my self-doubt and the sound of my voice talking. Though I have no idea what impression I made, it was a dynamic and painful experience of self-observation.

While efforts of this kind provide unusual data about oneself, they are followed by an inevitable reaction to what is seen. There's really a lot of stuff I don't want to know about myself no matter how often I vote for self-knowledge! The search for truth calls for such a re-examination of old assumptions and values that I had to ask myself how much uncertainty could I tolerate? And how devastated would I be by feeling I'm wrong all the time? I was no longer sure about what's right, and saw that at least one aspect of myself didn't like to be "caught out" or engaged in the "wrong thing." Yet it's the only path I know to reality. My every attempt at impartial seeing-what-is shakes up my rigid attitudes and notions of how things ought to be, replacing them with a deepening awareness of how things really are.

Why are we unable to stay present in the world? Gurdjieff said that we suffer from a lack of *being*. He spoke of different levels of being within ourselves and that each of us could live on many possible levels. He invited us to get out of the basement where we are caught up in desires and creature comforts. Down there in the damp and dark, we are slaves to our loves and our hates; we are caught in endless reactions to what's going on in and around us. We are mired in whirling thoughts that invent a world lived entirely in the head.

◆

Toward a Three-Centered Being

When you look with one center you are entirely under hallucination; when with two you are half-free; but if you look with three centers you cannot be under hallucination at all. You must begin by collecting material. You can have no bread without baking; knowledge is water, body is flour, and emotion—suffering—is fire. — Gurdjieff

The possibility of living in all three of our parts at once, simultaneously present to mind, feeling and body, is the true inheritance of a human being. When I am "all there," cradled in the present moment, I'm available to joy of another quality, rather than the pleasure of getting what I want. Contemplatives often experience this joy, although in the world's eyes they have sacrificed a great deal for it. In such moments, we can serve something larger than ourselves.

A moment of balance between the centers is a moment of presence. It connects us to a higher level of being than the one on which we usually live. Jeanne de Salzmann, to whom Gurdjieff entrusted the leadership of his teaching when he died in 1949, called it a science of being. She often said that the real purpose of human existence is to create "a link between two levels, to receive energy from a higher level in order to have an action on the level below (rather than) a reaction. Man has a special function ... (that of) becoming a bridge for certain higher energies." (Ravi Ravindra, *Heart Without Measure*).

If it's true, as Gurdjieff and de Salzmann say, that human beings are born to serve higher purposes, that we are sending/receiving stations in which energies of many levels meet or through which they pass, our primary job must be to avoid static or interference. But we usually live piecemeal, caught up in one or another center rather than operating as a whole. At one moment we obey the urgencies of the body, or find ourselves completely taken over by an emotional reaction. At other times we are, as we ourselves say, "lost in thought." Said Gurdjieff, "The failure of the three centers to coordinate means that there are, as it were, three different men in a single individual, the first of whom does nothing but think, the second only feels and the third lives only by his instincts and motor functions. ... These three men never understand one another, and unconsciously frustrate the plans, intentions and work of each other, and yet at the moment when he is in action each of them occupies a dominant position and calls himself 'I.'"

Further complications ensue when one of the three centers tries to do the work of another. For instance, every time we learn a new motor skill, the thinking center assumes control as we follow directions step by step. Then, when we get the hang of it, our automatic "moving center" takes over. Do you remember your first attempts to ride a bike? Or drive a car?

Imagine driving a car at 50 miles an hour if you had to think about every twist of the wheel or how much pressure your foot needs to exert on the gas pedal. Our centers switch duties and energy all the time although we are seldom aware of it. If you do something physical with unnecessary tension, you can be sure emotional energy is getting in the way. Or ask yourself why preparing taxes is such an emotional experience. Our feelings invade the work of thought.

Careful observation of ourselves in action provides living proof that these three basic centers and the energy that flows through them are uncoordinated and either unrelated to each other or habitually replacing each other's work in a haphazard way. We live all tangled up in one center or another. That may pass unnoticed in everyday life, but when facing an emergency for which our best intelligence is needed, we may discover with dismay that "there's nobody home."

In any case, we seldom know where home is! We have no base from which to take a new direction, to give the actions of our lives a meaning that represents more than the reaction of the moment. Victimized by habits or haphazard reactions occurring in one center or another, we are momentarily taken over until a new stimulus evokes a new reaction, perhaps in a different center. Each calls itself 'i' and takes charge in my name, making decisions and writing checks for which all of me will have to pay.

Gurdjieff used an ancient analogy, comparing our three parts to a horse (emotions), a carriage (the body) and a driver (the mind). He explained that the horse, which is where the motive power is stored, has never been properly educated. It only responds to harsh tugs of the reins telling it to go left, right or stop, or else a whipping from the driver. The carriage, designed with a shock-absorber and oiling mechanism made for irregular country roads and rough terrain, no longer functions properly because it's only used for short rides on smooth city streets. As for the driver, who feeds the horse straw and uses its feed money for drinks at the local pub, he prefers to spend his time with his chums, dreaming happily about all the interesting trips he might make.

The missing element is the owner of the equipage. For though the usual driver is a cabby at the service of every chance passenger or small "i" who summons him for a brief ride, he could be at the service of a permanent occupant, a permanent "I." For that to happen, the driver's work is clear. He must turn his back on those long hours fantasizing at the pub, educate the horse and buy it real feed, polish up and oil the carriage and be ready to roll at the call of the Master.

I discovered firsthand the effect of three-centered balance the year I graduated from college. The Gurdjieff movements and sacred dances were to be privately presented for the first time that spring at the recently acquired Gurdjieff Foundation in New York City, which my parents and a dozen or so others had contributed money to buy. Fresh from a junior year in Paris where I had relished taking several movements classes a week, I was desperate to take part in this first U.S. demonstration since the 1920s. Having escaped to New York for a long weekend twice a month to work regularly with the class, I planned to cut school for the two weeks in March when Madame de Salzmann would work with us. As soon as she arrived in New York, I begged her to allow me to join in the demonstration. The answer was yes, on condition that my grades didn't suffer.

Those two weeks were also my first intensive experience. Because I took part in all but the men's movements, I was on my feet and in action for three to four hours every evening, amazed that I never felt exhausted or even breathless. My mind was clear, the youthful roller coaster of my emotional life had smoothed down to soft hills and valleys and I was filled with joyous energy.

We quaked before the demonstration, but after it was over we felt light and free and unafraid. While we were changing back into real-life clothes in awed silence and hanging up our flowing white costumes, Madame de Salzmann entered the dressing room. We gathered quietly around her. With an authoritative glance at me, she told us: "You are both more and less than you think you are." Then she added, "From now on it will be your task to connect all three parts of yourselves whenever you practice." I returned to college ten pounds lighter, knowing these dances would forge a new relationship among my three centers. Thirty years later Madame de Salzmann repeated to Ravindra: "Do you see what you lose when you are in pieces? The Work is to bring these centres in harmony, so that there will be higher intelligence." (*Heart Without Measure*).

◆

Uncovering Buried Conscience

It is indeed possible ... (for people) to perfect themselves, yet this can proceed exclusively only ... (through) conscious labors and intentional sufferings. — Gurdjieff

This higher intelligence can lead us toward change and a new understanding of the meaning of our lives. But how do we connect with it? At the heart of Gurdjieff's message is the awakening of conscience, not the pseudo-conscience formed by education and the environment in which we grew up, but the true conscience that is an essential part of every human being in all societies. He affirmed that this conscience is still quite pure in us, but seldom influences our lives because it's buried deep under layers of protective, defensive and even perhaps atrophied psyche.

Uncovering real conscience can be a devastating experience. We've all known what it's like when a parent or close friend dies or something terrible happens. Something similar takes place when some of the buffers that protected us from seeing our real situation disappear, and we come face to face with how we think, feel and behave. In either case, when buried conscience awakens, a new suffering flowers deep inside us, along with remorse for the careless way we usually live. Our values shift. Things that used to seem so important, the little affirmations and disappointments of daily life, seem totally irrelevant in the light of the huge experience we are going through.

There we are, suddenly connecting, without much preparation for it, to another level of reality, struggling through each naked moment, recognizing the fragility of our lives and our relationships. Life is experienced minute by minute because we are no longer able to conceal it or ourselves behind our personal colorations, explanations, defenses and ego affirmations. It's a harsh time because, as T. S. Eliot, a sometime student of the Gurdjieff ideas, said in *The Four Quartets:* "Human kind cannot bear very much reality."

This painful work of resuscitating conscience can't be left to portentous life events if we are in search of freedom from our "automaton" (Madame de Salzmann's term for the habitual, mechanical part of us that runs us on autopilot). We need to practice daily to be present to ourselves. It will help keep our eyes and hearts open to what's going on. Only then can we observe ourselves and begin to create a new attitude that opposes our tendency to let ourselves off easily, to avoid the responsibility of our actions and seek comfort rather than pursue understanding at any price. As Ouspensky put it clearly more than half a century ago: "You cannot live on gold you find in the streets. You must learn to mine your own."

Such a new attitude can be reinforced by a careful investigation of one's personality and the effort to separate its manifestations from essence or the essential nature we were born with. "Essence," said Gurdjieff, "is a child." It was never given room to grow or proper education in Western civilization, where personality has almost entirely taken over, except in people who still live close to the earth and the turning seasons. Balance is always the key, because those who are closer to nature may have a more developed essence, but their personality may be underdeveloped. Both a grown-up, developed essence and a well-functioning personality are needed for our evolution into "man-without-quotation-marks."

But how can we discover how we really are when ego and reaction quickly move in to deny the truth of it? Gurdjieff advised us to find ways to go against our habits, suggesting that we intentionally interfere with our automatic pilot by inventing alarm clocks to disturb our sleep. Or that we purposefully place ourselves in situations which force us to be aware of ourselves no matter what happens. Such efforts can be as simple as assuming an uncomfortable physical position and staying in it, or as difficult as finding a new relationship with someone whom we can't stand, whose manifestations we can't bear.

One well-known task he gave his students was to "like what 'It' does not like." This immediately provoked a separation between my comfortable go-with-the-flow persona and my determination to experience the present moment. When I accept to go against what's automatic in myself by placing a small crowbar in the constantly turning wheel of my mechanical habits of thinking, feeling or doing, I know I'll be forced to make an effort. As soon as I go against my usual comfortable adaptations, and do what 'It' doesn't want to do, a whole series of reactions appears, revealing all my stories and excuses.

While rigorous self-observation began to show me the mechanical and inefficient way I usually lived, it wasn't a comfortable pursuit. However, in tandem with the unpleasant sightings of "my beauties," a new taste of the meaning of my life began to appear and my burning question became loud and clear: *What work could I undertake to awaken objective conscience?* Gurdjieff said we're abnormal, that we see everything upside down. That made sense to me. He also said that if I wanted to be responsible for myself, and anyone who might depend on me, I must first become like "the Good Householder," the honest and hardworking person who perhaps wasn't interested in spiritual quests at all!

Gurdjieff often taught in parables. One that guided me for years was that of a large house with many servants and an absent master. Everything went wrong after the master went away. The gardener took the butler's job, the cook worked in the stable and the housemaid ran the kitchen. Suddenly the news came of the master's return. Panic set in. How quickly could the servants prepare the house for him when everything was in such confusion? In desperation, they met together and decided to elect one of their number "Deputy Steward," promising to obey his commands if he'd get things turned around fast.

◆

Leashing the Wandering Mind

I am where my attention is. — Gurdjieff

Sooner or later each of us has to appoint a Deputy Steward to deal with our own personal house-in-disorder. We may have found the ideas intriguing, disturbing, challenging, and done our best to think our way through or around them—either to dispose of their grip or to understand better what they mean. But once committed to serious study, we have to address the quality of our thinking center.

According to Gurdjieff, there are two kinds of thought. He compared our usual associative or automatic thinking to a careless secretary at the front desk, who sends out randomly any messages that come in. She files papers in the wrong cubbyholes, misconnects and disconnects the lines of communication among the executives (the three centers) and seldom listens to what is asked, intent on polishing her nails and reading cheap romances.

He said we are suggestible and uncritical because we "believe any old tale." We hear or read opinions and, liking their tone, we repeat them to others. Having opinions inflates our self-esteem, gives us authoritative positions about subjects we know very little of. We let others think for us.

Until we recognize that this habit of "collecting" points of view that aren't ours, or thinking vaguely about things, is insufficient, real change will never appear. As Madame de Salzmann wrote many years ago in her personal journal: "Objective thought is a look from Above. ... Without this look upon me, seeing me, my life is the life of a blind man who goes his way driven by impulse, not knowing either why or how."

Gurdjieff students are required to bring their minds to group meetings. New people are asked to investigate whether they possess all the powers they think of as theirs, such as a real will, freedom to choose and a focused power of attention. They're given tasks to help them see the reality of their waking moments and explore whether this is an accurate picture of themselves. An unpleasant list of attributes of man-as-he-is provides groundwork for ways to explore, chew and digest this picture.

As I studied, little by little I came face to face with my own "beauties:" lack of sincerity about myself, my tendency to lie, to obfuscate, to prevaricate. I began to see how much of my waking life was dissipated in unproductive imagination, and how negativity and complaint played into my personal relationships. I learned what Gurdjieff meant when he said that we "identify" with everything, becoming a broom when we sweep rather than a person consciously wielding a broom. I also saw how I identified with people—which he called "considering"—wondering, fearfully, what others were thinking about me or annoyed that they didn't appreciate my "finer" qualities. Even the exaggerated physical tension of my body blocked me from more objective "seeing" and from gathering attention for the central work of remembering myself, or the practice of presence in my daily life. Most difficult to accept was that my own rigid attitudes kept me imprisoned in habitual ways of thinking, feeling and doing.

Reading kept the ideas in the forefront of my mind. I had a whole cosmology to piece together and the "chemical factory" of the body to study. Self-observation—taking snapshots of myself reacting to the ebb and flow of daily life—helped me recognize the importance of developing a higher level of attention. I learned that it was possible to focus some attention briefly on myself rather than yielding to the attraction of everything outside me.

Yet, in spite of my best efforts, the clarity of my vision came and went, because, as it was explained to me, our level of understanding fluctuates with our level of being. That's why sometimes, in a special state or under special circumstances, I perceived something very clearly and understood something about myself I thought I would never forget. "From now on," I'd say confidently to myself, "everything will be different." But the next morning I'd wake up in an old familiar corner of myself—that moment of larger clarity only an exquisite longing or a memory, if it was recalled at all.

When I brought my complaints to Madame de Salzmann, telling her about my repeated inability to do what I'd intended and how hard it was to *live* the precepts of the Work even when I knew it was what I wanted, her response was always the same: "Stay in front of the lack." As she explained years later to Ravindra: "When you see active attention losing itself in passivity, it is important not to try to do something, but to stay in front of it and to suffer. That seeing is what produces new knowledge."

◆

Awakening the Intelligence of the Heart

Only understanding can lead to being, whereas knowledge is but a passing presence in it. — Gurdjieff

Thinking about ideas, reading the great thoughts of wise guides or talking about the meaning of life will never satisfy the longing for understanding. This was beautifully expressed in Gurdjieff's adventure-tale *Meetings with Remarkable Men*. Father Giovanni tells the story of Brother Sez and Brother Ahl, two ancient itinerant monks who travel from monastery to monastery, giving sermons. The highly anticipated, once-a-year visit of Brother Sez made a tremendously strong impression while he spoke, but soon evaporated and the monks forgot his message. By contrast, what Brother Ahl said in a low, cracking voice made little impression at the time but affected them more and more each day, gradually becoming "instilled as a whole into the heart, and remains there for ever." Why? Because the sermons of Brother Sez "proceeded only from his mind, and therefore acted on our minds, whereas those of Brother Ahl proceeded from his being and acted on our being."

If the knowledge we gather from books or conversation is only a passing presence, what can lead to real change in our level of understanding? The answer is that direct work is necessary. We need to see ourselves as we are and be touched to the heart by what we see. But there's more to learn: how can we open to impressions of another level, which feed the growth of our being? According to Gurdjieff, three kinds of influences are available to us, which he labeled A, B and C. "A" influences come from a higher level and can only pass from person to person. This is direct teaching. "B" influences originated in that higher level but are now found in sacred books, myths and fairy tales. They nourish our search for understanding and help orient us toward the discovery of a living teaching. Finally, "C" influences manifest in ordinary, worldly life.

One way to be open to "B" influences is to practice conscious listening. This way of listening bypasses the inner interpreter in oneself who puts labels on everything that's heard, or wanders away down a winding road of associations. My first experience of this took place as I sat in discomfort on the floor of the big hall at the Gurdjieff Foundation with a hundred people, listening to a chapter from *Meetings* about the Seekers of Truth and their long journey across a desert.

My wandering mind suddenly anchored in the midst of a sandstorm that could wipe out a caravan in minutes, but only blew five or six feet above the ground. The Seekers had cannily crafted stilts on which they climbed when the storm suddenly appeared. There, in its raging chaos, they walked and spoke to each other above the roar. The stars above, the storm below. Goose pimples covered me as I shivered at this vision. There it was, as quiet as the night sky above the seekers-on-stilts, the message that if I could rise just a little above my own devastating emotional storms, the air might be clear.

The recognition of my need for psychic stilts remained engraved in my heart, a true moment of self-remembering. How did it burn so deeply? Perhaps it was a combination of growing discomfort of sitting on the floor, my renewed effort to listen with attention and the quality of the message itself. It seems that although we desperately need to receive conscious impressions from a level of heightened understanding, we are only able to approach them indirectly, because so much of the baggage we carry is in our way.

As mentioned earlier, our efforts in this teaching lead to direct work on buried conscience, which means direct work on our emotional center. As Gurdjieff wrote in *Meetings With Remarkable Men*, our aim should be to "work so that … the desire of your mind should become the desire of your heart." A difficult proposition, because even my best efforts seemed inadequate. However, if I could stay in the emotional fire generated by the recognition of my inability to do what I intended, rather than losing myself in habitual self-attack at my inadequacy, the suffering engendered produced a new level of feeling, directly connected to the reality of my own presence.

It's a very slippery place to be and I'm seldom able to stay in that cauldron where the dross can be burned away. As a young woman I confessed to Madame de Salzmann how shallow I felt I really was, and she immediately responded: "It is true." I was shocked and hurt, having expected her to contradict me and tell me what an unusual, deep person I was. But once she had devastated my ego, she added a few words that changed my life: "You see this now, very young, what many people only see toward the end of their lives. Stay with the pain of it. This is the fire that can create a new possibility for you."

Over the years, I saw that if I could stay with the recognition of my inadequacy at remembering myself, a change in my state resulted from this confrontation between the desire and the impossibility. But at such a moment I usually lost myself in self-congratulation at the new feelings unfolding in me, or felt so much pain at what I was seeing that I escaped into theory, justification or explanation. It was as if a door opened, but I slammed it shut. How could I keep it open?

My mother, who led groups in New York and Canada, used to exhort us "to be available." She asked us to accept that there are different stages or levels of being, and that we can only go one step at a time. She would smile and say that we longed to *Be* with a capital *B*, but were not yet able to Be, so why not work first on our *ableness*? The path to this *ableness* lay in the attempt to be available—right here where I am—to another level within ourselves. Pauline de Dampierre, one of the elders of the Gurdjieff group in Paris, also spoke of this subtle effort. "Remember," she would say, "there is a level just a little higher than where you are right now, and you can open yourself to it."

Gurdjieff often told his students that we cannot *do*, cannot make happen what we want to happen, even with our sincerest wish. No matter how hard we try, we are seemingly powerless against the tremendous forces of habit and mechanicality that keep us imprisoned at the level where we are. It's because we are too full of ourselves, he would often say, ever under the sway of our principal psychic companions, Madame Vanity and Mister Self-Love.

But he also informed us at the end of his cosmic epic, *Beelzebub's Tales to His Grandson*, that another possibility exists for us. We have two natures. He used the analogy of a river that divides into two streams. Each person is like a drop of water in the first, passive stream, sometimes deep down near the bottom or at other times in a ripple near the surface. That's why our life is sometimes easier and sometimes more difficult, but each drop has the opportunity to take advantage of the current when it's closer to the surface, in order to jump into the other stream, which is governed by different laws. The water of one stream will finally disappear into the earth, but the other river ends its journey by pouring into the great ocean of being. Our choice is either to be slaves of Great Nature or, with conscious attention, to learn to be servants. We must serve "willy-nilly" in any case, he assured us. But that could be as a slave, a servant, or even, for a few gifted souls, a son.

Madame de Salzmann clarified the mystery further: "Remember that our aim is to be able, one day, to maintain ourselves consciously *between* our two natures. It is the relationship that we create that will form our individuality." If human beings are meant to serve as a bridge between these two natures, what is required of us? Somehow we must find a way to make ourselves more available to participate in this service, bringing the practice of presence into our daily lives, emptying ourselves of enough of our small preoccupations so that the energy of another level of being can find, even temporarily, a resting place in us. Madame de Salzmann assured us that although we would not be able to "do" it, "it can be done in me, and I have a part to play."

◆

Seeking a Sensation of Presence

*Your body is not only yours. You need to work to relate the
higher with the lower. That is the purpose of human
existence.* — Madame de Salzmann

The body is where everything happens, where unconscious
forces play, where intelligence vies with habit, where comfort
competes with ambition and where personal likes and dislikes
rule the kingdom. Not that our bodies should be blindly
dominated or punished, because we need to remember our
whole life takes place in the body. It's where both our functions and our possibilities lie. Most important is to make a
new relationship with it, a conscious one that replaces our
automatic assumptions. According to Madame de Salzmann,
"higher energies are *in* the body, but they are not *of* the body.
… Our attention is so scattered that it needs to be trained to be
contained in the body, to relate with it, to remain anchored."

The primary effort in work on the body is to anchor the
attention of all our parts here in the flesh. When we try, the first
thing we notice is the constant state of exaggerated tension.
Even though we often complain about it, we don't realize how
deeply it imprisons us. Work with only one center drains our
energy. Why do I use so much force washing dishes that the
glass in my hand breaks? Why am I more exhausted after a day
spent solving a problem at the computer than if I had been
out chopping firewood? It becomes clear that I am holding in
or holding on to something. What would happen if I let it go?
Can I let it go? How?

Self-observation ushers us to the threshold of self-remembering. The practice of sitting still can lead us further, if we can

silence the chattering mind by focusing attention on awareness of the body and everything that's going on in it. I delighted in the Buddhist term for this shift in concentrated attention from the "monkey mind" to the "Buddha mind."

I was introduced to the practice of sitting just before I left for my first year at college, when I nervously asked Madame de Salzmann what I could do so as not to lose myself in the hurly-burly of the "outer" world. She advised me to sit very quietly before I left my room every morning, to become aware of the parts of my body and listen to what was going on inside my head. Perhaps, after fifteen minutes, I could make a wish for myself for the day. I have always been grateful to her for initiating this habit, which has become an integral part of my life.

At the beginning of each morning I take the time to sit quietly, intentionally become aware of my physical tension wherever it may be, notice where it is strongest, and investigate limb by limb and part by part. When the body is invited to a deep relaxation, a real change may take place. But it's not a question of forcing a release. I place my best attention on my physical parts and enter into a dialogue with them. This sitting is also a practical preparation to noticing the many times during the day when I'm hyper-tense in action, when I use my hands with much more force than needed for a particular job they are doing; when my shoulders are a couple of inches higher and tighter than they need to be.

We see the world upside-down, explained Gurdjieff when he spoke to his early Russian groups about the critical relationship between the body, heart and head. Who's the boss? I thought often about the arrows Ouspensky drew for *In Search of the Miraculous*, to express Gurdjieff's comparison of the way a normal human being, the "man-without-quotation-marks," lives and how most of us live. In the first case, the arrows went from Real "I" or the Master to the head, then to the heart and only last to the body because "I" should direct the head, the powerhouse of emotional energy needs to follow, and the body should respond or obey. But our topsy-turvy life is lived from below. We are motivated by how the body feels at any moment, which leads into emotional reactions to which the head adds its formulations, reasons and explanations. The arrows are reversed. They run from body to heart to head. There is no Master. Everything obeys the body, which obeys outside influences.

What, then, is the right place of the body? We were told that it should be a servant. This possible direction from higher to lower constitutes an authority, literally a new order in us. Such a hierarchy is reflected in two prayers that were sometimes spoken in a movements class or at the end of a sitting. *I-Wish-To-Be* and *I-Am-Here* lead us from "I" to the head, heart and body, or from "I" to the place "I" dwells.

At the same time, everything in us and outside us is in movement. Madame de Salzmann reminded us that our degree of availability to serve something higher varied. "Sometimes it is one part that leads my wish and sometimes another," she explained. "Sometimes it is true that *I am-here-to serve*, but sometimes what is true is that *here-to serve-I am*, and at other times it is another way: *to serve-I am-here.*"

The classes of sacred dances and movements—a royal road to noticing how upside-down or one-centered we often are—awaken us to our habitual ways of thinking, feeling and moving. They engage these parts or centers of ourselves every time we are asked to take unaccustomed positions, in unusual or conflicting rhythms, breaking the chains of habit. According to Gurdjieff, "a man can never get away from his repertory of intellectual and emotional postures until his moving postures are changed."

He had a very effective way of surprising or shocking us into a new experience of ourselves, which he had used

frequently at the Institute in the 1920s and again in the movements classes I attended in the winter of 1949. It was the Stop
Exercise. Sometimes he would suddenly shout "*STOP!*" in the
midst of an exercise and we would freeze where we stood. Woe
to those who moved after the command or were caught in
the wrong position and fell victim to his scathing comments.
Other times he would scatter litchi nuts at the class during a
break, and call "*Stop!*" after the orderly rows of dancers had
dissolved into acquisitive individuals trying to catch one.
People would freeze instantly into whatever position they
were passing through as they fought for physical balance. It
happened once when my stepfather was reaching out for a nut.
He froze instantly with both hands outstretched toward the
ground and one foot high in the air. I watched, breathlessly, as
Gurdjieff got up from his chair and walked slowly around him,
commenting quietly, even admiringly, "Ah, Doctor!"

Madame de Salzmann often returned to the crucial
connection between the head and the body and the need for
us to maintain an equal attention between them. Without it,
she said, the centers cannot function harmoniously. "Put the
mind on the body and a new feeling will appear," she repeated
on many occasions. "Neither one should be stronger than the
other. They need to have equal force. Then real feeling will
arise." When people told her they couldn't make this connection among the centers, she exhorted them once again to "stay
in front of the lack."

Her call to evoke balance in the psycho-physical relationship by paying attention to the relationship between the head
and the body was one of the primary reasons that, years later,
I came to study the Alexander Technique. I was intrigued by F.
M. Alexander's emphasis on the key role played by freeing the
neck from tension, so that the head rests lightly poised atop
the neck/spine, rather than being crunched down into it, as

the rest of the body releases. I also discussed the head/body relationship with Pauline de Dampierre, who often spoke with me by phone from Paris in the years after my parents died. She invited me to work with greater simplicity, saying that the problem is that the body is not tuned to what is higher. "Stay with your impression of the body, without flinching from its coarseness or wishing to be different," she exhorted me. Heeding her words, I discovered that it was possible to stay present in the body a little longer as soon as I saw my tendency to focus away from it towards an imagined "better state." When I stay with how I really am at a given moment, two sides of myself are simultaneously present: something coarse and something finer, watching.

"Gurdjieff said work is awareness," she reminded me. "We have a sensitivity we always use for the purpose of things coming from outside, but we should become sensitive to this other *something finer*. We can find it if we stay with our awareness of the body, just as it is. The body is a fact. Our challenge is not to always want to be different, but to have an inner awareness of the body. Be aware of how you are, and then *stay in it*! Don't change anything."

♦

My Encounter with Gurdjieff

Only what cannot be shaken is your own. — Gurdjieff

My first memory of G. I. Gurdjieff was not of a man but of a bed covered with candy. We must have gone to meet him when I was very small, and my mother must have led me into a bedroom where I was told to choose from among open boxes of every kind of candy a child could imagine. All I can remember is how excited and amazed I felt. Those who knew Gurdjieff were familiar with his custom of distributing candies and chocolates to both children and adults on many occasions. It was as integral a part of his direct teaching methods as his angry shouts, his caustic commands, or the quiet comments he made in a low voice, whose often-devastating message was only recognized by one set of ears in the crowd around him. Whatever his aim, he made a lasting impression.

During World War II, my brother and I became aware of another life led by our parents. They went to lectures of P. D. Ouspensky several nights a week and often disappeared on Sundays to work for the day as farmhands in Mendham, New Jersey, at a house Rodney Collin-Smith and his wife had donated to the Ouspenskys. Madame Ouspensky lived there and had turned the house into a place of practical work for Gurdjieffians, along the lines of the former Institute for the Harmonious Development of Man. Franklin Farms had permanent residents, some refugees from wartime London and some Sunday visitors from the city who came for a day of farm labor. This "work in life," an opportunity for people to observe themselves while functioning under demanding conditions, is still one of the essential practices of the Gurdjieff teaching.

In December 1948, Gurdjieff made his first postwar appearance in New York, and I met him for the second time. My brother and I were brought to the Wellington Hotel for dinner at his invitation ("Bring *resultats*" was his command and his way of referring to his students' children). "Can he read my mind?" I asked nervously as we prepared to go to the hotel. "Of course," answered my stepfather lightly and rather callously, I later felt. I was consumed with fear of this unknown man, wondering how I could hide my thoughts from him.

We entered a large rectangular living room almost empty of furniture. A few people were in chairs against the walls but most sat cross-legged on the floor. Gurdjieff was seated in a chair at the center of an end wall. Almost immediately someone began to read a chapter from his unpublished book, *Beelzebub's Tales to his Grandson*. Everyone but me listened attentively. I sat against the long wall with my legs stretched out in front and couldn't stop myself from staring at him. There he was, the magician who had my parents coming home at three and four A.M., the cause of their getting up tired and crabby every morning, the reason they practiced strange dance positions during the day.

During the reading, Gurdjieff's great bald head turned in a slow, implacable arc from the person sitting beside him at his left all the way around to the right side, as he studied his listening students one by one. Every time his gaze passed over me I shrank back inside and tried to think the right thoughts, whatever they might be. His deep look was all the more overwhelming because it seemed to take absolutely no notice of me and my terror, nor did his face change expression as his head swiveled inexorably on.

Later, in the dining room, my fear was refueled by one of his well-known displays of anger. Dinner had ended and coffee was being served. My godmother had brought him a bowl of sugar lumps, which he liked to put in his mouth to sweeten his coffee as he drank it. But she had been unable to find the small square ones he liked, so these lumps were large rectangles. On seeing them, his shouts of outrage filled the room. Suddenly my godfather stood up and said in a quaking voice, "Mr. Gurdjieff, you cannot speak to my wife that way!" Like a snuffed candle, Gurdjieff's rage disappeared instantly, as he quietly said "Bravo!"

On January 13th, 1949, I made my second trip to the

Wellington Hotel for Gurdjieff's yearly celebration of the Russian New Year. All the children had been invited and were introduced to another of his favorite teaching methods: that his students make difficult choices, decisions from which there was no turning back. Shortly after we arrived, I was put in charge of a deep dish brimming with silver dollars, while a younger girl was handed a bowl of crisp new ten-dollar bills. Then he asked each of the children to choose, as "a gift from Mr. Gurdjieff," either eight silver dollars or a ten-dollar bill. We politicked among ourselves as to which would be the better choice while the adults watched, amused and curious.

I championed a pragmatic approach, arguing that $10 was more than $8 any way you looked at it. I don't remember why I tried so hard to convince them, but in looking back I now think I was trying to drive the herd rather than be a part of it. In any case, most of the boys immediately agreed with me, and when the fatal moment came to choose, all the boys but one opted for the ten-dollar bill, while the girls carefully selected silver. Finally only the bowl-holders were left to make a decision. The other girl took a bill from her bowl, and I was about to reach over and do the same, when an unbidden thought stopped my hand. A ten-dollar bill would be quickly spent, but the silver dollars were solid treasure, as well as a memento of this enigmatic man who had such an influence on my parents.

My head was now pitted against my heart. Embarrassed to expose such impractical weakness in front of eighty or ninety people, I quickly reached into my own bowl to count out eight silver dollars. I've always been glad I did. I set them in a necklace I sometimes wear on January 13th, but the part of the story that Gurdjieff would have enjoyed most is that each coin is now worth $20-$30. Who knows how much they would bring on eBay as a gift from him!

Later that evening Gurdjieff asked Katherine Hulme,

author of *The Nun's Story*, to tell the children a story. She sat down next to him and painted a melodramatic picture of a refugee child traveling alone on a plane. She went on and on about how terribly sad it was not to have parents and how lonely the child must have felt, in a whinier and whinier voice. Although we were bored, we remained politely attentive. I wondered whether this was part of the Gurdjieff "show." The adults were also getting restless. When she finished, Gurdjieff leaned toward us where we were sitting on the floor at his feet and said slowly with a smile, rolling out every word: "Now, children, you understand what means Crocodile Tears!" The room reverberated with laughter as we looked at each other, relieved that these grown-ups *did* have a sense of humor!

Later, when we left with my parents, I said goodbye to him like the good girl I was, giving him a quick peck on the cheek. "Aha!" he said, turning to congratulate my parents: "Never been kissed!" This struck me as incomprehensibly rude, but my parents assured me that I would understand better when I was older.

♦

A True Inheritance

Dances are for the mind. — Gurdjieff

Soon after, I was taken to a movements class at Carnegie Hall Studios and told to join a few other children in the back, behind twelve or thirteen rows of taller and taller adults standing in six files. Music began, and we tried to imitate the arm gestures and foot rhythms of the elders moving in front of us. What was going on? It was both interesting and laughable. The people nearest us obviously didn't know what they were doing as they waved their arms in the air, so we tried to figure it out for ourselves. To be on time was obviously important, and to take correct positions. But so many people in front of us were making mistakes that we were sure we weren't getting it right. Later, our parents helped us understand the positions and I went to the classes as often as I could.

From the beginning, I loved the challenge of the dances and exercises, even from the back row. So I attended the classes several evenings a week in spite of school early the next day. One evening I was summoned from the back of the class by an angry Mr. Gurdjieff. In no uncertain terms, he told me to sit on the floor in front of him and learn the positions correctly from my stepfather in file one of the front row. From his scathing tone in language I could hardly understand, I realized I was accused of having "spoiled" some of the positions. I smoldered at this unjust attack, knowing exactly who in front of me had messed up. But a pleaser rather than a fighter, I sat down quietly at his feet and watched the class until everyone was ordered to sit down on the floor and rest.

Gurdjieff then handed me his hat filled with chocolates and told me to pass them out to some twenty visitors and students behind him, watching the class. Always the good girl, I jumped up and began to thrust it at each of them in turn, so they could choose their favorite kind. Instantly Gurdjieff was on his feet shouting at me, but I couldn't understand what he was saying. Realizing this, he went into an elegant mimicry of me heedlessly handing the hat around at arm's length, not caring who chose what. Then he shook his head sternly, pantomiming how he wanted it done. Holding an imaginary hat in front of him, he examined its contents gravely and chose a chocolate with great care. He presented it with exaggerated politeness to the nearest person, then elaborately selected another chocolate for the next person. He passed the hat back to me and gestured for me to do likewise. I was now angrier than before as well as humiliated by all this exposure. Not only had I been falsely accused of taking wrong dance positions, but I was now being forced to make decisions for adults who probably would hate me for giving them the wrong chocolate!

After I had offered the chocolates one by one to the visitors and returned Gurdjieff's hat to him, my public ordeal came to an end. He sat back in his chair and signaled the class to get up with a big upward sweep of his arms and the command "Allez-ooop!" I was allowed to take my place in the 14th row of the 3rd file again, to carry on as best I could. I made myself as invisible as possible—grateful, for once, that a forest of adults towered between me and the front of the room.

Twenty years later I went with my children to the Russian church in Lima, Peru, on the anniversary of Gurdjieff's death. Smelling the incense and thinking about him, I realized with a shock what he had wanted me to understand. Because I was desperate to please others, I always clung to a middle-of-the road position and assessed how the wind blew before making decisions. Gurdjieff forced me to make my own choice. I, the waffler and pleaser, should not let others decide what they would take from me. I must choose what to give. Unpleasant as it was, I recognized myself and was grateful.

Although I continued to attend these wonderfully enlivening classes, I avoided notice as much as possible. One evening he stopped us for a rest, as was his custom, because these classes lasted several hours. We sat with our feet stretched in front of us on the floor, hands on our knees. Gurdjieff took out a bag of litchi nuts, and began to throw them in every direction at the class. My hidden anger resurfaced as I said silently to myself, "If you're so great, I dare you to throw one all the way back here!" Almost immediately, one bounced into my lap.

On another evening I sat on the floor near the piano when the class ended and watched everyone stream out, followed by Gurdjieff. His umbrella was still hooked over a pipe on the wall near me. The good girl in me grabbed it as I rushed across the room after him. "Mr. Gurdjieff (breathlessly), you forgot your umbrella!" He turned back slowly, like a great cat stretching in slow motion. He looked at me pensively and then said formally, with a smile, "You *very* kind!" I preened. He continued to look at me, adding an afterthought, his voice quieter and his attention more withdrawn. "Sometimes." Somehow this didn't offend me. I realized he knew my inner quakings and strivings, but I was no longer frightened by him. It was as if the grandfather I never knew had spoken.

After Gurdjieff left New York in early 1949, having given orders that we prepare a demonstration for his return in the fall, his students continued to gather several times a week to practice the exercises he had left with us. But, in October, instead of coming back to New York he died in Paris, leaving everyone dismayed.

Classes continued in preparation for a future demonstration, which was felt to be even more important now that his students were responsible for keeping his work alive. While Gurdjieff remained a mystery to me, both fearsome and beckoning, the movements and sacred dances that he had brought back from his years of travels with the Seekers of Truth had an immediate effect on my life. Filled with a new sense of independence, I finished my homework early those nights and hurried to Carnegie Hall Dance Studios on the Fifth Avenue bus. Wrestling with the exciting demands of the rhythms and positions, I was undisturbed, even unaware, that besides myself and one other young girl (William Segal's daughter Elizabeth), there were no other children in the class. There I was, along with rows of grim-faced adults making efforts, I supposed, to save their souls. But my aim was quite different. I went there full of expectation, hungry to be challenged, gleefully pitting myself against what often seemed impossible odds, experiencing the joy of movement.

For these dances and exercises demanded a total commitment of attention from the performer, far beyond our usual capacity for concentration. The first dilemma I met with in each new exercise was how to remember the unusual rhythms, the sophisticated combinations of foot, leg, arm, head and torso positions and displacements and the order in which they came. My teachers at that time, Alfred Etiévant and Jessmin Howarth, left us no time to think it out ahead of time. We were called into immediate action with little time to integrate one or two of the aspects of the exercises before we were asked to bring all the parts together as best we could.

To add to the complexity, the positions of one part of the body often came on different counts from those of another, or appeared at unusual places in the rhythm, usually maintained by the feet. To catch them on the fly and bring one's body into action, making the right movements at the right time, demanded complete attentiveness. But a clear head, though essential to keep order and direct oneself into the necessary positions, wasn't enough. The struggle to move swiftly and accurately from one pose to the next also called for an immediate receptivity in the body. So on the one hand, I had to remember the various rhythms and positions, and on the other, I had to be available to move instantly, trusting the body's experience to know what came next. I couldn't withdraw in my usual way to figure it all out first and "get it right," because there was no time for my mind to be sure before my body was called into the next position.

If I forgot a sequence or became distracted by a sense of success at finally "getting it right," I'd find myself trailing ignominiously behind the rest of the class. By then it was too late to catch up. Worse still, I might end up standing frozen in confusion at too many signals. Yet I headed home from those classes brimming with joy, unable to sleep. Something new was singing inside me—a new sense of special alertness and a kind of happiness at just being there that would stay with me for days. It was my first experience of the *practice* of presence.

Although I didn't join a group at that time, I sometimes attended readings of *Beelzebub's Tales to His Grandson* and often joined the Sunday work at Franklin Farms in Mendham, New Jersey, sharing a day of farm work which ended with a movements class. As a city dweller who was once a country child, I loved working in the gardens best, and my favorite task was weeding artichokes. It was there that I tasted my first ripe peach, dangling off a tree over my head—the most delicious fruit I have ever eaten! As for the many house assignments, the most challenging for someone who loathed making decisions was the team that separated tomatoes into categories: good (for sale), on the verge (for today), going bad (for cooking up into sauce), and rotten (to dump in the compost heap). Those decisions, made working side by side with people who would get twice as much done in the same time, seemed like Suffering with a capital "S."

But the real nourishment came from the movements classes, which provided me with a totally new kind of food, food for *being*. Some essential flavor of Gurdjieff's Work entered me through the dances and exercises and created, on some underground level, a non-verbal understanding of the teaching. For these dances embody a three-centered experience. Calling for simultaneous effort from head, heart and body, they shook me from habitual ways of moving, often awakening me from a somnambulant state. Most important, they gave me a taste of sharpened awareness. My longing for this awareness and my dissatisfaction with a life that does not include it are my true inheritance from my parents and from contact with G. I. Gurdjieff and his Work.

Even as I enjoyed a new sense of self-importance after college as a reporter at *Time* magazine, I harbored a secret wish to participate in one of the movements films that Madame de Salzmann made from time to time. One day, while she was in New York on a late winter visit, I learned that she was about to make a new film in Paris. I told her I wished to come for three months and take part. She replied that I could certainly take part but not with time reservations. If I signed up, I had to be there until the end of the film production.

Having spent a lonely year in Paris during college, I hesitated to commit to an open-ended stay, and wrestled with my decision for weeks. Once, walking toward Madame de Salzmann down the long corridor at Franklin Farms, determined to say "yes" as soon as our paths crossed, I remained speechless. She looked at me with sympathy and passed by. Finally, during a long dark night just before she returned to Paris, I came to a clear place in myself where I knew I would turn down this unique possibility. The decision was not intellectual, but came from deep within me after weeks of inner torment. It was led by the force of a new truth that blossomed in my heart like a gift: doing this or that wasn't going to change my life. Only *being* was important.

I went to see her the next morning to tell her how unhappy I was to turn down the opportunity. "It would change every-thing!" I added sorrowfully. She nodded sympathetically at my pain: "*For a little while*," she corrected me gently, emphasizing the words, "things would be different." Her message settled into me like another new truth: no single effort or experience can change everything, except for a short time. As it turned out, the spring filming was unsuccessful. The following September, just as a new effort at filming began in Paris, I left New York for Lima, Peru, to teach movements classes to a new South American group. There I met my future husband and a new installment of my life story began.

♦

Connecting with the Gurdjieff Work

The Way begins above the level of ordinary life. — Gurdjieff

Gurdjieff never claimed to have invented his teaching. He said his ideas came from a great oral tradition kept hidden by its devotees throughout the ages. It was still alive during his lifetime in obscure and isolated desert monasteries.

Even in childhood, he had restlessly pursued answers to major questions about the meaning of life. As a young man he joined a group of men and women who called themselves "Seekers of Truth." In a riveting mixture of myth and storytelling in *Meetings with Remarkable Men,* he told how they searched for twenty years in deserts and mountains in the Middle East and Central Asia for traces of lost knowledge. In 1978, Madame de Salzmann made a film, directed by Peter Brook, about this epic search for the meaning and aim of human existence. It is now available at many video stores and at *www.Parabola.org.*

My stepfather, Dr. William J. Welch, attended Gurdjieff in October 1949 at the American Hospital of Paris, during the last days of his life, and was present when Gurdjieff said to Madame de Salzmann, "Do not build larger than you understand. The essential thing is to prepare a nucleus of people capable of responding to the demand which will appear." After his death, groups were organized by people who had worked directly with him or with his students. For more than forty years these groups remained related to each other through Madame de Salzmann, who led the development of the Gurdjieff Work until she died in 1991 at the age of 101. During that time, study of the Work spread all over the world.

It's important for those interested in understanding Gurdjieff's message today to recognize that he taught directly, person-to-person. No books were available to explain what he meant. Everything had to be paid for by one's own effort. The students who listened to him, or heard his manuscripts read aloud, treasured every new disclosure, forced to wrestle with the many contradictions intentionally provided. For Gurdjieff permitted nothing to be taken for granted, but insisted that his ideas be put into practice at once. The work of his followers included the effort to assimilate an enormous quantity of ideas and material into their minds and hearts, knowing they might never have a chance to hear it again. Even after the books became available, the music written with Thomas de Hartmann and for the movements exercises passed from group to group through careful hand-copying until its publication a few years ago.

All this made a student's path both rich and difficult. Gurdjieff, the man, was never easy to understand because he always gave his messages in two or three different, often conflicting, ways. At one meeting he might announce that "Man is a being who can do," and at the next explain how we can do nothing, that man is a machine, completely automatic, a sheep to be shorn. Clearly his intention was to force his students to critical evaluation and self-examination. They would have to deal with contradiction by putting the separate pieces of the human puzzle together in new ways. Obliged to make major efforts to hear and remember the readings, and to seek answers to questions wherever they could, their task was to re-create the authentic teaching in their own minds and hearts, and thereby make it their own.

At Gurdjieff's death, his students were left with the manuscript of his great allegory, *Beelzebub's Tales to His Grandson*, a mythic history of humanity on the scale of the universe. Two other books carry his voice: *Life is Real Only Then, When "I Am,"* which he never completed, and *Views from the Real World*, compiled from notes taken during his lectures and group meetings. That same year the first book about the teaching was published. *In Search of the Miraculous: Fragments of an Unknown Teaching*, by P. D. Ouspensky, was a faithful account of his years in Russia as Gurdjieff's student.

The current situation of the Gurdjieff Work is very different. Hundreds of books about his teaching are now available as well as Gurdjieff's own writings and those of his immediate followers (see Bibliography). But books can only give you a preliminary taste of this Work. Many of them simply recap earlier Gurdjieff literature, trivialize and oversimplify it or are inventions like those of a purported "Mr. G." who propounds what he calls "The Fourth Way Circle." There are also personal inventions like the recent studies of the Enneagram. While the Enneagram is an ancient and very real symbol rediscovered by Gurdjieff and spoken of in his teaching, it has recently been dressed up as a vehicle for personality analysis—a use totally unrelated to its real esoteric meaning or to his teaching. Like the astrological system, the enneagram offers enough complexity to mirror the complexities of human nature, but such use of this symbol falls outside the Gurdjieff teaching and would have to be judged separately on its own merits.

As for an Internet search, it produces more than 130,000 references and a host of websites, many calling themselves "Gurdjieff groups." Despite all these written resources, it's well to recall that this is a largely oral teaching. Like the practice of presence, the understanding of this Work cannot be acquired through books and talk, but only through repeated efforts and work with others who follow the same path.

Authentic groups usually meet once a week with the intention of bringing active and conscious inquiry into everyday life. Gurdjieff's ideas are discussed and experiments related to them are suggested, There are weekly classes of the movements and sacred dances as well as physical work and creative exploration in arts and crafts, generally organized for Sundays, and week-long intensive work periods in the summer.

These studies and exercises engage the student in an effort of special attention that can lead to a more balanced state. Progress in one's understanding depends not only on renewed weekly work with others in groups, but also on daily efforts of self-observation and the practice of presence in the midst of one's own life conditions. Quiet work is also important. It seeks a silent mind and is somewhat comparable to Zen meditation, or to the "prayer of the heart" practiced by the Desert Fathers of the Philokalia (see Chapter Five on Prayer and Meditation).

The search for groups with a direct lineage to Gurdjieff may not be easy, because there are many claimants. Some now call themselves "Gurdjieffian" or "Fourth Way" groups. Some are study groups based on secondary sources. Others organize their students to visit bookstores and slip bookmarks advertising their meetings into any and all books about Gurdjieff and the Work. One factor that can help you discriminate between them is that real groups don't "market" themselves. Gurdjieff always made it difficult to glean his message so that people would have to make efforts, and those who followed him continued to feel that the teaching was of most value to those prepared to work seriously to discover it.

So if you run into enigmatic and charismatic "gurus" who tell people what to do with their life and how to live it, who promise the moon and wisdom—guaranteed in a very short time—you can be sure they are not true Gurdjieffians. Active engagement in a path of self-development is not a quick fix, nor is it synonymous with turning oneself over to another person. When monks go into seclusion or East Indians lay their hearts, minds and bodies at the feet of a guru, they do it for a very specific, voluntary reason, related to the study of obedience, to giving up their petty willfulness in order to serve something higher. Conscious obedience can be a path toward developing presence and the capacity to hear the true voice of the Master within oneself.

As for those who seek the sacred through drugs, they may throw away their best discriminatory capacity, not to mention their common sense, to follow a dream. As Gurdjieff said when he was asked about it, the danger of experimenting with drugs is that forcing one's way into the "fourth room," the place of the Master, may come at a high price to one's organism. And the room may be empty.

Several questions are worth raising with a representative of a group before you commit to it. Why do they advertise (if they do) and what is the cost of attendance? If, as in some cases, you are asked to give a tenth of your salary or a large sum of money, I can only say *Buyer Beware!* You may well feel that you would pay anything required, which shows a real valuation for the most precious nourishment on the planet, the food for *being.* But such groups are not authentic. True Gurdjieffian group leaders may be enigmatic and sometimes even charismatic, but they don't market the Gurdjieff Work or sell what they believe to be precious material to all who ask. It's up to the seeker to find a way to earn it.

Real groups don't ask for contributions until new

members have worked for several months or even a year in a preparatory group and demonstrated that this is an appropriate path for them. At that point a small monthly fee will probably be requested of those who can afford it, to help provide upkeep for the non-profit foundation. For those interested in investigating further, a website providing information about the location of authentic Gurdjieff groups can be found at *http://www.gurdjieff-foundation-newyork. org*. Another useful source, which includes an overview of key books and a wealth of other material, is the Gurdjieff International Review (www.gurdjieff.org).

Don't go back to sleep.
People are going back and forth
Across the threshold
Where the two worlds meet
The door is round and open.
Don't go back to sleep. — Rumi

Two

INVESTING IN LOSS:
THE TAO OF T'AI CHI CH'UAN

*In the pursuit of learning, every day something is
acquired. In the pursuit of Tao, every day something
is dropped.*

— Lao-tzu

Nurtured by the ideas of Gurdjieff's teachings from an
early age, I was awakened to the spirit of inquiry and a growing
hunger for a state more connected with my own authentic
nature. The possibility of bringing self-awareness to birth in the
sensation of the body must exist. It seemed that for this it was
necessary to develop a *conscious intending* to discover what was
happening "below the surface." While I had already experienced
moments of an entirely different state, I longed for more,
yearning to live on another, higher level of consciousness.

Unfortunately, those few precious momentary gifts seemed
to be wrapped in a demand for objective self-discipline. After
all, one of my most revered Gurdjieff teachers had said, "Very

good is not enough." I thought I had to be perfect to "get there," that spiritual success was one more thing to add to my long list of strivings—to be a good daughter, good wife, good teacher, good friend. As I continued to study and practice the Gurdjieff Work, I often felt I was reaching for the moon. I wallowed in self-disapproval even as the movements and sacred dances called me back into balance and sent new energy coursing through my blood.

In 1960, I went to Peru to teach the movements. There I met and soon married a Peruvian in the new group that had formed. A few years later, when I visited New York from Lima, Madame de Salzmann suggested that I study T'ai Chi Ch'uan. I had often heard her speak of the importance of developing a conscious relationship between the head and the body, so I was eager to see for myself whether T'ai Chi might help me come alive in a different way.

To my great good fortune I shared my mother's private classes with Master T. T. Liang, who had just arrived in New York from Taiwan. A diminutive man in his early 70s, Liang had suffered through a dangerous illness some twenty years before and felt that his life had been saved by learning and practicing T'ai Chi. He spoke almost no English at that time and the many books now available hadn't yet been written, so I struggled to understand what was going on, opening myself to the wordless experience. There were no easy explanations to interrupt my active inner questioning.

However, information was available about Taoism, so I began to study the ideas behind the exercise, discovering a world that didn't call on me to perform as an aggressive achiever. The origins of T'ai Chi Ch'uan (literally the "Supreme Ultimate" Boxing) stem from an ancient path of relationship to the natural world, which celebrates the power of the yielding to overcome the firm and the liquid to overcome the rigid—just as water flowing over rocks will gradually wear them down. It was a path of inner balance through active engagement with the cosmic forces that rule us and of which we are a part. The "True Man," according to the Taoists, is one who consciously fills the space he occupies between heaven and earth with his own presence. His feet are firmly planted on the earth, which nourishes him, while his head reaches into the heavens with an awakened mind, through which finer energies can enter him.

The word *Tao* is usually equated with *way* or *path*, but in ancient times it was called The Great Meaning. Richard Wilhelm, who brought several key Chinese texts to the attention of the Western world more than seventy years ago, referred to it as "a track which, though fixed itself, leads from the beginning directly to the goal," indicating that although the Tao itself does not move, it is the source of all movement.

Tao is the original ground of being out of which Nothingness (*Wu Chi*) gives birth to *T'ai Chi*, the One, the Great Movement, or primordial spirit. T'ai Chi divides into two as the principles of light (*yang*) and darkness (*yin*) begin their complementary dance, interrelating with each other to produce on earth the Ten Thousand Things, including humans. And in us there is also both stillness and movement.

Over time I saw that although radically different in speed and style from the Gurdjieff movements, T'ai Chi nevertheless contained a similar principle, that one's finest attention be continually directed from the mind onto the body, or rather, as Madame de Salzmann corrected me, onto the energy in movement. The slow pace and endless repetition of this meditation in movement helped bring my high-soaring spiritual ambition back down to earth as my conscious intention shifted from earning another step up the ladder of spiritual evolution to rooting my feet in the ground.

What were these movements? You have probably seen T'ai Chi in a film or on TV—a group of people, usually in a park or at the seashore, turning rhythmically to face every direction in a synchronized slow movement of arms, legs and torso. With their legs firmly planted on the ground like tree trunks, their torsos turn and bend while their arms wave like willow branches responding to every wind. You are looking at a meditative exercise and martial art dating back into the mists of Chinese legend.

According to legend, Ta Mo, an Indian monk, came to China in the early 7th century to practice meditation and invented an exercise to improve the physical well-being of the monks at the Shaolin Monastery, who were in poor condition. Next, sometime around AD 750, a woodcutter named Hsu Hsuan-ping performed the Long Boxing Exercise, which includes some positions recognizable in contemporary T'ai Chi Ch'uan. However, credit for the development of the exercise closer to what it is today seems to rest with "the Immortal" Chang San-feng, who lived in the 13th century.

Chang, a magistrate who retired from his job to travel all over China, studied meditation techniques and martial arts wherever he could find Taoist teachers. He was a dedicated student of the *I Ching* or *Book of Changes*, perhaps the earliest known spiritual document. One day, the story goes, he watched a snake and a crane fight each other, attacking and feinting again and again. The snake always managed to twist away out of reach as the crane's sharp beak came after it, then it turned and darted at the crane's long legs, which the latter protected by lowering his wing against them. Finally they both gave up the battle, unconquered.

Here was living proof that the best way to defeat force was by yielding, a central message of Taoism. What Chang had just witnessed was an incarnation of the interplay between *yin* and *yang*, in which the strong became the yielding until the yielding became strong again. He went on to develop a series of movements based on the principles of the *I Ching* and on his studies of the natural world, in combination with some of the Shaolin exercises he had learned in his years at that temple.

Today there are a number of schools of T'ai Chi. I studied the Yang style—by far the most popular in China and around the world. It is practiced in a series of movements linked together. Some versions are called "Short Forms" with fewer sequences, taking some ten minutes to perform. Other versions are known as "Long Forms" which have more or repeated movements, taking perhaps twenty or thirty minutes to go through depending on how slowly you move (the slower the better). Some teachers develop their own personal style, so don't be surprised if you discover several Yang versions in the same town.

Whatever style is available, it's important in the beginning to learn from a teacher. Studying from a book or videos is impractical for several reasons. First, the subtle, flowing movement between positions is an essential element of each form, difficult to improvise without following a living, moving example, and second, words or diagrams can't really describe how to focus the attention. The presence and way of moving of a senior teacher communicates a lesson in itself. Third, while it may help to watch a video and attempt to move with it, it's difficult to know when your positions may be off-track without a teacher's objective eye to point it out.

◆

Dancing In the Field of Cinnabar

In resting, be as still as a mountain; in moving, move like the current of a great river. — Wang Tsung-yueh

Because I've always been a busy person, it was a new experience to stand still without doing anything. I grew to love it. When I worked in a doctor's office I often had to wait in a darkened room for X-rays to come out of the developing tank. As I stood there, I became aware of my body—its weight, its balance, its uprightness, as well as the downward pull of gravity. Then I'd begin the first few movements of T'ai Chi, loving the fact that from the horizontal view of time, these movements were rooted in practices that were centuries old but that, from the vertical view, they could only exist in me in the present moment. There I stood between earth and heaven in the back room of a doctor's office, feet firmly planted on the ground, mind alert to the sensory perception of my body and open to the world of spirit above.

To sense the T'ai Chi experience, imagine for a moment that you've already learned the Yang Solo Exercise from a Chinese master and you practice it every morning. Each day you get out of bed, throw cold water on your face and proceed to a quiet space at least four feet square. There you stand, still foggy with sleep or agitated by the night's dreaming, with your feet shoulder-width apart. Before you move, you send your not-very-awakened thought all the way down to the floor, trying to figure out how your weight is distributed. More on soles than heels? More on the inside than outside? More on one foot than the other? Sending your thought down through your legs and feet and into the floor below, you root yourself in the earth as your feet wake up little by little and send messages back to your brain.

Soon energy may begin to flow upward, starting at *Yung-ch'uan* (Bubbling Spring), an acupressure point at the center of the indentation in the middle of your soles. But even if you don't feel it, you turn your thought toward that flow as if the energy were rising up from the floor, through your legs, flowing up into the spine and then to the top of your head. Now you are ready to place your heels together, to swivel your toes diagonally apart, to invite your thought energy to flow back down from the crown of the head, through the body and into the right leg and foot as your weight shifts onto it. Then you place your left foot to the left side, shoulder-width apart, bending your knees to begin the introduction to T'ai Chi Ch'uan.

As you move, you consciously scan your body to see what's going on inside. You may discover that your thoughts have been turning like quick-flying birds or more like clouds slowly drifting across the sky. Or you may be fired up with an emotional reaction. Were you in an argument? Are you angry at your boss for making you get up so early, or anxious about finishing a task? Or you may be just plain tired. All this and more can fill your body with tension, which is why general relaxation (*sung*) is the very first effort.

Notice any tension? You invite it to melt away as you bring your attention to the belly region, clear your head of thoughts, let go in the shoulders and empty the thorax. It may help to imagine that your tensions are slowly liquefying, starting at the top of the head, as if your body were an iceberg that the warm sun is melting. Thus the *ch'i* or vital energy moves down to its resting place a couple of inches below the navel and inside the belly.

In China this central pool or source of vital energy, *ch'i*, the focal point for meditation and energy, is called the *tan-t'ien*.

The term literally means the "Cinnabar Field," which refers to crystals of mercuric sulfide or a vermilion pigment sometimes called Dragon's Blood. The Japanese word for this location in the belly is *hara*; the Sufis call it *kath*. You sink your thought, your energy, your *ch'i* so it can accumulate in this place of power, ready to give you the speed or force you need when required.

Now you are moving without resistance or hesitation as your weight shifts from one foot to the other and your arms make slow circling motions through the air—your hands continually aware of each other and of the space between them. Each position melts into the next in a continuous flow, so that an observer wouldn't know where one form ended and the next began.

But since you do this every morning, it's easy for your mind to wander after the first few attempts at concentration. There are a million things to think about as the day begins and you know these movements well. That's why you may have to remind yourself that T'ai Chi is not just an exercise for the body although it's highly recommended for health, improved circulation and staying power. Your teacher explained that its purpose is to unite body and mind, and for this it's necessary to concentrate on every moment of every movement.

From the Taoist point of view, your body represents a unity that is part "full" and part "empty" at any given moment. For example, when you shift your weight from one foot to the other you are emptying one leg and filling the other as if you poured water slowly from one glass to another. If you are attentive, you may become simultaneously aware of the leg that's emptying and the other that's filling up. The next step would be awareness of both of them as parts of the greater whole that is "you."

During these movements, the spine should remain straight as a plumb line. The vertebral column is the "pathway of the soul" when it is truly vertical, a ladder between earth and heaven. The head is poised delicately at the top as if it hangs from the ceiling on a string. The flow of movement should be easy and regular. So you monitor it to be sure you are neither hurrying nor slowing down, but at a steady pace, as if you were pulling a silk thread from a cocoon, taking care not to go too fast or too slow so the thread won't break.

Each movement begins from the floor, passing up through the legs to the trunk and on to the arms, which are light and free like the branches of a bamboo tree swaying in the wind. You feel power coming up through your legs and slightly bent knees as you repeatedly "root" your feet into the earth. You may have to recall your wandering mind to focus on your movements—not only the physical changes but, more subtly, the experience of your energy in motion. Although a hundred thoughts call your attention away, you return to center your mind again on the *tan-t'ien*, as if grasping the string of a floating balloon before it moves too far out of reach.

Gradually the fog lifts from your waking-up mind and you begin to experience a sense of lightness, a kind of opening up in all your joints, as if there's more space between the bones. Your thought becomes clear and alert to every tiny change of circumstance in mind and body. The air blows softly against your skin. Perhaps when you first began to move, you had to concentrate to keep your attention on the slow-moving positions, but now your mind freely accompanies them. You are attracted to a new and delicious sensation, result of the connection between two parts of your nervous system. Your mind and body are listening to each other.

Since you no longer need to struggle for concentration, your movements flow like the current of a river. Feel the heaviness of the air as if you were swimming underwater. In fact, many T'ai Chi masters recommend what they call "dry swimming." When you imagine that you are moving through water rather than air, it brings awareness of the substance you move through and the lightness of your own body by comparison, reinforcing the impression that the body is buoyant and pliable.

The river image is a good one. Although you feel you move easily, this freedom is not a rebellion against the forces of nature but a joining of your current to the greater current of energy of which you are a part. To achieve it, you may have to give up your expectation of how you want or imagine it to be and enter into relation with whatever's going on. It's not easy to stay in that current. You move and allow yourself to be moved at the same time, without the constriction of thought or ideas about results.

Your mind, so full of scattered plans and worries a few minutes before, is now calm and clear, as if the quality of the water has changed. The stirred-up motes of dust and mud that clouded your mind when you began are now settling down onto "the riverbed." The structure of the forms you move through does not impede this flow but channels it, as riverbanks provide a channel for the flowing water so it won't be absorbed into the earth and disappear. Any sense of confusion or agitation present when you woke up has come to rest in the *tan-t'ien*, where it can convert into latent energy and then begin to move within you in the meditative dance through the Field of Cinnabar.

◆

Giving In and Letting Go

Although we do not see power in a glass of water, once it is turned into steam, it will drive the pistons of very powerful engines. — T. T. Liang

The study of this martial art can lead you to philosophy, psychology, meditation and a physical exercise workout, all in one. You will be joining in a millennial process that will affect your state of mind and body each time you perform the Solo Exercise. However, before you decide whether or not to study T'ai Chi, you'll want to know whether it's right for you. You might ask yourself what you expect from investing the time to learn it. Will you feel better, be more present to yourself, more grounded, more balanced, even literally not trip over things or fall down so much? Possibly you wish to be less confused by life or subject to emotional ups-and-downs. For me it was all the above and, above all, that I wanted to feel more centered in my body and in my life.

T'ai Chi is especially valuable to people who live with a general sense of stress, who feel tense all the time because they are trying sincerely to do all they believe is required of them. Some hold on tightly through fear and others because it seems to them an expression of strength not to give in. They exhort themselves to "get a grip" even when their body or mind cries out for rest. Such a continual sense of pressure makes us wonder what parts of ourselves need to relax in order to free us from stress. We may discover that letting go of the body's tension is easier than letting go of what's holding onto the body. T'ai Chi offers a path towards this deeper release. As Master Jou Tsung-hwa put it, "by reflecting outer calm, one's inner self will become quiet and still like the water in an old well."

Then there's our unconscious conviction that we need to hold ourselves up because gravity is pulling us down. But the fact is that we are already "up" because of our muscles and bones and, above all, our life force or *ch'i*. Our joints are constructed to let go into balance, even though we often keep them stiff through fear of falling down (see the *Posture and Balance* section in Chapter Four). We do better, feel better and move better when we allow for space between ankle, knee and hip joints, and in the shoulder, elbow and wrist joints as well. As for the spine, it's not a fixed structure but a series of flexible joints separated by gelatinous inter-vertebral discs which protect us from pain unless they're compressed. Arthritis in the spine or other joints, the commonest complaint of older people, might be slower to develop in a body that allowed itself more freedom to move and often shifted the relationships between its parts. T'ai Chi helps to do that.

Apart from the bones, tendons and muscles that mechanically bind our structure together, one thing links all our parts. As Deepak Chopra pointed out so beautifully in *Quantum Healing*: "The material body is a river of atoms, the mind is a river of thought and what holds them together is a river of intelligence." Any time I attend with all my attention to whatever I'm doing, my intelligence and my presence are brought into play. If I try to do something but at the same time think about what I want for dinner, the argument I just had with my spouse or the threat of an immediate deadline, I can't be present with all of my faculties engaged.

This is an essential concept, well known in the orient but little understood in the West. We assume we can walk or do pushups or weight-lift or work on exercise machines or even sweep the floor while chatting, reading a book or watching TV, without giving what we do much thought or attention. It's true that if you exercise regularly muscle mass will change and weight will be lost or gained, and, yes, there's that great feeling of "I did it! I did my exercise for today and I feel better." But what's the price we pay? When you lose the sense of your wholeness, your integrity in action, something radical and essential is missing: *you*. When your movement lacks your *presence*, your whole self is denied its soul-food.

Perhaps presence or lack of it is what makes our search for inner balance so enigmatic. We want an immediate solution to every problem, but find that we alternate between losing connection with ourselves in habitual movements, on the one hand, and spreading our attention too thinly over a million thoughts and a thousand things to do, on the other. Rather than allowing our awareness to flow from one moment to the next, we dam up the flow of our energy by fixed concentration and excessive tension toward situations as they occur. T'ai Chi invites us to include *ourselves* in our "program," to exercise our inner person along with the muscles, joints and tendons that hold us together.

Relaxation as we know it, although it may be the opposite of tension, is not what's needed here. Too often it becomes a kind of collapse, a loss of tone, the surrender of any effort at all, which also relinquishes awareness. True, sometimes a soak in a hot bath is just what's needed to dissolve the tension caused by what I held onto in a dedicated effort to fulfill my obligations. However, in T'ai Chi a different form of relaxation is sought — a release of tension like that described in Chapter Four about the Alexander Technique. It's more like poise in movement, ease of body, yes, but also mentally very aware: a sense of presence cradled in a balance between mind and body. This combines minimal physical effort with maximum performance.

Master Liang said the word *relax* was an inadequate translation of the Chinese *sung*, which he defined as loosening the muscles, releasing tension, giving up external energy but preserving internal energy. Master Cheng Man-ch'ing called it energy conservation. He said that you are learning "to throw every bone and muscle of the entire body wide open (for the *ch'i* to pass through) without hindrance or obstruction."

◆

Sinking the Ch'i

The body follows the mind as the shadow follows the substance. — T. T. Liang

What is the *ch'i* in T'ai Chi Ch'uan? It's a different word from the "Chi" in T'ai Chi and is usually interpreted as intrinsic energy or vital force. Like *breath* or the Hindu word *prana*, it represents a subtle, invisible substance, nonetheless very real. To sense your *ch'i* energy in movement, you might try this experiment. Stand comfortably with feet shoulder-width apart and observe the rhythm of your breathing. Without altering it, when you next breathe in, let your arms rise very slowly to a low diagonal position on each side. As you breathe out, allow the arms to sink down. Do this a few times. Then, with your next few breaths, float them up to the horizontal. After you have done that several times, let them ride on the in-breath all the way up until they are above your head and descend slowly down on the out-breath.

Be careful not to alter the natural rhythm of your breathing as you move your arms slowly in tandem with it. You may begin to imagine that they are swimming through the invisible substance of air. So as you move, your energy flows through the air in continuous movement with your breathing. Now, if you observe how each out-breath rolls into an in-breath and vice versa, you can apply it to your arms so that when they settle down at your sides they aren't abandoned, flopping loosely. Then tension eases as you prepare them to return upward and the downward movement quite naturally converts into an *up*. Each time the arms change direction you remain related to your energy or *ch'i*. Instead of disappearing when your arms come down, like water flowing into sand, it will gradually increase as if, little by little, you were filling a pool.

If you tried the arm-raising and lowering experiment attentively, you will have noticed that you weren't making a simple muscular exertion. Your arms rose and fell with the invisible force of *ch'i*. In the same way, the T'ai Chi practitioner sends his thought down to the *tan-t'ien* so that his vital energy can accumulate as he moves through the forms. Cheng defined it as a "mass integration of conserved energy," advising us to breathe deeply and slowly as we let the *ch'i* sink down. Jou suggested that gathering *ch'i* was like depositing money in a bank.

Don't think of this pool, the *tan-t'ien*, as an immovable point in your belly on which you fix your thought, because just as your blood, breathing, mind and energy are in constant ebb and flow, so is the rest of your body. To center yourself in activity, a moving relationship is needed between all your parts. The best way I know of achieving this is to harness your thought to the belly region while simultaneously following your shifting weight and limbs. More important than thinking about moving the limbs is to sense and follow the flow of the energy that moves through you, gently powering each movement you make.

The theory behind this movement of energy or *ch'i* takes us back to the image of a river, which although it seems to flow in silent ease within its banks through the landscape, will assert its power the moment it is blocked or dammed. Like the river and the movements of T'ai Chi, our energy follows curving, circling, spiral patterns, building up force in the midst of its gentleness. However, where there is injury or even unnecessary tension in the body, the flow may be blocked or impeded and we may feel pain, heat or swelling as *ch'i* tries to find its way through to continue circulating.

This energy *will* find a way. Just as the river adapts its current to flow around rocks and branches, so will our inner structure adapt to allow the energy to flow. The musculature is arranged in spiraling and crisscrossing lengths around the bones, and the spiral patterns of bones shift and develop in response to stresses from the weight they carry as well as from how we move them. In fact, recent studies of body language have suggested that our shape is as much a result of the way we have lived as the body we inherited. If this is true, we need to accept that in spite of the fact that most of our movements are hypothetically under conscious control, we haven't lived or used ourselves consciously. Once this is acknowledged, something can be done about it and, happily, the structure of the body will change as we use it more wisely.

Thought and care as to diet and exercise can alter shape and habitual posture. Mind intention can produce even deeper results. Regular practice of T'ai Chi helps integrate and coordinate the expression of the sympathetic and parasympathetic nervous systems, as it stimulates and relaxes the whole being. Students are helped to develop patience and persistence along with greater strength and suppleness, a freer, well-regulated respiration and circulation, and a growing sense of tranquility under stress. Then, after long and dedicated practice comes the stage Cheng called "propelled movement," which he compared to a car moved by the gas feeding into its engine. It's also a state of presence in movement.

In someone with a high level of expertise, the *ch'i* energy builds up and becomes absorbed and stored in the bones, which become as hard and resilient as steel, according to Cheng, as it transforms itself into essence (*ching*). At this point the *ch'i* has overflowed the *tan-t'ien* and moved into the blood. When the student connects to it with the mind intention, heat is generated at the base of the spine, creating even more *ch'i*. Tendons and sinews conduct this heat to the bones and humidity congeals it into marrow. Body and functioning are no longer separate but joined and rejuvenated. The end result of developing and concentrating the *ch'i* is the level of expertise called "needle inside the cotton," in which the master's strength is invisible but present—the body as pliable as that of an infant, the outer appearance soft as cotton, the inside hard as steel.

Like the growth of essence, these changes take a long time. Liang compared the time it takes for them to occur with the period needed to refine steel, from melting iron ore into cast iron and then into wrought iron to its purification into steel. As the *ch'i* sinks repeatedly to the *tan-t'ien*, movements become light and the body sensitive and alert. Feet, legs, waist, arms, all move together or rest attentively. Once the postures or forms have been mastered over time, the rhythm, the movement, even oneself, merge into a state of presence which he called "meditation in action and action in meditation."

T'ai Chi masters have offered several interpretations of what makes up the *ch'i* and how it works to produce inner calm, better health and a happier, longer life. Master Da Liu, who taught at the United Nations in New York, described it as the product of joining mind, breath and sexual energy. He explained that two ideograms form the word; one indicates respiration in the usual sense of air coming into the lungs and the other indicates essence (*ching*), which includes sex energy. This is transformed into steam (*ch'i*). Thus there are two kinds of breathing: the ordinary or "post-natal" breathing through nose or mouth and the "pre-natal," or the breathing of the fetus in the womb as it receives oxygen through the mother's blood. Long-term work in T'ai Chi produces a combining of the two called the "Union of Fire and Water."

The experience of the *ch'i* in action can be astonishing. A friend of mine accompanied his wife, an ardent student, to visit Da Liu in his apartment. "What is this *ch'i*?" he asked, rather skeptically. "Come, I show you," said Da Liu, leading him into a small room with a mattress, obviously his bedroom. He picked up the mattress, placed it vertically against the far wall, then gestured to my friend to stand a few feet in front of it. "He barely touched me on the chest," reported my friend. "But all I remember is that I was flung instantly against the mattress and crashed down to the floor! Da Liu laughed glee-fully and announced 'That *ch'i*!'"

However, not everyone whose blow can split a brick is honored by the masters. Linda Lehrhaupt's insightful book, *T'ai Chi as a Path of Wisdom*, described a young Chinese martial arts troupe that strutted their expertise for several hours in Madison Square Garden. As she marveled at each amazing feat, an elderly teacher sitting next to her muttered: "very pretty, but not *ch'i*." Then, just before the show ended, an old man brought the crowd to its feet by splitting a stone that no one else had been able even to crack, with a quick blow of his head. The master expressed his satisfaction: "not pretty, just *ch'i*!"

As Liang explained it, mind, intention (*li*) and *ch'i* are three inseparable elements that work together. When the mind moves, intention is aroused and *ch'i* will follow. But he warned that if one part moves and the others are still, confusion results. And if the mind becomes confused, intention will disappear and the *ch'i* will move upward—away from its resting place in the *tan-t'ien*—because the *ch'i* can't move well by itself. It needs the well-focused mind to direct its circulation through the body. The mind follows the flow of movement through the series of postures and the body comes to rest for a millisecond at the end of each small segment. In that instant the intention of the mind fills the gap until the next segment begins. Mind intent and *ch'i* are the principles, said Liang, while the positions or forms are the method or technique.

◆

Gaining Through Loss

It is only from the greatest pliability and from yielding completely that you can attain power and ascendancy.   — Wang Tsung-yueh

Another central principle of Taoism is *wu wei*, variously translated as non-doing, effortless effort or gaining through loss. When we move with *wu wei* we become part of an easy, curving flow of energy moving like a river, as it flows under, over or around obstacles. But it's not easy to free ourselves, to center ourselves in the practice of presence, when competition and inner conflict compromise our energy with fixed attitudes and physical, mental or emotional tensions. Yielding in order to follow also contradicts the Western "can-do" attitude toward solving problems as well as our conviction about the importance of self-expression. *Wu wei* is an alternative to the fight-or-flight stress reaction which so often accompanies our way of dealing with life's challenging moments.

You then might ask, if the aim is to free the student from tension, why is it necessary to follow the circling movements of T'ai Chi with such precision? Wouldn't it be better to "go with the flow," to express oneself in a kind of free dance? Not according to Taoists, who believe that surrendering to the untrained mind confuses the *ch'i,* while carefully following the form, shape or outward manifestation (*hsing*) guides it. Also intrinsic to *wu wei* is surrendering one's own assumptions, tendencies and prejudgments, as well as the need to have things one's own way. Cheng called this effort "no foregone conclusions, no arbitrary determinations, no obstinacy and no egotism."

I often found this difficult to accept. It was hard to sacrifice "knowing" and "preferring" in order to discover the truth of each moment. The need to know before moving is very strong, and sometimes necessary for self-preservation. But I finally realized that without letting go into present attention and awareness, I wasn't in touch with where I really wanted to live. The repetitive movements of T'ai Chi gradually broke down my resistance, inviting me to trace and retrace a circular path with the whole body/mind continuum in this ancient ritual, exercising sustained attention on precision of movement even as I sought to release excess tension. T'ai Chi wasn't mine to reinvent, just as my body and mind aren't my own creation, but mine to follow into a new world of experience.

You have, no doubt, seen the T'ai Chi symbol of a circle divided into two equal, curving spaces. One is black and the other white, with a tiny dot of the opposite color at the center of each. Some call it the *yin-yang* symbol. If you bend your mind to take this symbol into movement, you may appreciate the Taoist view of life, in which one extreme constantly flows into the other and then turns back toward itself. Each curving half of the circle moves toward its opposite, leaving behind a tiny circular trace of itself which, instead of disappearing, initiates a gradual return to a new but momentary position of power. An elegant illustration of this shifting dominance is the sun which, seconds after high noon, begins its decline toward evening. In the same way, the darkest hour before dawn gives way to the first light.

As you learn the forms of the Solo Exercise, you can experience for yourself this interchanging flow of forces as your energy moves out in thrusts and kicks and returns quietly back in the withdrawals—*yang* melts into *yin* and *yin* again becomes *yang*. This exemplifies the heart of the Big Taoist Riddle: how can the gentle and pliable conquer the firm and powerful? We often hear that dripping water gradually wears away stone, but Cheng wasn't satisfied with that explanation. He insisted that change can be instantaneous, comparing the gathered power of *ch'i* to what happens to water and air when they enter into what he called the "mass integration" of a tidal wave or a tornado.

Taoists claim that the development of this mysterious life force leads to an optimum state of health—that it clarifies the mind, increases vigor and prolongs life. How does this come about? Liang said that the stimulation of the *ch'i* produces inner heat and activates circulation. He called *ch'i*, which circulates with the blood, "the master," and blood "the assistant." One protects, the other circulates as it nourishes the body.

Da Liu explained that the slow T'ai Chi movements of arms and legs "guide" blood circulation, cleansing and repairing the tissues, while muscular tension prevents blood flow to both coarse and fine arteries, such as those of face and hands. Practicing T'ai Chi "corrects this condition, pouring color and life into neglected parts as water to a flower." Cheng said that loosening the muscles and releasing pent up tension by sinking the *ch'i* is a good way of conserving energy. He also told his students that by putting their bodies to rest in this way, they were learning a practical method to control and reduce the over-reaction of the nervous system.

T'ai Chi masters claim that other beneficial effects accrue over time, such as better regulation of circulation and ease of breathing, a reduction of habitual anxiety and even of habitual weariness. Cheng explained that while the internal organs of animals are suspended from a horizontal spine so that they are exercised by every movement they make, the organs of upright humans are bunched closely together and experience much less movement. However when the *ch'i* sinks to the *tan-t'ien*, the inner organs have more space to expand or contract or vibrate. He urged his students to keep "the mind and the *ch'i* in each other's company" whether they were walking, riding the subway, waiting for a bus or just resting.

My own experience has been that all these good things are true of T'ai Chi, and I've benefited enormously from it. When the *ch'i* circulates freely throughout the body, one's feelings, perceptions and touch become very sensitive and one's mind clear. Decisions can be made intelligently, in a state of alert attention, rather than compromised by emotional reaction. Over time, the combination of relaxation with awareness creates a new sense of security. The balance that T'ai Chi creates between mind (*yang*) and heart (*yin*) parallels the balanced connection among the centers—head, heart and body—that I studied so assiduously in the Gurdjieff teaching.

Jou likened the body to a car carrying the inner organs and nervous system as passengers. For their comfort, the car must be driven smoothly, just as the well-focused mind should direct the movements of the body with emotional calm and mental quiet. The idea that anyone could consider T'ai Chi remote from the modern world amused him. Although today's technology-driven life appears light-years away from ancient Chinese philosophical ideas, he liked to point out that computers function with a binary system using two numbers—zero (*yang*) and one (*yin*)—the mathematical symbols for yes and no. Could there be a clearer example of the presence of the *Tao* in our daily lives?

◆

Yin and Yang

T'ai Chi ... is the source of motion and tranquility and the mother of Yin and Yang. — Wang Tsung-yueh

Yin and *yang*, darkness and light, passive and active, feminine and masculine, solid and empty are always in movement and constantly changing into each other, just like our psychic states. *Yin* characteristics include cold, stillness, and centripetal force, while *yang* energy is represented by heat, motion and centrifugal force. When the kettle boils, steam and power are produced—that's *yang* energy. When water freezes and becomes firm and still, *yin* has taken over. All that is light and firm is *yang* energy, is male, represents the sun, heaven, the head, while all that is heavy and yielding is considered *yin*, such as female, the moon, the earth and the belly.

When we are full of energy, active in mind and body, we function in a *yang* mode, but when we feel tired or cold, pessimistic or confused, we are enmeshed in the net of *yin*. Jou recommended that in a *yang* state his students remind themselves that nothing lasts, and when in a *yin* state that they watch for the turning point, because *yin* will always turn into its opposite. He used the history of the transportation system to illustrate the inevitability of such changes on a larger scale. In its *yang* stage, faster cars and super highways were built, revolutionizing mobility. But as more people bought more cars, previously unimagined problems appeared, such as air pollution, traffic jams and a scarcity of parking spaces. *Yang* turned into *yin*.

The play of *yin* and *yang*, representing together the duality of nature and the movement of energy, was first studied in the *I Ching*, an ancient Chinese book of divination. Legend has it that in 3000 BCE the emperor/sage Fu Hsi, China's first historic ruler, took combinations of broken or *yin* lines and unbroken or *yang* lines to create the eight basic trigrams on which the ideas of the *I Ching* are based. The emperor held that the eight combinations formed by these two kinds of lines were symbols of the fundamental nature of the universe.

Since man and universe obey the same laws, Taoists believe that the individual human being is a microcosm of the universe, that human life reflects outer events and that the future is contained in this present moment. Every phenomenon, every relationship, every moment in time contains six stages, and the *yin* and *yang* forces direct the process of changing from one stage to another, as well as from past to present to future. From the emptiness of *Wu Chi* appears *T'ai Chi*, the One. As soon as manifestation begins, it divides into *yang*, the active principle in any phenomenon, and *yin*, the passive or receptive principle. An illustration of the one becoming two is that both poles are needed to create the flow of electricity. Neither a positive nor a negative charge can generate light and heat by itself—electrons must flow from one pole to the other.

The movements of T'ai Chi Ch'uan were based on the trigrams of the *I Ching*. An inner trigram represents one's state of mind and an outer the condition of one's body. Both of them—the visible and the invisible—are in constant fluctuation under the influence of *yin* and *yang* forces. It's easy to see how the shifts in movement during the T'ai Chi Solo Exercise express this duality. For example, advancing into a punch is *yang*, while retreating is *yin*.

A good way to experience these shifts is by studying them in the simplest of movements—the T'ai Chi walking exercise. Stand evenly on both feet and send your conscious thought down to the center of gravity in the belly region. Because you are standing "like a balanced scale" the *yin* and *yang* have momentarily become one. But you are ready to move instantly, defending yourself from attack on all sides like a horizontally turning wheel or the fighters in a martial arts film. As soon as you even think of moving, the *yin* and *yang* separate into opposing forces as the whole body responds.

Alert to the physical sensation of your weight in the lower abdomen and legs, you begin to "empty" one leg—passing its weight slowly into the other as you take a small step forward. It helps to imagine that water is moving from the "full" leg to the "empty" one. It passes up the leg into the lower belly—the *ch'i hai* or ocean of *ch'i*—from which it pours out into the "empty" leg, gradually filling it. Next you raise the "empty" foot and bring it down a little in front of the toes of your weight-bearing foot, at first just letting the heel touch the floor then gradually the rest of the foot, as your weight flows back into that leg. Once all your weight is on it, the other foot is free to take a new step forward. The movement should be gradual, your thought totally engaged in measuring the shifting of your weight in kinesthetic sensation—first 10%, then 20%, 50%, 70%, 90% and finally 100% comes off one foot and onto the other.

◆

"Work on What Has Been Spoiled"

What has been spoiled through man's fault can be made good again through man's work. — I Ching

We have seen and even sensed in the walking exercise how the One develops out of stillness into *yin* and *yang*. These two then double into four: greater *yang*, lesser *yang*, greater *yin*, lesser *yin*. Greater and lesser *yang* are recognizable in the T'ai Chi symbol as the large white "fish" and the small white circle within the black "fish," and greater and lesser yin as the large black "fish" and small black circle within the white. Da Liu explained in *T'ai Chi Ch'uan & Meditation* that practicing the movements of T'ai Chi as a whole calls on greater *yang*, but it is always accompanied by deep inner quiet or lesser *yin*. Sitting in quiet meditation calls for greater *yin*, accompanied by an active, lesser-*yang* interior state.

The alternation of these two states is the essence of Taoism and, in either case, the one prepares the way for the other. For example, several T'ai Chi teachers told me they meditated before practicing T'ai Chi. I preferred to begin my day with T'ai Chi before meditation because it helped me become alert in the early morning. As I worked, the *yang* energy of the T'ai Chi exercise finally settled into quiet, and the intense stillness of my meditation was filled with inner movement. Over time, it is this alternation of *yin* and *yang* in active movement with a restful interior state, or in restful quiet with an active inner state, that brings better physical health and mental and emotional balance. An active interiority in stillness or a quiet inner state during exterior movement is central to the practice of presence.

These four *yin-yang* combinations expressed in various formations make up Fu Hsi's eight essential trigrams. Their names and functions offer a wide range of meaning:

Chen: Thunder, the arouser; life breaking out of the depths; the beginning of movement.

Sun: Wind, wood; the gentle, all-penetrating.

Li: Sun, fire; the clinging, lucidity.

K'un: Earth, the receptive; the *yin* principle receiving heaven's seed and nurturing it.

Tui: Lake, mist, serenity; the joyous.

Ch'ien: Heaven, the creative, strength; the *yang* principle which fertilizes *K'un*.

K'an: Water, the abysmal; the moon, opposite of *Li*, the sun (their marriage produces the child, the new man).

Ken: Mountain; keeping still; the state of meditation which, by quieting the outer, enlivens the inner world. (Life and death meet here.)

When these trigrams are stacked two by two in every possible combination of six lines, they form the 64 hexagrams of the *I Ching*. Accompanied by commentaries written by sages in centuries past, the hexagrams have been used since time immemorial to obtain oracular advice and predictions for the future. If you seek predictions you will need guidance from someone who knows how to interpret the random fall of yarrow stalks, to evaluate the advice given in the hexagram as a whole and the relation of the trigrams to each other.

Western pundits who studied translations of the *I Ching* in the late 19th and early 20th centuries were surprised at the extent to which Chinese philosophy was based on chance because, in their opinion, chance was irrelevant. However, the Taoist sees the present moment as a window into what is really going on, even though that may include a jumble of different and confusing factors. Psychiatrist C. G. Jung celebrated the importance of chance in his introduction to Wilhelm's *I Ching* translation: "Every process (in the natural world) is partially or totally interfered with by chance ... the irrational fullness of life has taught me never to discard anything, even when it goes against all our theories." Jung also noted that the ancient Chinese view of the cosmos is comparable to that of the modern physicist as he praised the book as "one long admonition to careful scrutiny of one's own character, attitude and motives."

But how do you apply the divination power of the I Ching to your own life? Here's an example of how I used it in the midst of writing this chapter: Discouraged at how slowly it seemed to be proceeding, I decided to see if the book had any advice for me. It certainly did! Although the ancient official method is to throw 49 yarrow stalks down six times, interpreting their fall for each line, I used the simpler method, tossing three old Chinese coins onto my living room rug. The inscribed side represents yin (a broken line) and the other side yang (an unbroken line), so each throw will either be all yin, all yang, one yang and two yin or one yin and two yang. When you stack up the results of all six throws from bottom to top, one of the 64 hexagrams is indicated.

My six throws brought hexagram # 53, "Development" or "Gradual Progress," made up of the trigram Sun—"the gentle, wood"—on top, interpreted as adaptability; and Ken —"keeping still, mountain"—on the bottom, interpreted as calm. The text explained that the quality of stillness in a mountain and the penetrating nature of wood provide together the image of the slow growth of a tree firmly rooted on a mountain. The commentaries informed me that hasty action is unwise and that the appropriate way of proceeding would be to root myself in "inner calm combined with adaptability to circumstances." Needless to say, I continued to write without so much anxiety to finish or pressure to "get it right."

Sometimes the voice of the I Ching can be a little unnerving, and I confess I have seldom experimented with it since my first attempts. I started off armed with my customary journalist's incredulity, like many people who feel that these messages-that-appear-from-the-present-moment are accidentally arrived at and without special meaning. But my first few experiences silenced my doubt and evoked respect for the uncannily accurate formulations. They also made me hesitate to play with this particular brand of psychic fire. For example, over a period of eight years, I received the same hexagram three times in answer to an urgent question. That's a highly improbable statistic.

At that time I was running the United Nations preschool, International Playgroup, in Lima, and hexagram # 61, "Inner Truth," popped up in response to each crucial decision I had to make. The book seemed to be repeating "Hey, wake up, pay attention, and do what I'm telling you!" as it advised me to trust my own intuition rather than the advice I was getting from all sides.

On two other occasions my inquiry resulted in # 9, "The Taming Power of the Small" and # 18, "Work on What Has Been Spoiled." The latter especially attracted my interest because it seemed to represent what Gurdjieff called "Objective Hope." Made up of the trigrams "keeping still, mountain" on top and "the gentle, wind" below (the reverse of Hexagram # 53), it offered the Image of a bowl in which worms are breeding. According to the ancient interpretation: "the gentle indifference of the lower trigram has come together with the rigid inertia of the upper, and the result is stagnation."

I was deeply touched by this message about stagnation, and the possibility of transforming it through new efforts. It came at a difficult moment in my marriage. There I was, in a stagnant place, like many people in midlife, shot through with guilty feelings about what I had done or not done and the trouble I had loaded onto others. Shaken to the core by the oracular pronouncement, I was relieved by the two words immediately following, which often appear in the *I Ching*: "No blame." In other words, a guilty attitude doesn't help and may hinder. Getting down to work is better than indulging in self-attack.

The section called the Judgment contained an interpretation appended to the ancient text a century before Confucius worked on it. It stated that: "It is not immutable fate ... that has caused the state of corruption, but rather the abuse of human freedom." I felt summoned from the depths of primordial wisdom to render myself accountable for what I had failed to do. I was invited to take a personal stand against my own abuse of freedom. But I felt dismay at the "gentle indifference" and "rigid inertia" in my life. How could I oppose it? The missing element was "work on what has been spoiled." The *I Ching* was telling me that there hope lies, no matter how much of a mess we've made of our lives. Yet what kind of work could change our lives? Surely not the usual tensing into an effort, as we tilt at the windmill that blows away our resolve, days after our latest New Year's resolution.

Work in the Taoist sense means total *engagement*, a wholehearted effort rather than the usual half-hearted try that comes from a lack of commitment and is soon abandoned. I told myself I would have to deal consciously with the pecking and cawing of the birds whose noise usually filled my "monkey mind," as well as the ebb and flow of my emotional reactions and the passivity of my body. I would also have to separate myself intentionally from all the borrowed and half-baked attitudes that informed my view of life. It was time to accept my hidden possibilities and to make them actual.

So if you, like me, have decided to undertake the effort of serious renewal, you will want to know that, according to the *I Ching*, the first step to prepare for the journey "across the

Great Water" is to recognize the enormity of t
ing. It's a decision not to be made lightly. It will
painful to recognize and accept what one has sp
lifetime avoiding or blaming on others. So how can you forge a
steely determination, a commitment to sincerity that will not
be easily melted? How do you prepare to taste the raw new
wine of unrelenting truth?

◆

The Secret of the Golden Flower

If the thoughts are absolutely quiet so that the Heavenly Heart
can be seen, the spiritual intelligence reaches the source unaided.
— The Secret of the Golden Flower

In 1920, when Richard Wilhelm obtained one of the 1,000
privately printed copies of an ancient Chinese document
called *T'ai I Chin Hua Tsang Chih* or *The Secret of the Golden
Flower*, renamed by its Chinese publisher *The Art of Prolonging
Human Life*, the seeds were sown for a profound change in
modern Western thought. This esoteric teaching, taught orally
to only a secret few from the time of the Tang Dynasty in the
8th century, is said to have originated with Lu Yen. Wilhelm,
who translated it into German in 1929, thought it dated back
to Master Kuan Yin-his, the person for whom, legend goes,
Lao-tzu wrote down his *Tao Te Ching*.

Wilhelm was fascinated by the specificity of the exercises
described in the text, which purportedly allowed whoever
practiced them to meet death "as a conscious spirit" by
bringing psychic influence on the endocrine gland system:
"to strengthen, rejuvenate and normalize the life-processes,

so that even death will be ... a harmonious ending of life." Though its complex images are difficult to grasp, the book suggests specific ways to work on essence.

It tells us that people dissipate their intrinsic energy or *ch'i* in external activities, instead of valuing and "guarding" this energy for inner development. A metaphor from the *I Ching* explains our ignorance of this danger: "Even if a man lives in the power he does not see the power, just as fishes live in water but do not see the water." However, *The Secret of the Golden Flower* assures its readers that by applying intelligence, clarity and calm while collecting the thoughts daily in the recommended mental exercises, one may develop over time a "spirit-body" within the carnal body. The Golden Flower is the light (*Chin Tan*—literally the golden ball or the golden pill—also translated as the Elixir of Life). By practicing such exercises as "the circulation of the light," "melting and mixing," and "the backward flowing movement," we may live longer and with greater vitality.

To learn how this may be achieved we must first understand what is meant by "the place from which essence and life originally spring." When a human being is conceived, primal energy divides into essence (*hsing*) and life (*ming*). After this separation, "if the utmost peace is not achieved, essence and life never see each other again." All through our lives, our energy will flow outward as its power "leaks away and life consumes itself."

Ming, the "conscious spirit," represents our destiny, our level of vitality and length of life. It dwells in the heart, the place of feeling and is in a continual state of flux, reacting to all the impressions coming toward it. Dependent on the world, it becomes easily hurt, enraged and overcome by emotions, behaving "like a strong, powerful commander who despises the Heavenly ruler because of his weakness, and has seized for himself the leadership of the affairs of state." *Hsing*, the "primordial spirit," essence or Heavenly Heart, does not move. It rests immobile in the "square inch" between the eyes—also known as the upper *tan-t'ien*. Here "dwells the splendour," says the text, "... the god of utmost emptiness and life. The Confucians call it the center of emptiness; the Buddhists, the terrace of life; the Taoists, ... the dark pass, or the space of former Heaven."

Once the essential creative energy divides into these two at birth, each individual is activated by two natures. One is a feminine or *yin* soul (*p'o*)—described as dark, heavy, turbid, seeking death yet at the same time "loving life, ruling it with blind passions." It typically dominates the masculine soul (*hun*)—"the power of lightness and purity." We can think of them as the animal/emotional part on the one hand and the mental part on the other. But the former almost always drags the mind along with it. Both energies exist in each of us, but if they never find a relationship with each other, they will have different fates when we die. The masculine spirit will rise up and evaporate or pour into the river of life, while the feminine energy will decay into the earth.

The Secret of the Golden Flower offers an alternative outcome at death if we can reverse the situation and make the Heavenly Heart our "strong and wise ruler." In that case, the mind will be released from passionate attraction toward the external and "all those rebellious heroes will present themselves with lances reversed ready to take orders." That will allow the higher centers to receive the nourishment they need. Everything depends on development of the ability to circulate the Light throughout the body and create the "backward flowing movement" that opposes the outward flow of energy, transforming it into spiritual energy independent of the body at death.

The emphasis on maintaining thought in the Heavenly Heart may seem to contradict what was said previously about the importance of sinking thought to the *tan-t'ien*. But these exercises represent a lifetime of work and we can only begin at the beginning. The first stage is "wakening seed power" in the lower *tan-t'ien*; then comes "crystallizing spirit" in the solar plexus and finally "gathering thoughts" in the upper *tan-t'ien*. The text specifically states that working on all three of these parts is essential to develop "the spirit-fire." One is not more important than another. For example, concentrating one's thought at the point midway between the eyes—the location of the "third eye" often mentioned in other religious traditions—is only one third of the practice. Such an effort "means only what the plumb-line does to the mason."

I was saddened to learn that when the conscious spirit rules the human heart, the primordial spirit loses its place, and turns its power over to our reactive animal/emotional nature. I was attracted by both "the Primordial Spirit (which) loves peace and the Conscious Spirit (which) loves movement." But the oracular pronouncement was unequivocal: "Day and night it wastes the primal seed till the force of the primordial spirit is entirely used up." This meant "if one wants to protect the primordial spirit, one must first not fail to subjugate the knowing spirit … through the circulation of the Light." In other words, the Taoist's task is to learn how to distill the feminine, earth or *yin* energy within oneself so that it becomes imbued with Light or *yang* energy. Then life energy, instead of being wasted, will help create a center of gravity independent of the body.

Taoists believe that this special work of reuniting essence and life force is our purpose here on earth. Our work is to set "the Light in circulation by reflection in order to make manifest the setting free of Heaven. … If then the true seed is born, and the right method applied in order to melt and mix it, and in that way to create the Elixir of Life, then one goes through the pass. The embryo, which must be developed by the work of warming, nourishing, bathing, and washing, is formed." In other words, if we could incarnate or embody the energies we received at birth, which need a suitable container in which to incorporate themselves, they would become distilled over time into the Elixir of Life.

◆

The Circulation of the Light

When the Light circulates, the powers of the whole body arrange themselves before its throne ... just as when the master is quiet and calm, men-servants and maids obey his orders of their own accord, and each does his work. — The Secret of the Golden Flower

In such mysterious formulations, *The Secret of the Golden Flower* tells us what we are and what we can become. We are two-natured, composed of an animal/emotional conscious-ness that guides us to want or dislike, avoid or prefer, protect, attack and escape; and another, higher consciousness. The first, located in the heart, reacts to every impression coming from the outside by making immediate, programmed, superficial choices using whatever data has been previously acquired by instinct or past experience. It constantly changes and adapts in reaction to what's coming from the outer world.

The higher consciousness resides in the head, and the tragedy of human existence is that often no connection exists between these two natures. However, esoteric teachings in many religious traditions offer a path of practical exercises to re-unite them. This is the practice of presence. In Taoism, the "Circulation of the Light" attempts to link the world below, the earth or animal level which is an inescapable aspect of who we are, with the world above, the divine which (and this is important to acknowledge) already resides within us. God, Allah, the Self, the Great Spirit, whatever you choose to call that higher power, is everywhere and in us, only we are seldom related to it.

Of all animal life, only human beings have this possibility to actively create a relationship between their two natures. Through the power of consciousness—by engaging in self-questioning and by developing an objective recognition of what is just and unjust—we can experience ourselves as both animal and divine. Then, if we long for it enough, we can commit to undertaking the necessary exercises to link them.

Such inner work should be repetitive because we are creatures of habit, so daily effort is necessary. The aim isn't to slough off the body and become pure spirit, but rather to engage in regular efforts that deepen a living channel of energy in ourselves so that spirit can incarnate in flesh and the two become one. This mental commitment must find a way to anchor itself in the body. It is fueled by the true wish of the heart, which in turn needs to learn how to attend without wavering. An intentional circulation is required because energy, whether divine or animal, is always in movement. What's more, the Chinese text states that once some success in circulating the Light has been achieved, "a man must not give up his ordinary occupation in doing it." I rejoiced that this, too, was work for life-in-the-world! Indeed, that segment of the text ends with the affirmation that the circulation "has just this meaning: To live in contact with the world and yet in harmony with the Light."

At the time I read *The Secret of the Golden Flower*, I had young children to care for and serious financial problems to resolve. My central question was "how to be?" It seemed that my sense of "being" fled as soon as I started to "do" something.

It was as if I lived in two different worlds. Now unknown Chinese monks reached toward me across the centuries to help me in my private "Holy War" to find inner presence in the midst of an active life. Although complex and difficult to absorb, the book's message reaffirmed my study of Gurdjieff's work on our two natures, and revitalized the Christian image of earth and heaven that had influenced me as a child. There were others on the same path, practicing secret exercises to wrestle with the same challenge that often overwhelmed me: how to "be" in your life? How to practice presence in the midst of an active day? Readings from *The Secret of the Golden Flower* gave me new energy to continue to practice T'ai Chi every morning before six, when I had to wake my children for school and the long active day began.

The result of the gradual forging of this connection between our two natures is a growing sense of centeredness. The practice of T'ai Chi provides this experience of participation in an ongoing current of energy. A quiet mind is essential to the task. "All methods take their source in quietness," says *The Secret of the Golden Flower*. Da Liu referred to it as "concentrated quietness," and asked students to develop it both in meditation, "in which the outside moves inside," and in practice, "in which the inside moves outside."

When such a connection takes place, the breathing becomes slow and steady without my holding on to it or controlling it in any way. Although some teachers give breathing exercises to new students, these efforts may produce tension and interfere with inner quiet. If the Solo Exercise is done correctly, an easy, lengthening rhythm of breathing emerges, natural to the performance of the forms. It flows out with the quiet unfolding of the movements of legs, arms and torso as you advance, while those of retreat, turn or withdrawal invite the in-breath. The play of *yin* and *yang* becomes visible in the breathing as well as in the rhythmic circular movements of the body.

Liang listed three primary conditions for success in T'ai Chi: concentration of the mind, relaxation of the body and sinking the *ch'i* to the *tan-t'ien*. He suggested that when I went back to Peru I should start teaching right away what I had learned from him. "That's the best way to make it your own," he said. Back in Lima, I soon had two classes, one with several Karate black-belts, who were fascinated by this totally different martial art. They soon discovered how much these gentle movements could support and transform their Karate practice and raise it to a subtler level. One of them went on to study and develop Aikido in Peru and now leads the national chapter.

A few years later I returned to New York, hoping to learn more, but Liang had moved to Boston, so I went to see Master Da Liu, who worked in a different way. Before beginning the Solo Exercise, he asked me to sit on the floor in an erect posture and to focus my thought-energy first in the *tan-t'ien*. Once my thought had gathered into a clear sensation, he wanted me to engage my mind in moving the *ch'i* slowly through my body step by step, gradually linking all of the vital organs. I was to move mind-intention and *ch'i* from the front of the body, which represents the *yin* or "Functional channel," to the back, up the *yang* or "Governor channel" to the top of the head, and down the front. This exercise, the Microcosmic Orbit, begins its focus in the belly and moves down to the coccyx, then slowly up the back to the crown of the head, then to the upper *tan-t'ien* between the eyes, then down to the chest and solar plexus, and finally returns to the belly. *The Secret of the Golden Flower* called this "circular course" *fixation* and the Light *contemplation*, saying that "Fixation without contemplation is circulation without Light. Contemplation without fixation is Light without circulation." Body and mind are equally essential to the opening of the Golden Flower.

Da Liu explained that the aim of this meditation is to convert sexual essence or *ching* into intrinsic energy or *ch'i* and then refine or transform it further into pure spirit (*shen*). When I center my attention in the belly as I sit in meditation or stand quietly to begin T'ai Chi, I sense a direct connection with the earth and its forces. It's as if concentrating my attention there provides my whole being with firm ground to stand on. Once this centering takes place, not only does the body move with relaxation and a sense of being anchored, but whatever emotional reaction is present tends to diffuse itself. Even the seat of emotion, the solar plexus, seems to be rooted in the belly, like an exquisite water lily that flowers in the chest, its long stem grounded deep in the nourishing mud of the lake bottom.

◆

T'ai Chi for Self Defense

When attacking above you must not forget below; when striking to the left you must pay attention to the right; and when advancing you must have regard for retreating. — Chang San Feng

T'ai Chi is the least flashy of the martial arts. Da Liu explained that it's more balanced between the *yin* and *yang* forces, pointing out how quickly you can shift from defensive to aggressive action. *Kung Fu* (the Skill of Man) and *Karate* (the Empty Hand) are aggressive, attacking *yang* modes, while *Aikido* (the Path of Unity) and *Judo*, (the Gentle Path) are receptive, self-protective *yin* modes.

T. T. Liang urged students first to improve their health and balance through daily practice of the Solo Exercise before learning self-defense. He divided the study of T'ai Chi into the principles of Tao (internal development of mind), and the martial art (techniques and external discipline). Stating that T'ai Chi is based on *intrinsic energy*, he roundly criticized those martial arts schools that teach students to use external muscular force for strength and swiftness. He called on his own students to give up "weak, ineffective and limited" external muscular force in order to develop "powerful, strong and limitless" internal energy. The latter will appear, he said, as the *ch'i* begins to "permeate the bones and become marrow." Thus, the fighter's most important task is to develop intrinsic energy, not muscular force.

Cheng Man-ch'ing agreed, saying that according to the masters, "tenacity is alive; force is 'inert.'" Tenacity is the resilience or tone of living muscles however relaxed they may be. He compared force, which derives from muscular tension and binds the bones tightly to give "a mighty blow," to a rigid stick. Tenacious strength, on the other hand, hits like a "pliable cane, with all one's bones at ease and resilient muscles in a state of complete relaxation."

To study the difference between these two kinds of strength, Master Liang had his students read three T'ai Chi classics, later published with his own commentaries in *T'ai Chi Ch'uan for Health and Self Defense: Philosophy and Practice*. One of the classics is attributed to Chang San Feng sometime in the Tang Dynasty and the other two to Wang Chung Yueh during the Ming Dynasty. These writings claim that while other martial art schools rely on strength over weakness or swiftness over the slow, T'ai Chi has a different approach to fighting: teasing the opponent into attack, then neutralizing his power, no matter how great. Wang Tsung-yueh insisted that a slightly built or elderly fighter can dominate a strong young athlete by "deflecting a thousand pounds with a trigger force of four ounces."

How can four ounces topple a thousand pounds? Obviously

not by brute force. If someone comes at you with a mass of a thousand pounds of combined body weight and movement force, instead of meeting him head-on, at the last moment you step away. To take advantage of his impetus, you enter from the side to pull or push him and thus increase his momentum until he loses his balance. His own force defeats him. Even if you don't knock him over, your lack of resistance as you dodge and move away gives him no focus for his attack.

When you are ready to experiment with "Pushing Hands," there are four important concepts to learn: *chan*, which means to adhere and lift; *lien*, to support and prevent from falling; *t'ieh*, to stick to the opponent horizontally; and *sui*, to attach to him or her from the rear. Two students come together in the "Ward Off" position, touching each other with opposite forearms or the back of their hands. Each tries to maintain contact without resisting pressure from the other. They are alert to any response, so if one presses forward, the other yields; if one retreats, the other follows, never losing contact. Gradually they learn to sense the oncoming movement of their partner until one becomes a shadow of the other. However, it's easy to lose your centeredness if all your attention is on the contact of arms or hands. Unless you are also rooted firmly in your feet, as Liang said, "your waist will not obey your orders."

The cardinal rule is to *follow* the opponent, which isn't as easy as it sounds. To follow, you must give up your aggressiveness, your impatience, your high opinion of yourself and your assumption that you can figure out what will happen next. There is no inevitable next movement. You follow Confucius' commandment to "subdue the self" or, as your T'ai Chi master would say, "invest in loss." That means neutralizing the opponent's attack without resisting or using force against force. Only when you've mastered the art of complete yielding can you study counterattack. In the words of Lao-tsu: "When you want to expand, you must first contract; when you want to be strong, you must first be weak; when you want to take you must first give. This is called the subtle wisdom of life." (*Tao Te Ching*).

Since the body's weight should be centered on only one leg at a time, the other is free to move instantly in another direction. That way you can adapt and shift your balance with lightning speed. Liang called "double weighting"—keeping your weight on both feet at once—a "ready-to-be-beaten posture," because your opponent can easily push you over or sweep your feet out from under you. The use of the hands follows the same principle. An expert will never put both hands on the opponent with equal strength—one hand pushes, pulls, twists or lifts, while the other is ready for the opponent's next action. If he kicks, that hand is free to grab his foot and topple him over.

The quality of the hands is very different from Western fighting. They are never totally soft or totally rigid. To improve their use, one beginner practice during the Solo Exercise is to make the palm hard at the final moment of the punch and soft when retracting, in a gradual shift. Another is to harden either the bottom part or the belly of the palm (just below the four fingers). The aim is to have the whole hand appear soft but be energized from within. Every part of you needs to be tuned into the action because each part has its duty in defense or attack. According to Chang San-feng, "The energy is rooted in the feet, develops in the legs, is directed by the waist, and moves up to the fingers."

As soon as you learn how to yield and to avoid double weighting, you are ready to learn a series of withdraw-and-attack techniques: folding; finding your opponent's defects and your own "superior position;" locating your opponent's center of gravity in order to upend him; and concentrating on one point.

Most of us think of tranquility and action as opposites, but in T'ai Chi they are complementary, the one associated with guarding and protecting watchfully while the other is expressed whenever needed. In Wang's words, "*Yang* does not leave *yin* and *yin* does not leave *yang*." It is the coordination between them that develops intrinsic energy. A true master can throw his attackers off as they touch him. While standing still, he sends his energy into circular movement against them. According to Jou, he can meet a challenge in three ways, either by disappearing like fog, resisting like a mountain, or fighting back like a tiger.

Action-ready quiet and concentration are visible in a cat watching a mouse. Frightened, the mouse stays absolutely still. The cat seems totally relaxed but entirely focused on the mouse. The instant the mouse breaks for cover, the cat springs. Another T'ai Chi-like example is the bullfighter, who neither meets the bull head-on nor runs away. Concentrated on watching the bull charge, he merely steps aside at the key moment to avoid contact, and then attacks as the animal thunders past him. To strike at the moment of withdrawal is what Taoists call "the *yang* among the *yin*."

The dance of *yin* and *yang* energy comes into play as soon as you are attacked. If from right or left, you withdraw with a twist to the opposite side so that your enemy has no one to hit. This is called becoming *insubstantial* or empty. You dodge your opponent's attack by *yielding* or *withdrawing*, dissipating his energy until you can move back to *dominate* him. Then you close with him, said Liang, "like plaster adhering to his body, giving him no chance to escape."

This move is related to one of the first forms you learned as a T'ai Chi student—Roll Back—which is also known in its fighting mode as "opening the door and welcoming the robber in." Until you entice "the enemy" towards you, you may be unable to catch him. But when he moves toward you and strikes, you yield completely until he has used up his propelled force reaching for you. Then you can strike from the side or from below in his moment of weakness, upending his center of gravity. At all times you follow your opponent's speed, moving slowly when he does then swiftly as he speeds up. The idea is to interpret and anticipate the enemy's intentions—to read his thoughts just as he begins to move. That way, your counterattack will be underway before his attack reaches you. In *The Art of War*, Sun-tzu referred to this as "dispatching troops after the enemy but arriving before he does."

◆

The Enemy Within

If a man were to conquer in battle a thousand times a thousand men, and another conquers one, himself, he is indeed the greatest of conquerors. — The Dhammapada

Every day we meet other, less physical opponents that tire our body, consume our energy and confuse our minds. The practice of T'ai Chi can also help us to defeat these. In gesture and broken English, Liang told me that whenever you do the Solo Exercise an enemy is present. It was up to me to find out who the enemy was.

Gradually, I discerned several of them. One major opponent was a hidden attitude that interfered almost every morning with the quality of the Exercise—a preference for taking it easy because no one was watching. I had to acknowledge that I paid better attention to the continual flow of my movement when I was teaching or giving a demonstration. Both annoyed at myself and grateful to discover the real enemy, mind wandering, I confronted this tendency to carelessness every day. Each time I reminded myself that there was no reason to do this voluntary meditative exercise at all if I couldn't give it my best attention.

Another discovery developed from the question: Was I leading or following the movements? Always a consummate "do-er," I began to notice in quiet moments of practice a subtle version of the same aggressive mode I needed to get through all the tasks of the day. It didn't seem to matter whether I did T'ai Chi in the morning or the evening, although in the evening I was perhaps a little more relaxed, my energy used up. At either time, I saw how I pushed my body along rather than letting myself be propelled by the *ch'i* energy.

The only way to reduce the pressure I put on myself was to recognize it as it happened. Each time I forgot to pay attention, the mode shifted back to pushing. Endlessly useful, this discovery called me to be present throughout practice of the Solo Exercise, and also alerted me to watch for pushing during the day. I uncovered a subtle form of propelling myself on to the next task without awareness of what I was doing at the moment.

Other questions arose from these discoveries, such as: What is important? Is the discovery that you're not paying attention the ultimate BAD? Self-accusation finally revealed itself as a barrier to deeper relaxation. Every time I noticed myself pay inadequate attention to what I was doing, the judge and critic in me were triggered. They were full of self-disapproval that I wasn't engaging all my faculties. I saw that I couldn't accept myself unless I gave 100% to the task at hand. The demon of perfectionism was fully present even when I wasn't!

Here's how it would work: When I performed T'ai Chi in a distracted state and noticed a lack of appropriate intensity, an inner alarm would sound as I condemned myself. There I was, wrong again, once more inadequate to the task. I discovered that there was a choice at that point. I could wallow in self-disapproval or move directly to make a more centered effort at presence. This meant letting go of the self-attack. Sometimes that was impossible, in which case I simply concentrated my attention on the shift of weight from one leg to the other. This would produce a shift in my state, so that I could work more quietly.

Sometimes the slow, steady movement of the Solo Exercise evoked irritation and impatience, but it could also cure them. When I was in a hurry or emotionally distraught, I often felt annoyance rise as I practiced—the same irritation which often appeared when I was doing one thing and thinking of another. Something in me resented taking the time for this and wanted to get on to the next thing. I tried to ignore or "deal with" this rising sensation of leashed anger by telling it to go away. Fat chance! What helped me was the realization that this anger didn't correspond to the moment. It was primal energy that lived in me but wasn't under my control. I could neither suppress it nor allow it to consume me. I was not in charge! At the same time I knew I must make some effort, perhaps just to recognize that this primal energy expressing itself was my own energy in movement.

This stirred up a question in me about the "Enemy Within" worth everyone's attention. When criticized, do you react by attacking back? Does the conflict develop further until both of you get angry? Or do you say nothing, i.e. retreat, and feel hurt and ill-treated? The T'ai Chi principles suggest that it would be more useful to send your thought down to the *tan-t'ien* as you listen carefully to an accusation, weigh it, decide if it's true and accept or dismiss the tirade without getting caught by the other person's reaction. If the universe is made up of energy, why react? We could just watch with amazement as these cosmic forces move through us.

During the performance of the Solo Exercise, the student studies his or her own movement from within, acutely aware of the shifts from punch to withdrawal, from aggressive to receptive, from closed and hard to soft and open. The ability to focus quietly on the body for a few minutes, then move into T'ai Chi practice, can gradually transform your experience of yourself over the years. It can provide a deeper sensation of your weight, of your feet on the ground and of your arms swaying like young branches in the wind. Your inner world slows down. Your movements become less like an exterior moving of limbs and more like the slow current of a river that carries everything with it. As the ancient *Song of the Thirteen Positions* says, "The mind and *ch'i* direct, and the flesh and bones follow."

How much did the study of T'ai Chi help me toward the practice of presence? That's an impossible question because it's so integral a part of my life. I certainly had difficulty creating a place for it every morning once my first enthusiasm waned. So I would often resist the call to practice, but finally submitted, reminding myself that I didn't know much, and perhaps T'ai Chi could help me. But during difficult periods of my life, especially at the end of my marriage, it was T'ai Chi that brought me out of early morning despair into an active day. I would wake with my heart drowning in sorrow and a sense of failure. But as I dragged myself out of bed and into the forms, the flow of their movement quieted my anguish, steadied my resolve and reminded me of a larger world than my own. The call for inner stillness, this sense of presence that is at the heart of T'ai Chi, has graced my life for many years, and still does so every morning.

Who can make the muddy water clear? Let it be still, and it will gradually become clear. — Lao-tzu

Three

The Way of Individuation:
C. G. Jung

*The requisite for real life is not that life should happen in
and for itself, but that it should also be known.*

— C. G. Jung

You may wonder why I would undertake Jungian analysis
if the Gurdjieff teaching had "all the answers" and T'ai Chi had
helped me to center myself below the mind. I confess it was
only gut instinct that led me from "reading about" to plunging
into what seemed like such a radical pursuit. However, it led
to a significant change in my understanding of the reality of
the emotional life, so I thank my guiding stars that I dared this
leap into the unknown.

My parents and childhood teachers had taught me not to
be negative. As a Gurdjieffian, I was encouraged to see negative emotions more clearly, note their immediate causes and
sources in order to create a pathway to another level of feeling

response. But instead of really doing this, I repressed them so that I could think of myself as a "good Gurdjieffian" and a "good girl." Since psychic energy is a reality—if you push it aside in one place (the conscious mind), it will appear somewhere else (often the body)—I developed symptoms of indigestion long before I questioned their cause. In any case, some years before going into therapy, I began to read about Jung's ideas of the unconscious, and it brought many insights to my situation. I learned that there was a lot more going on in my psyche than what I consciously understood.

My mother introduced me to Jung, just as she had been my passport to Gurdjieff and had brought me to her T'ai Chi classes in the early sixties. In the late seventies, she explained for the first time why Jung's books were on her library shelf. "When you were just a baby, Patty, and your brother almost two years old, your father deserted us. I suffered a serious depression and turned to a Jungian analyst for help."

Soon afterward I returned to New York from Peru as a single mother with three children. There I was, entering the second half of my life, feeling I had made a mess of the first half. This was the time, according to Carl Jung, to begin a new search for meaning. While I had always considered myself a seeker, my studies had been based on the development of consciousness. Jung appeared to call for quite the opposite—an exploration of the frightening world of the unconscious, out of whose depth we are moved into action by forces we aren't aware of. That seemed quite different, even dangerous.

Did I dare look into the dark side of myself? Up to this point, I had a superficial impression that psychology, with its rats running in mazes and silly statistical proofs, was irrelevant. And as for personal therapy, I assumed it was a one-on-one encounter between an "expert" and a mental basket case. On top of that, it was my understanding that psychologists convinced their patients that a search for meaning through spiritual development was simply sublimated sexual frustration.

I read Jung's *Modern Man in Search of a Soul, Psychological Types* and *Civilization in Transition* slowly, finding them both difficult and enigmatically exciting. It seemed there were tensions, drives and *archetypes* at work, invisible to me in a life of what had seemed a reasonable dedication to being a "good daughter," a "good wife," a "good mother" and a "good Gurdjieffian." How did my avid pursuit of consciousness and perfection relate to this underworld of obscure forces and influences? For example, what were these archetypes he spoke of? In his words, "Archetypes ... are living psychic forces that demand to be taken seriously, and they have a strange way of making sure of their effect. Always they were the bringers of protection and salvation ..." I felt drawn to this prophetic pronouncement concerning the inner world of my psyche. Something deep inside was trying to communicate with me.

◆

Myth and Image — Our Primordial Inheritance

*Whoever speaks in primordial images speaks with a thousand voices
... transmutes our personal destiny into the destiny of mankind,
and evokes in us all those beneficent forces that ever and anon have
enabled humanity to find a refuge from every peril and to outlive the
longest night.* — C. G. Jung

Having done some reading, I felt I wanted to investigate further and attended several courses and Saturday seminars at the Jung Foundation. It became clear to me that far from being a glorification of how the unconscious dominates us,

Jung's psychological approach called for a development of consciousness through becoming aware of what is buried in unknown parts of ourselves. I associated this with Gurdjieff's statement that our true "conscience" is buried in what we call the subconscious. But following the path to it seemed a new and frightening endeavor, a letting go of the light of reason to explore the dark unknown of the unconscious.

Jung considered myths and images a primary path to explore the hidden parts of ourselves, and his interpretation of the story of Adam and Eve eating the fruit of the tree of knowledge of good and evil provides an example of his point of view. He saw it as the psychological representation of the growth of a human being, its message being that the development of consciousness brings the paradisiacal innocence of childhood to an end. According to Jung, eating that apple was necessary for human growth!

Many spiritual guides interpret the Bible through metaphor. For instance, concepts of heaven and hell may refer, not to the afterlife, but to the quality of our lives in this world. Our beliefs and attitudes can create happiness or unhappiness. Jung spoke of the Last Judgment as a projection after death of our continuing encounter between ego and Self. Our ego must sooner or later take second place to our larger, transpersonal being.

It made sense to me that the myths and fairy tales I had loved as a child represent the hidden forces that drive us and that attending to their messages could help us understand who we are and why we do what we do. Jung thought that the interpretation of myth and image could clarify our personal conflicts and even be applied to humanity as a whole, exposing what is buried in human memory, in what he called the *collective unconscious*. Though we relegate such stories to the remote past too often, they do, in fact, carry important messages about how we live today.

From this point of view, stories and myths can help us understand what goes on in our psyches right now. How? Because we sense that we are not alone, that we are connected to a larger reality. Listening to their message creates a breathing space between the whole of ourselves and our small but powerful personal reactions; a link between the agony or confusion of our private inner world and the myth or image shared by many others through the ages. If we can connect our consciousness simultaneously to our suffering and to the myth that represents what we are going through, we access a more objective place in ourselves, as well as sharing the experience of the human condition with those who came before us. The Greek tragedies are sterling examples of this; as full of death and dramatic suffering as they are, the stories they tell of the human condition offer catharsis to the theater audience.

This made so much sense that I played with interpreting some of my favorite fairy tales. *The Princess and the Pea* was an obvious first choice. Even as a child, I knew that only someone true and pure could discern the tiny falsehood in an expert lie, just as only a real princess could spend a sleepless night on twenty mattresses if a prince had placed a tiny pea under the bottom one to test her quality. Then there was *Rumpelstiltskin*, who inevitably lost his magic power to spin straw into gold as soon as the queen, desperate to keep her baby, discovered his name (i.e., who he was). And the frog, who could return to his life as a prince only if someone had the courage to confront and kiss his ugly, moist mouth without flinching.

And what about that ubiquitous third son whose ignorance, simplicity, generosity and true-blue trust in his fellow man (or in friendly animals or trolls) protected him from harm and won the hand of the princess over his rude, smartypants, unfriendly big brothers? I paused to consider how often the hero loses his opportunity or his girl because he sleeps through the moment of danger. But don't give up on him yet! After many years of travel in search of his heart's desire and enduring all sorts of difficulties, he may yet slay the dragon or monster of the psyche. That fearsome being who protects, with magic power and fiery rage, the treasure or the princess may even be transformed into a bewitched prince or princess when freed from the wicked magician's curse.

In addition to taking a closer look at fairy tales, I began noticing my dreams and recurring images in waking life. One repeated dream image, in particular, was filled with raw emotion. I would find myself standing in the middle of a crossroads and see that all four roads were blocked by high wooden barriers. No road was open on which I could move forward. Even in the daytime, my sense of frustration brought me back to this imaginary place where I felt imprisoned in the confines of my life. Finally from somewhere deep inside came the suggestion that instead of trying to force my way through one of these barriers, all I needed was a helicopter. I could move in the one direction that hadn't occurred to me: up.

From that time on I would often search for an image or myth to clarify whatever dark mood I felt caught in. It was one of the most helpful ways to invite awareness of a larger world and could get me out of the inner swamp in which I seemed so often to be stuck. The explanation for this phenomenon in Jungian terms is that the ego becomes identified with a mood or a person or an archetype. Finding a mythical image to express it can sometimes set the psyche free. Even though the pain remained, a new understanding of how I was imprisoned transmuted into a sense of release. I knew I was not alone, for others had experienced this "prison" as well.

One of my first all-day workshops at the Jung Foundation introduced me to Edith Wallace, a well-known therapist who trained with C. G. and Emma Jung in Zurich. In the morning session she spoke of the importance of myth to the Jungian way of studying ourselves, adding that each of us carried within ourselves our own personal myth. She invited us to ask ourselves what it might be and then write it down. The morning passed in writing and discussing, and in the afternoon session we expressed our myth in collages by tearing up and pasting colored tissue paper. It was my first experience of artwork from the unconscious.

Years later, analyst James Hillman clarified further for me in *The Soul's Code* how finding out what our own myth is, and then trying to live it consciously, would help our search for happiness and meaning. He explained that this personal myth may be connected with an actual legend or fairy tale deposited in our memory in childhood, one we have cherished or lived out or perhaps, on the contrary, denied in ourselves. One way to uncover it is to study the longings and gut reactions that have been erupting in us since our own personal tale on earth began. Whether we are aware of it or not as adults, this hidden myth is still close to our hearts and entwined in our unconscious drives.

As soon as I asked myself "What is *my* myth?" it startled me by appearing in my mind whole and immediate, without any question or doubt, although I hadn't thought of it in many years. Its power and influence had fired my imagination as a teenager, later to become hidden from my conscious awareness. Clearly here was my ideal, what I had tried to live by in the years of study, search and practice, reflecting a life-long hunger for purity and truth.

My myth came from Talbot Mundy's East Indian spy-thriller, *OM*, which told of a mysterious valley beyond the great mountains in Northern India, guarded by a savage tribe whose members would kill without mercy anyone who was hardy enough to survive the terrible climb over the Himalayas.

In this valley lived the Masters, legendary wise men who, since the dawn of time, kept the ancient knowledge alive in order to save civilization whenever it began to destroy itself.

At the heart of this kingdom of higher beings was a stone or great jewel of extraordinary properties, set in the ground at the center of a circular gathering place. All who had the courage to look into its depths would see themselves reflected. But truth can be dangerous. Those who looked into it would at first see (to their horror) exactly what they were, including all that they could not bear to accept in themselves—their faults, their lies, their devils, their wickedness. Only a very few pure mortals who had not already died or fainted from the shock of that first glance could continue to gaze into the stone, where, deep in its depths, they would discover the other side of themselves—their essential being and potentiality.

The Priestess was the only person actually born in the valley apart from the savage tribe, for the Masters had learned the secret of perpetual life and lived there for thousands of years. She was born just as her father and mother were dying, he of wounds from an attack by a band of robbers before he escaped with his pregnant wife over the mountains, and she in childbirth, of exhaustion from the journey. The baby was found by the savage guards and brought to the Masters, who determined that this was a unique opportunity to educate a child untouched by the destructive influences of society, from birth to perfection as an adult. They would share with her their secret knowledge, and then send her out into the world to transmit their understanding and thus introduce a new vision of human possibility. So they brought from all over the world some twenty other abandoned girl babies to be raised as her companions.

All of them grew to be extraordinary young women, highly developed in intelligence and endowed with multifaceted talents—true, honest, discriminating, well-educated, talented in the arts and languages—all that we would long to be. An integral part of their education had been the ritual obligation to look periodically into the stone, and accept and correct any faults they saw reflected there. However, even though they could be considered nearly perfect, these girls were forced to look into the stone at night by the gentle light of the moon. Only their leader, the girl born in the valley, a kind of high priestess to the stone, could look into it in the full light of day.

I felt that I had secretly identified myself with that girl who was able to face all aspects of herself. My longing for perfection, accompanied by a rather grim search for truth, was a laudable determination but, like every stick, the search for truth and perfection has two ends. Gradually, over the course of a Jungian analysis, I became aware of a tremendous anger raging in me against my own imperfection and unfortunately, often anyone else's.

Yet on the other side was something even more fearsome. As I began to look into my own jewel/stone, a profound need for self-justification and superiority over others was exposed. It called to mind one of Gurdjieff's father's aphorisms, "I am up because you are down." In the seductive fantasy at the heart of my favorite myth it was I who was the priestess. Deep in the underworld of my secret ambitions and intentions, the wish for perfection had imperceptibly shifted its focus from a simple longing to be better (more this, more that, more what?) to a secret satisfaction at how special I was to be driven by such a wish.

♦

Encounters with Shadows

Everyone carries a shadow, and the less it is embodied in the
individual's conscious life, the blacker and denser it is. At all
counts, it forms an unconscious snag, thwarting our most
well-meant intentions. — C. G. Jung

I attended a five-lecture introductory course at the Jung
Foundation that detailed the step-by-step progression of
self-discovery in analysis, from the first sight of one's Shadow
to recognizing the Animus projection to the discovery of
the Self. I peeked over my shoulder to see if I could catch a
glimpse of them without too much risk. Not so easy, I decided,
and plunged into my first contemporary Jungian book, *The
Wounded Woman*, by Linda Leonard, whose all-day seminar
I attended. Though dozens of unread tomes awaited me at
home, and I was already saturated with words that didn't seem
to diminish the anguish I felt, I soon realized *The Wounded
Woman* was my entry ticket into a scary, shadowy circus of
images and personality fragments which, over time, I slowly
began to discover in myself. Later readings of Jung clarified the
advantage of seeing parts of oneself as separate mini-person-
alities. Like Gurdjieff's idea of many "i's" that inhabit our
personality and that we identify with, this discovery helped
me to recognize that I could be in the grip of a *complex*, that
these personas weren't "me." However, while it was fine to
think about such things, it was entirely different to *withstand*
the encounter with one's own fragments!

Leonard described her experience of such internal characters as the "Armored Amazon" and the "Eternal Girl," easily
recognizable in myself and in others. It suddenly dawned

on me that the inner critic whom I had always attempted to obey without question might perhaps be only a fragment of myself and not the head honcho at all! I figured it was formed by a childhood spent with a science-minded stepfather who worshiped at the altar of critical thought and a mother who lived by incredibly high standards of personal consciousness and conscience.

I was too experienced a psychological warrior to think that either of my parents could be held accountable for my problems, or even to point the finger of blame at the harsh reality of the Gurdjieffian view which I had ingested as a child. At the same time there was no question that the high level of demand from both parents and teaching provoked the growth of this judgmental fragment of my psyche which, armed with the disappointment and self-accusation that accompanied the failure of my marriage, had dominated my waking and sleeping hours.

In order to understand this better, I tucked another new book under my arm and went off to visit a friend in Maine. Reading Marion Woodman's *Addiction to Perfection* every day made for an incredibly painful vacation, only partially solaced by walks in the sweet-smelling pine woods and swims in the pristine lake. There was just no getting away from these critical voices in me, which harried me by day and turned into nightmare messages or threatening figures in my dreams. I gradually had to accept that nothing and no one matched up to my standards and that even I, myself, could never please this inner judge. No matter how hard I tried to succeed (and in fact my life could be considered something of a success story against major obstacles), I knew I fell short of the implacable ideal that I myself had forged. Only later did I understand this to be what psychologists call the *superego*.

In the end, I accepted the fact that I had been in a depression ever since I left Peru, though I was still fully functional; I maintained a demanding job and provided for my children. It was time to take action against this dead-end emotional situation, so I decided to risk a Jungian analysis, hoping to put at least some of my demons to rest. At a reception at the Jung Foundation that fall I met a therapist and began to work with him. I hoped that with his expert help I might separate myself from these domineering fragments.

But anyone who has undergone an analysis knows well that it is no quick fix. Gurdjieff had said we were ruled by an Inner Tyrant—and how right he was! As a child I had taken on an unforgiving attitude from the demands of the Gurdjieff teaching—phrases I had heard from adult conversations or readings were ingested as facts, such as "very good is not enough," and "all pleasure is shit." Because I had no life experience at the time, I soaked all this up like a little sponge. The message to myself was always, "*You* are not good enough!"

My father left my mother when I was about six months old. With the help of my analyst, I began to understand the secret weight his desertion must have carried, reinforced by our few early encounters which indirectly informed me that I was somehow not worth keeping, because I was "only a *girl*." By the time I was a teenager, I had accepted that while my brother was the apple of his mostly absent eye, I was a disappointment to him. After that, I was busy with college and my father was preoccupied with his third and fourth wives.

So my perception that Gurdjieff and my parents demanded perfection, along with my birth father's rejection of me, had perhaps created the unconscious attitude that I was generally unacceptable. Fanfare of trumpets. Enter my *Inner Judge*. This is the voice we all carry around inside our heads, criticizing us and everyone else. Self-hate is a terrible wounder of psyche, spirit and even body, I discovered, and my *Judge* used a sharp knife that resulted in tremendous anxiety and serious indigestion. Happily, this hateful judging voice has transformed itself today into a relatively decent, if picky companion, who often points things out to me, but without so much scorn and rancor. My digestive system celebrates with relief.

At that time, in an effort to defuse its power over me, I tried to imagine this critical part as a black crow sitting on a telephone pole, high up and dominating the foreground. Though it was only a segment of my inner landscape and I couldn't stop its cawing, at least from time to time I recognized it as separate from what I called "the real me." Weekly meetings with the therapist continued, and writing down and discussing my nightly dreams led me deeper and deeper into the dark side of my being, which Jung had referred to as the Shadow. Rather than cleaning up my act quickly, as I had hoped, this analysis seemed to nudge me downhill into further frightening and painful experiences.

Our shadow side begins to develop very early, when we, as small children, are encouraged to act in certain ways and told to avoid or suppress others. These "unacceptable, shameful or sinful" manifestations differ in various societies and even in families within the same culture. As children, in order to survive, we hide and reject what's "naughty" in the name of pleasing others. But of course nothing really goes away. What is nasty, shameful and inadmissible to the growing young person's self-image is deposited in the dark side of his or her personality and functions autonomously, unconsciously—sometimes surfacing to wreak havoc on any conscious intentions. As Connie Zweig and Jeremiah Abrams pointed out in *Meeting the Shadow: The Hidden Power of the Dark Side of Human Nature*, the shadow in us " is dangerous, disorderly, and forever in hiding, as if the light of consciousness would steal its very life."

In analysis, this Shadow is the part we usually meet first. I desperately wanted to clump all those shadowy parts of myself together and just get rid of them! But stuffing my shadows into a closet wasn't going to work. Even more disturbing, further reading and exchanges with my analyst informed me that while on the one hand this repository obviously included infantile demands, "shameful" thoughts and violent emotional reactions, on the other hand it also harbored a great deal of energy, undeveloped talents and unexpressed human potential.

Finally, I decided to cooperate with this exploration instead of resisting it. I had already uncovered a part of me that could not tolerate how I presented myself to others, how I tried to please everyone. I began to suspect that it was destroying me in some way. With this awareness now front and center, I decided not to bury the devil deeper and began to remember that I had known this shadow side, even as a small child.

My earliest and most frightening dream was of running as fast as I could from the house one dark night down a pebbled drive, with a great, black, formless monster in pursuit. It was infinitely bigger than I, so I knew that in seconds it would be on top of me and I would be engulfed by it. So I finally decided in the midst of my terror that I might as well turn around and face it. Hopelessly, but gathering all my courage, I turned to confront it and die—and then I woke up. Reading Jung's *Memories, Dreams, Reflections*, I discovered that he had had a similar dream. While carrying a candle in the night, he had become aware of a great dark figure following him, and knew he had to keep that small candle of his own consciousness alive although the light it cast was the reason for the great shadow behind him.

I also remembered how often as a child I had turned to an exciting and frightening photograph in a book called *The*

Poet's Camera, which captured a dark and terrifying woods in early evening with gnarled and twisted trees whose branches seemed to writhe and reach out. The caption read: "*Enter these enchanted woods, ye who dare!*" Even when I was a little older, my "dark self" maintained a mesmerizing attraction, at least in daylight. My brother and I, often left alone on Sunday afternoons when our parents went to Franklin Farms, would tune in at five p.m. to a forbidden radio program, *The Shadow*. Here was someone who had the power to "alter men's minds so that they cannot see him." We shivered deliciously at the opening lines as a sepulchral voice asked: "Who knows what evil lurks in the hearts of men? The Shadow knows … " Fade in the horrid, eerie, meaningful laughter, which is as alive in my ears today as it was when I was eight years old.

So, after fifty years of a virtuous, almost blameless life of being a "good girl, good wife, good mother," that mysterious evil-seeming presence was assaulting my private world again. Gradually some aspects of myself that I didn't like, and had refused to admit to consciously, came into clearer view. I began to recognize them through noticing my strong reactions to similar attitudes in other people. In psychological lingo that's called *projection*—you attribute to someone else an attitude you can't admit is yours. It reminded me of Gurdjieff's advice to be alert to what irritates you in other people if you want to know yourself better. Even though it led to painful admissions, this suggestion was very helpful.

♦

The Myth of Family

All this unraveling of parent-child stuff may have nothing to do with why we are crazy. — James Hillman

My life as an adult was primarily shaped by my deification of the idea of family, perhaps due to the fact that my mother didn't have one. Her mother had died when she was two and her father when she was ten, but she barely knew him because she was raised by cold grandparents, who claimed they were her parents. She grew up feeling as if she didn't belong. *Family* was very important to her, so even as a single mother with no financial assistance, her courage kept us all afloat throughout the Depression.

I began to understand how I had mimicked her situation— keeping my own husband and three children going, as I held on to an untenable financial situation and refused to give up. The *family* represented almost everything that I cared about, driving me to heights and depths of emotion, giving meaning to my life and crowning my sense of usefulness. Finally, my dedication to "keeping the family together" led to illness, depression and a lot of suffering before I could separate from my husband and begin life again.

Even afterward, as I tried to raise and support my children alone in New York City, driven by constant service to what I perceived as their needs with little thought for my own, I felt intense guilt at having shattered this ideal. My recurring image, whenever I recalled those last years in Peru, was of an ineffectual effort to keep my finger in the hole of a dyke at whatever cost to myself, hoping to hold back the inevitable flood that would carry us all away. It took an encounter with

James Hillman to help me see the dark side of my dedication to family.

Hillman, an erudite revolutionary in the world of psychology, trained in both the Freudian and Jungian camps, first riveted me at a Jung Foundation seminar on the *Puer Eternis*, or Eternal Youth archetype. I began to read his books, embracing his uncompromising thought and radical invitation to re-enter confusion in areas which other psychologists were trying to clarify. For example, in *The Myth of Analysis*, he pointed to a basic flaw in our attitude to therapy, saying that psychology had become "a massive yet subtle system for distorting the poor psyche into a belief that there is something 'wrong' with it." Since I had recently assumed that *I* was the basic flaw in my marriage and my life, this sounded like a possible escape out of the self-condemnation I so often felt.

When I learned that Hillman was giving a day-long seminar entitled "The Myth of Family," nothing in my over-crowded life could have kept me away. (Despite suffering from cholestatic hepatitis, I worked at *Fortune* to keep the family in food and lodging and would race home in the evening to cook healthy dinners for the kids and try to get enough rest so that I could return to my job the next day.)

Hillman's words shocked me. Having been totally "identified" with my own family, blaming its breakup on my inability to handle my life, I was startled to hear that family was largely a myth created by our culture and reaffirmed by therapists. Was it possible that my blind dedication to keeping the family together had been overkill, perhaps even detrimental to my own and my children's psychic health?

Getting right down to destroying our illusions in the first five minutes, Hillman provided a series of grim 1990 statistics: one in four Americans lived alone versus one in seven twenty years before; two-thirds of the children born that year lived in one-parent families, one in five with unwed mothers; and three percent of all adult males were in the correction system. How could we see the family as the norm, he asked us, if the lives of 75% of Americans were a departure from it?

He then explained the probable cause: the idea of family evokes warmth and comfort and the child archetype in us longs for it. Then he exhorted (was he looking straight at me?): "Break out of the ideal of family! Let go of what you held onto and cherished, and see what your imagination produces. You have created an imaginary story out of your past life with family, but it isn't what really happened. Marriage is a heavy-duty, dirty-diaper, realistic thing. Home is the most dangerous place to be, with the most homicides and the most hurt."

This was harsh stuff! Continuing his attack on my Number One Identification, he added: "If the dress no longer fits, is it your fault? What is the guilt you are feeling doing for you?" I began to feel pressure in my sensitive gut. Was my guilt at breaking up the family the reason my relations with my teen-aged children were so tense? It had certainly turned me into a too-permissive mother and an inadequate substitute father!

Family therapy became Hillman's next target as he pointed to what he considered the flawed approach of trained psychologists who might tell you that you are a result of social causes, that not you but the family is at fault if you are dysfunctional. He also decried the underlying message they were giving society that we should all adjust, that people who were odd, different or strange should feel guilty and ashamed of their strangeness. Instead, Hillman said, "the individual *should* be odd and shouldn't fit into anything else. Individuation means differentiation. It's *important* that we are different."

Finally he reassured everyone hanging on his words that, "You are never going to figure it all out or untangle it. You will just exchange one fiction for another. We are always in a play, always making drama. But we need to let go of the error that we are victims of our culture." Here was a powerful invitation to let go of my total identification with my family. I rejoiced at the idea that I could put my consuming guilt away forever. At least it seemed possible in the heat of recognition, but as my stepfather often liked to say, "Things usually get worse before they get better."

◆

My Cast of Characters

The first person singular—that little devil of an I—is neither first, nor a person, nor singular. — James Hillman

Over the next few years I focused on understanding my feelings of anger, shame and guilt, seeking to discern hidden 'shadow' figures through the study of my reactions towards others and the people in my dreams. Little by little, I discovered my own cast of characters. Who's in charge? I wondered. My daytime hours were dominated by frequent forays between *The Slave-driver/Judge/Critic* in me—a scolding parental figure lodged mostly in my head—and *The Forgetful Child* who didn't want to be bothered and dreamed of wandering through the woods picking flowers.

This is how I described the two figures in my diary:

> The child is whining, crying, desperate, at wit's end sometimes, and at others mindless, happy, gushing with good feeling, delighted in the moment of warm sensation, happiness. The child forgets, leaves things behind, allows gaps to appear. The child is warm, loving, spontaneous—

wanting everyone to be happy, wanting to please. Or
sometimes annoyed, wanting to have its own way, wanting
what it wants NOW, not later, and annoyed at anyone or
anything that gets in the way.

Then there's the critic, who's also the judge with no
face or sex, the attacker, accuser, faultfinder, pointing
out how I have once more fallen down on the job, failed
myself and others, and, above all, failed to live up to
the performance expected of me. I suppose it's also the
perfectionist, who hates me because I can't measure up
to such high standards and makes me feel royally hated,
desperately inadequate, a Disappointment.

From time to time I would meet new personages, like
Mrs. Rigid, a lady who liked to have things *one way and no
other*. I noticed her on the beach in front of my birth father's
Gulf Coast house in Florida where I visited him near the end
of his life. I was harried and exhausted from the Manhattan
treadmill—trying to keep up with both my work as a journalist at *Fortune* and my duty as primary caretaker of my elderly
mother and stepfather. I had planned to recuperate during a
relaxed vacation week, but my psyche had other ideas.

Mrs. Rigid began to dominate that beautiful seaside setting
by interminably organizing my activities. She told me when I
should take walks, when to go swimming and even when to
have a cup of tea. I didn't seem able to make any comfortable
choices as this organizing demon sent me thither and yon so
that I would "use my time well." In her limited and narrow-
minded way, *Mrs. Rigid* was also quite recognizable as a part of
myself. I began to see that I needed to help the panicked person
in me learn to weigh decisions and shift plans in midstream
rather than be so darned RIGID!

A year later, I met her again at my father's house. When she
reappeared, I felt as if I were locked in a suit of armor. During

my first walk on the beach, *Mrs. R.* told me to program it, exactly one half-hour going and one half-hour coming back. In other words, she couldn't let things happen as they happened. She had to plan each detail, occupy every moment with sterling usefulness. My problem began to clarify: if she weren't around to tell me what to do, who would make decisions for me, caught as I was in a jungle of *oughts* and *shoulds*?

This question still burned in me the next day as I walked along the beach, until I suddenly felt an inner shift, as if I were walking hand in hand with *Mrs. Rigid* on the seaside and a *young child* on the other. As I walked, it felt as if something was passing through me from one to the other, connecting them, changing my whole internal landscape. That was when I first I realized that I could be the bridge between them. The disapproving adult kept the child feeling scared and incapable, perpetuating the situation, rather than lovingly educating her so that she could grow up into an intelligent, sensitive human being. The child reacted and wanted to run away. But as soon as I attended to both of them at the same time, an exchange was possible. A prayer rose in me after this epiphany: to remember that communication between my *child* and my *critic* could only appear through my own presence to both of them at once. I later heard Jungian analyst Marion Woodman call this strange psychic experience "holding the tension of the opposites." She described it as "life's greatest challenge." As we begin to integrate the tension between two parts of ourselves, a new consciousness emerges.

Nevertheless, it was some time before I realized that *Mrs. Rigid* was rigid not because she knew better, but through fear and loneliness. She planned things carefully so they could always safely remain familiar. *Mrs. R.*, like the *child*, needed help, affection, a sense of security, which she only felt when every free moment was organized ahead of time. I began to notice, once plans were in place, a subtle sense of relief that I wouldn't be alone with nothing to do, no way to fill the next hours.

Later *The Editor* in me appeared, at first only in business meetings. She was always sure of herself, passing judgment on other people's suggestions, disposing of them, denying them, affirming what she knew were the right views, full of opinions and self-assurance as if she knew everything. Suspicious of her, I kept an eye open for her at other times and saw that she also edited *me* when I was alone.

Finally *The Ferret* made its entrance, late to the game because I was convinced for a long time that this was the real *me*—the seeker of truth, the pursuer of consciousness. But gradually this personage who was always hunting down answers and trying to figure out what was going on became visible as just another fragment, one that was always asking questions. Why was there pain in my abdomen? What did I just say to someone that made them angry? What was the meaning of this or that, which might make all the difference to my understanding? This dominant pursuit of answers often led me away from being present to the moment I was living through. *The Ferret's* rule ended when an authoritative voice at the end of a dream announced: "*What you seek doesn't have to be looked for.*"

I would like to say that from then on *The Ferret* disappeared, but habits, whether mental, emotional or physical, don't disappear so easily. What raises hope about such epiphanies is that when you acknowledge that a *persona* you thought of as *you* is simply one artist in your cast of characters, a deep inner shift toward freedom takes place. The exposed fragment is forced into a corner because, once recognized by a more central identity, it can no longer steal the show.

Other techniques lead to self-discovery in Jungian analysis. As my first attempt at paper collage in Dr. Wallace's seminar had already proved, artistic expression is one of them. After three attempts, my fourth collage became the *"enchanted woods"* of my childhood poem, with a strange serpent-like being rising above it and a bright sun beaming down. Some time later my eldest daughter, who was studying art therapy, invited me to an intensive workshop at Pratt Art Institute. We worked all day on a variety of creative artistic constructions, then, in the last period of the afternoon, we were told to make a collage by choosing from a pile of thousands of cutout magazine pictures and photos.

Already tired of pursuing "ghosts," I started without much enthusiasm, but soon was taken over by a kind of concentrated, driven energy. It led me to select forms and colors which my hands glued swiftly to the paper as if without my help. The result was a rectangle divided into four quarters with a central figure. On the upper left I had placed a photo of a frightened deer running rapidly away off the paper, and scribbled the words *RUN! RUN!* below it. I didn't understand it at the time but a few years later I connected it with a state which sometimes overcame me, of feeling overwhelmed and wishing to flee as fast as possible from whatever difficult situation I was in. I called this new personage *The Frightened Deer*.

Once I recognized the frightened creature, it seemed my only way to make a relation with this state was to befriend the deer rather than condemning the fear. It helped to accept this fear as a fact, rather than to deny it. I tried to visualize taking the deer for a walk out into the street, keeping my hand reassuringly on its back and walking very slowly, never forgetting its presence beside me, or the fact that it was trembling with fear. That was how I re-introduced this country-woods fragment of myself to the city streets and the hurly burly of my life.

On another corner of the collage was a fiery explosion, and at the center was a serpent devouring a rose. A closer look showed me that even its own coils and the colored paper around it had added petals to the flower. The serpent and the flower became one. What was this serpent about? I'd seen it many times slithering through my dreams and in the image of *Laocoon*, the Trojan priest of Apollo who warned his people to beware the Trojan horse. The gods punished him for this, sending serpents to squeeze him and his children to death. A photo in a book I'd seen of the 2nd-century BC sculpture would appear in my mind's eye whenever I tried out Jung's suggestion to look for the image behind my mood. The man's body, with the serpent coiled all around him—torso, arms, legs—had burnt into my mind. Even my own aches and pains suggested that I was being slowly squeezed to death by serpent power.

Here before my eyes were a rose and a serpent, the serpent part of the rose and the rose being eaten by the serpent. This mysterious conjunction recalled William Blake's poetic image that had haunted me many years before: a rose sick from an invisible worm at its core. I felt threatened at the heart of my inner place of rest, remembering the end of his poem, "… And his dark secret love Doth thy life destroy." What love was destroying my life? At the heart of my wish and my longing, was there some destructive force at work?

I came to realize that Jung's answer would have been a resounding "Yes!" Since everything evokes its opposite, my wish for perfection brought shadow forces into play, represented in my case by an invisible worm at the heart of what I held sacred. Each time I found myself "making nice" to someone because I wanted to be liked and not from my own interest in them, I was angry with myself. On the other hand, when I did something "selfish" or put my own interest first while giving the impression I was thinking of the other, I attacked myself for selfishness. As usual, there was *NO WAY OUT!*

But my worst new experiences of the Underworld came through dreams. I had always resented the interpret-your-dream work emphasized in therapy, so incomprehensible and indecipherable to me, so far out and *unreasonable*. My dreams might be considered the Royal Road to integration by some, but to me they were more like a swamp of quicksand that sucked me under every time I looked their way. Since I could seldom remember them the next morning, I forced myself to write them down in the middle of the night. Yet I was so disconnected from that dream underworld of hidden meanings that they surprised me all over again when reviewed in weekly sessions with my therapist.

First to appear was *The Blonde Bombshell*, a loose woman with a cigarette between her over-rouged lips and a provocative hip sway. I could almost hear my stepfather's rude comments. She was all I refused to be and scorned as common or slut-like, while fascinated by such freedom from strict (and safe) morality. Jungian literature explained that same-sex characters in dreams usually represent the Shadow. That made sense given my strong disapproval of this character. But what good was this information to me? Was I supposed to tear off my clothes and dance naked on a café table?

As my nights became worse, repetitive dreams appeared of criminals and cops, of being tortured along with a group of friends by bad guys, of there being *No Way Out* of some war zone surrounded by enemy troops or infiltrated by spies. These dream figures and stories often had a simplistic, comic book nature, which might have allowed me to shake them off, except that when I woke up I was chilled or sweating and afraid to back to sleep. I tried to reassure myself with Jung's statement in *Memories, Dreams, Reflections* that "In the final analysis the decisive factor is always consciousness, which can understand the manifestations of the unconscious and take up a position toward them." But it didn't help much. I was on my own among threatening psychic forces.

A breakthrough finally came that left me with more respect

for what these violent, frightening adventures meant. One night one of the cops in my dream came into the room at the last minute, to my great relief, to save us good guys. I watched with satisfaction as he shot the bad guys who were about to kill us. But then the unbelievable happened: he coldly and quite intentionally turned his gun towards me and shot me point blank in the face. I was shocked awake. When my rapid heartbeat quieted down, I realized that not all that belonged to the "good guys" in me was necessarily trustworthy. My cops and criminals became two ends of the same stick. All these assassins and police and criminals were telling me something important, but I just wasn't getting it. A policeman shot me in the forehead when I gave him information about a criminal and expected him to turn his gun on the bad guy. A criminal shot me in the belly, just as I thought I'd convinced him I wouldn't betray him and expected him to pay me to keep quiet.

My own naiveté was getting shot both by *The Policeman*, who represented one side of me, and *The Criminal*, who represented another. What could this mean? *The Policeman* was needed to keep things under control, within the law, to pursue the bad guys, corral them and put them in jail. That was understandable, but who was *The Criminal*? Who, within me, was engaged in doing what some other part didn't want done? Was it a fragment that was hiding my real feelings from me, or someone who wanted me to express my feelings more? Did it want me to be nice, to be liked? Ready to shoot me if I strayed from the path? What should I make of the oft-repeated theme of betrayal? *Who* was betrayed and by what actions of mine? Finally, who was the innocent bystander getting it in the neck, always shocked by what she never expected to happen to her? Was being 'shot' a play on the word *shocked*?

The worst moment came like a stab in the heart when I realized that *The Nazi*, a sadistic torturer often present in my worst dreams, kept house in some part of myself. I had resisted the suggestion that all the characters in dreams are fragments of the dreamer, and was convinced that this *Nazi* was my most fearsome enemy, a terrifying phantom of the night. But it finally became apparent that—like every figure in my dreams—he owed his life to me. How could I learn to accept that it was a part of myself clutching the knife and twisting it with relish in the wound? Yet once I had assimilated the pain of this realization, he never came back.

◆

Dialogues with a Tyrant

We have in all naiveté forgotten that beneath our world of reason another lies buried. — C. G. Jung

One of the unique aspects of Jungian work is *Active Imagination*. When a dream figure haunts or frightens you or seems enormously portentous, your therapist may suggest that you try to dialogue with it in a daytime encounter. You sit quietly, evoke the image, then ask it questions and, if you like, write down the answers without judging or changing them. The usefulness of such an exercise seemed at first pretty far-fetched. Obviously it's me talking to me and I'm wide-awake, so what can happen that's new? When I tried it, I had two problems. My critical intelligence was affronted by the experiment itself and by the vulgar, sometimes violent responses that appeared. However I couldn't ignore the fact that, nasty as these comments might be, they often made sense.

These attempts to connect with unconscious fragments of

myself in a conscious state threw light on my hidden reactions, sometimes telling me in no uncertain terms what I had refused to face. Often the answering voice had the same outlandish quality of my dreams: childish, rude, angry or unforgiving. But when I thought about the message rather than the messenger, its relevance became clear. My analyst explained that repressed drives and attitudes can reappear in shockingly primitive forms until they become more integrated into the conscious personality. No matter how unpleasant, this was exactly why dialogues could be so important in uncovering what was going on below the surface of one's life.

When I began to dialogue with my dream characters, at first I felt attacked and disgusted. Then, over the years, I noticed that the answering voices were changing in tone, gradually shifting from primitive vituperation to thoughtful advice. I finally realized it was no accident that over the same period *The Tyrant* in my cast of inner characters had gradually become less accusing and more advisory. *The Black-Robed, Unforgiving Judge* had morphed into a kind of news commentator. But all that happened much later.

My first experiment with Active Imagination took place the day I woke up from a dream that ended with this scornful statement: "*Any price that has to be paid! You're available to pay it!*" This pointed to a deeply ingrained inner attitude: someone else's need or even just my perception of their need would impel me full speed ahead, all systems go, to help, save, pay or pave their way. When I asked the voice what it meant, the image that appeared was that of a fish darting with blind instinct at a temptingly baited hook. The message seemed to be that I was as driven as this fish in my role as savior or superwoman.

I sat at my computer, writing questions, eyes closed, body relaxed. I let my thoughts flow without inhibition and let any responses type themselves spontaneously without attempting to edit in any way. I remembered the dream voice telling me that I deserved to pay and pay hard! *"Take that and that and that! I'll show you what paying is 'til it comes out of your ears! You'll be sorry you offered!"* Suddenly it dawned on me that perhaps it was I who urgently needed help when I responded so dedicatedly to others' emergencies, putting myself and my own needs last almost with relish, with satisfaction, as if to punish myself by this readiness to "pay any price."

So, I asked the dream figure:

Who are you, who is saying "take that and that and that?"

What do you care?

I care. That's why I'm asking. I need to understand why you want to hurt everything gentle, vulnerable, fragile in me.

Kill the bird! Because it hurts, hurts, hurts! It hurts so much to listen, to love, to care for, to cherish. It hurts and hurts and hurts. So why not crush it before it gets a chance to hurt?

I don't know what to do or what to say to you. But I do believe a heart can break, and that my heart has seemed to come to the end of its possibility to survive several times, to hurt so much it felt it couldn't go on beating and sustaining life.

And yet you open yourself up to more of the same again and again. What are you, a masochist?

Maybe. I only know more and more that I can't be any different from what I am. So I guess I just have to learn to bear it.

That may be your idea of fun but it's not mine!

A few days later, a friend came around to visit me in late afternoon and four hours later she was still talking about all that had happened to her since we were last together. I was exhausted by her constant chatter, so when she finally left, I sat down at my computer to exchange with "whomever" might respond:

> I feel I'd rather not have anyone here than get so tired! Why do I allow myself to be so depleted by the person visiting me? Why do I make myself into an edible fungus that others can eat up at their pleasure?

> **Look how you listened to her ... concentrating eagerly on every word as if you were going to get an exam on it the next day. Why do you live so far from yourself?**

> Listen, you bum. I'm trying my best and it's pretty obvious that my best isn't good enough. But just how much do I have to dump on myself before I accept that I am the way I am and can't help it?

> **Sure! But look how resentful you are feeling right now about being used up by a conversation that brings you nothing and simply seems to serve as a cathartic to this other lady who's doing nothing for you. It's great for her! But what kind of a business are you in?**

More and more frequently I heard the voice of my inner enemy, whom I called *The Accuser* and then *The Tyrant*. What was the right definition for this character fragment? *Witch? Bitch? Judge? Critic? Termagant?* All these words failed to describe the screaming, stabbing, full-of-invective creature somewhere inside me. This creature attacked me in dreams and I began to hear its voice more often in broad daylight in the middle of what I was doing. I felt as if someone were attacking, punishing, stifling me, because there were so many things to be done and I wasn't doing them. My to-do list felt like bricks falling on my shoulders, weighing me down.

What could free me from the prison of this dark side, this angry, supercilious, arrogant, critical person inside me—attacking, scorning, putting me down until I felt like Orestes pursued by the Furies. A mighty force had been loosed in my consciousness, but defining it didn't seem nearly as important as surviving or connecting in some other way with this faceless negative being. I continued to carry on these dialogues with my newly surfaced enemies.

A new stage in my struggle to understand began when it occurred to me that *The Tyrant* might be as frightened as *The Child*. If so, that changed everything. If they were both afraid, each trying to find her own way, defending herself as best she could against what seemed threatening by commenting, criticizing, scorning, one-upping or running away, then it was their way of staying safe. In that case both *The Tyrant* who caused tension and pain and the fleeing, panicked *Child* were prisoners, each trying to care for herself, to defend herself in some way from the blows that came thick and fast.

Once more I tried a dialogue, even though I felt I'd had enough of this experiment.

Why do you hate me so, why do you attack me so?

Who's attacking who?

I thought it was obvious but maybe not. Can you shed some light?

To avoid being attacked you have to attack. Criticizing puts you on another level—above the other fella. Scorn does the same.

Is there a way we could live together, inhabiting the same body, and not destroying it or each other? I've expressed my view of you, do you want space to say exactly how you feel about me?

You are stupid, naive, bumbling, inadequate, idiotic.

Ughh! Was this supposed to be helpful? Thinking the results might be different if I approached a friendlier inner person, I tried a dialogue with *Mrs. Rigid*, asking her,

When will I be more whole? When will I be less fragmented, less victim, less turning in a vicious circle between the clarity and warmth of an inner relationship with myself and the circle of confusion of tongues, the rigidity, the reaction, the prison?

What is your prison made of?

I don't exactly know. My fixed beliefs that come from somewhere, my fears. I can sometimes feel actually physically constrained, as if I were tied down, or as if snakes were writhing around my body, tighter and tighter. Am I supposed to just accept that? Accept to be in prison? If so, why do I feel such anguish to get free of it, to live in a larger world where there is warmth and freedom, where I can breathe?

There is no freedom if there is not freedom from "results" and from right and wrong.

This exercise began to reveal more possibilities. It now often dissolved the tension that gripped me most of the time. I decided to challenge my unknown guide by evoking the two images that came to me most often, the Laocoon bound up in snakes that squeeze him to death and the crossroads where all four roads were blocked.

Where do we go from here?

Stand still and take stock.

But that can be a negative experience, trying to find a way out in passivity. Isn't everything in movement and shouldn't I find a way to move out?

Yes and no ...

That's helpful!

What is help?

Help is seeing a way out under or over barriers.

Help is letting go.

I asked my therapist why these more recent dialogues had changed so much in tone from my early conversations with *The Tyrant*. He replied that they could be effecting a gradual change in the very nature of my relationship with the unconscious, from a battleground to an exchange of information. The important thing, he said, was to listen. Marion Woodman said the same thing to me in different words: "Gradually the Unconscious opens up to you and becomes your friend."

That Christmas I received a poem from a friend that ended with these lines:

"May the wounded and the wounder
Find their way to one another,
As they are one."

I wept before I could think about it. The battle within me wasn't about choosing between a tyrant and a frightened child! In my effort to figure it all out I had forgotten I was both, that they came together in me. Yet all my suffering came from the clash between *The Accuser* who attacked with venom and *The Child* who panicked into fear and helplessness. If only the former could point things out, help make decisions, give hints and even, at times, orders without being so nasty. If only the child could bring me joy and freshness, lightness, softness and even good health without feeling so helpless in the face of attack. But for that to happen, the accuser would have to stop wanting to punish all the time, and the child would have to give up always wanting to be happy, stop expecting every minute to be an outstanding experience.

Some things couldn't change, I was sure. The accuser would always be critical, racking up lists of tasks longer than the length of a day. But it was up to me to decide when the lists should win my attention and when the child could be allowed to say "the hell with all this, now I'll have some fun." And sometimes maybe both of them could take a vacation from my inner landscape and give me a chance to ponder.

◆

Will a Child Lead Me?

In the individuation process, (the child archetype) anticipates the figure that comes from the synthesis of conscious and unconscious elements in the personality. It is therefore a symbol which unites the opposites; a mediator, bringer of healing, that is, one who makes whole. — C. G. Jung

Thus began a new level of exchange within myself as I started to believe in the existence of some of these psychic fragments.

Clearly someone inside me knew things that my conscious self was unaware of. *The Tyrant, Slave-driver* or *Judge*, along with *The Critic*—a milder version of the *Judge* who seemed to be replacing the others much of the time these days—had taken up most of my interest. Now it was time to pay more attention to that *Inner Child*, to relate to her, even to protect her from the ravages of life from which she suffered so acutely.

This unknown, yet well-known, part of me first reappeared at a friend's health resort in Maine, at a hypnotherapy session. It's an understatement to say I was reluctant to experiment with hypnotism—I *scorned* such nonsense but wished not to offend her, since she had invited me. So I lay on the purple rug in the exercise room while a weird, longhaired young man told me to count quietly from one to ten and that I was becoming sleepy. He then asked where I would like to go in my imagination.

"How ridiculous," I thought, perfectly awake with my eyes closed but going along for the ride. I chose the woods. "You are walking down a path through the woods," the guy intoned. "Who is coming to meet you?" To my surprise, my eight-year-old self appeared in my mind's eye, skinny and tough. She who loved to roam the woods and meadows, to fantasize in the garden and write poetry, had been left behind when we moved from the country, which I loved, to the city, which I passionately hated. Here she was leading me down the path a bit scornfully—after all, I didn't know where I was going!

With the help of Longhair's intermittent questions about what was going on, she took me to a house in the woods and into a room containing a large round table in the middle. "Who is sitting at it?" Longhair asked. Continuing my reverie, I saw with fascination that there were six or seven people, including a grim-faced judge in black. I couldn't tell whether the figure was man or woman, but it was a Cotton Mather type who never cracked a smile. Across the table a red-caped, muscular Superman (one of my favorite comics as a child) sat at ease, and next to him a pleasant, homey kind of woman.

The hypnotherapist asked me for details about each of them and ended our session with the suggestion that maybe Superman could defend me in my helplessness when scolded by the negative, hypercritical judge who was making my life miserable. That same Judge was thinking inside me that this was a pretty silly business as "Mr. Hypnosis" slowly counted backwards from ten to one and pronounced me awake. But neither I nor the Judge could downplay the memory of the house in the woods where my personality fragments sat in eternal conference, or erase the image of the child who had led me to them.

On reflection, I realized I must have cut myself off from this young side of myself. We moved to New York when I was eight and I had been mercilessly teased in fourth grade because I, the essence of an innocent country girl, didn't fit in. Perhaps I had been made so ashamed that I'd packed that side of myself away in my unconscious, and now, whenever aspects of my child nature appeared, the *Judge/Tyrant* accused *me/them* of being stupid and naïve.

It seemed urgent to understand the relation between these two fragments, *Tyrant* and *Child*. While it was possible to interpret *me as a child*, sometimes weak and forgetful in relation to more powerful forces, nevertheless I was an adult, and had spent many years successfully raising a family, running a school and, more recently, keeping a demanding job. Yet *The Tyrant* continually found fault, rejoicing at every opportunity to attack me and evoke a mountain of guilt about even the tiniest things. As I became more aware of this (and thus more *conscious* of it), I picked up other examples.

On one occasion I had pulled my address book out of my bag to look up a couple of telephone numbers, made a call and put it back. Then I remembered there was another call I had to make. At that moment an inner voice actually lashed out at me for having put the book away, as if I had committed a crime. "There you go again, stupid!" was the accusation.

Another time, when I was trying to cook dinner, I spilled millet all over the floor in my headlong rush. It spread in all directions, round, wonderfully rolling, the tiny pellets awakening me to the presence of the child. Then I remembered how many times I had tried to cook "special" things for my husband or my stepfather, and how often I ended up hurrying, spilling, burning, hastily trying to improve something that had already gone wrong. Was the child causing this, trying so hard to "do it right," but no matter how much she cared, she was all thumbs and making a mess as usual?

Something new had entered my life, caused, I felt, by the dialogues I began to have with *The Child*. Some ancient, buried hurt had been freed and now in daily life I began to notice more often the fears and excitements I could associate with a very young part of me. "What is needed of me? What is expected of me?" she seemed to ask as I went through my daily tasks, wanting to do whatever was needed, but feeling inadequate. The question hung there day after day until a kind of answer came: "*Being there, being present, being attentive is the only thing you can do.*" I began to accept that nothing else could be "done." I would always react, and I had to live with my fears in certain situations. In fact, *there was no escape from myself but presence.*

Not long afterward I had an acrimonious discussion with my daughter during which she walked away while I was talking. I erupted in anger and went after her shouting "I *insist* on being heard," and then burst into tears. This time, instead of controlling myself as I always did, I let all the pain and anger come out. "I *must* be heard! I *will* be heard! Why am I always refused a hearing?" There was clearly someone in myself to whom I myself refused to listen, some part desperate to be heard. "How could I be true to my*self?*" became my anguished question. To myself! Not to the image or the perfectionist. Not to the little girl wanting joy or the body wanting comfort. Not to the ego wanting to be praised or the inadequate person wanting to please; or the fabricator of my spiritual success story, who wanted to be top guru.

Finally, I turned to Jung's volume on *Archetypes and the Collective Unconscious* for help. Archetypes were as real to him as kidneys are to us and as physical in their basis. I learned that he considered the child archetype more than the human-child memory I had thought it was. He called it one of those "living psychic forces that demand to be taken seriously," and explained that these archetypes are activated when there has been a disconnection or conflict between present life and the past. For example, when there is a violent opposition between two parts of one's nature. Jung said that the loss of roots that might come about by denying certain emotional ties in the name of conscious thought would invite "an equally vehement confrontation with the primary truth."

His words clarified what was happening to me in this endless tug of war between *The Judge* and *The Child*. I began to think of it in his terms, as a battle between abstraction and rootedness. He said the child archetype is constellated when there is "a conflict situation that offers *no way out.*" (italics mine) That was a familiar phrase! He added that it was important also to understand that this child is not just a vestige from the past, but a present psychic reality "whose purpose is to compensate or correct, in a meaningful manner, the inevitable one-sidedness and extravagances of the conscious mind." Progress might supply us with many good things, Jung pointed out. But inevitably it evoked "an equally gigantic Promethean debt" as we became disconnected from our own deeper nature. Since the mind tends to worship at the altar of clarity, I could only guess that in my case the child represented a world of feeling that I cut off in my effort not to feel so much pain.

I want to make it clear here that my adventures with personality fragments, years raw with uncertainty and confusion, came long before reading about Jung's view of the Child archetype. Only later, freer of the grip of my warring parts, did I learn that in his view the child wasn't another partial *persona*, but represented the archetype of wholeness, potential and healing. I had been what Marion Woodman called "a *persona* person," trying to please, striving to figure out what I *ought* to do. Yet the fearless, capable eight-year-old that I had been, before our family moved to the city, could lead me to safety.

◆

Dancing the Soul

So long as power supersedes love, so long as the creative feminine and masculine energies are excluded from our personal and cultural lives, life on this planet is in jeopardy. — Marion Woodman

In recent years I've studied with Marion, who is currently reaching for a new approach to human balance in her seminal exploration of *BodySoul Rhythms*. During week-long intensive encounters, accompanied by dance professor Mary Hamilton and voice teacher Ann Skinner, she works in Jungian dream analysis, body movement, voice release and mask-making "to help women experience their own soul in their own body, expressed through their own authentic voice."

I had read some of her books years earlier, starting with *Addiction to Perfection,* so accurate a portrayal of me that I sometimes felt sick and had to stop reading. Another book that seared my psyche as it presented the "Father-Daughter Wound" was *Leaving My Father's House,* something I hadn't yet been able to do since I had returned from Peru into the family nest. I worked, raised my children and paid rent for a separate apartment in my stepfather's house, but he was an integral part of my support system and, as I began to ascertain, a model for the critical judge in me.

Marion gave infrequent lecture workshops over the years, which I attended without knowing that she was fighting cancer, as she later described in *Bone: Dying into Life.* When I learned about *BodySoul Rhythms,* a series of intensive courses available to a few prepared women already experienced in bodywork and Jungian studies, I joined her, Mary, Ann and 27 women for nine days on an island west of Vancouver, Canada.

The trip set a cosmic stage for studies of the unconscious—jetting across Canada and then transferring to a local, small bird of a plane to Vancouver Island just as the light faded on a stormy afternoon. We swooped low over a multitude of tree-covered islands as mists formed and dissipated around us, at moments seeing nothing until suddenly great panoramas opened up like a vision of the legendary Islands of the Blest. When we landed, a ferry took us to another island, where our hostel perched on a rocky shore, fronted in three directions by a great wide seascape dotted with islands.

Days started at nine and often lasted until 11 p.m. There was brief respite for meals and a short walk, if we were lucky, often followed by a study of something that had been touched on in the previous session. We began each day investigating the recent dreams of two or three of the participants while Marion and some of the others made comments on them. I often challenged her somewhat belligerently on the importance she gave those dreams, since mine were still a battleground of resistance and incredulity to me. She always responded with grace, openness and intelligence, telling me that they and our bodily symptoms inform us about what's going on in our depths. "Your dreams and your symptoms are your Unconscious at work," she would say. Her gentle firmness stuck pins into my "attitude," deflating it as she offered useful information on how to approach the understanding of dreams. She assured me that as an analyst she had refused any patient who wouldn't accept to dedicate an hour each day to dream-work.

A belated respect for my dreams grew out of my enormous respect for her. This lady was no fuzzy-minded, feel-good therapist but a clear, precise thinker. The demand she made both by her incisive intellect and the depth of her presence was as important as her verbal guidance, and focused us on the importance of both exploration and balance in all our expressive parts.

The afternoons of movement and voice-work, and evenings making masks, wove seamlessly together with the morning discussions, as we explored the hidden and ignored places in our individual psyches, to free the energy imprisoned there and move toward a new balance. "Analysis is about finding and reclaiming your own energy," she said. "Your greatest wound is your greatest gift." The voice and dance work was wonderfully freeing, filling me with nighttime energy. But it was the mask-making that brought me a confounding experience which demonstrated that the psyche has a memory and intentions of its own.

Several years earlier, when anger was just beginning to erupt from my volcanic depths, I had gone to a New Year's Eve party in which we were to mask ourselves in "what you wish for or plan to give up in the new year." My mask created itself swiftly, impelled by the hidden force of my then-unrecognized anger. Twenty minutes into a creative surge with paint and glue I was staring at the face of an angry Indian chief, which won first prize at the party. Recognizing this expression as my own anger and thinking it would help to study it, I hung the mask on my wall. But I soon discovered that frequent glances at it stirred up more anger and indigestion, so I had to put it away.

Now I was mask-making again, but in a different rhythm. Night after night the papier-mâché took on the shape of my own face, with no clue as to what the final result would express. When the time came to decorate and paint, a directed energy took charge of me for two hours, an intense intention to communicate from the bottomless depths how angry I felt. As I struggled to put together the scariest, nastiest, angriest face I could possibly invent, it seemed as though a repeat of the earlier episode were taking place, and indeed it became the face of another Indian chief.

But I was in for a very different shock. When I put on the mask and looked in the mirror at the final result, it was beautiful! Not horrible, not nasty, not unbearably ugly and frightening as I had tried so hard to make it, but serene and elegant in subtle pastel shades and decorated with beautiful feathers. Marion would call this another experience of "living within the tension of the opposites," active contact with two sides of myself at the same time. Back home, I was able to hang it on my bedroom wall where it still reminds me that there's far more going on in the underworld of my psyche than my conscious mind could ever understand!

Along with helping us study and release the energy imprisoned in our individual psyches, Marion's work always contained a call to recognize the urgent need for changes on a worldwide scale. I recently asked her to explain her future vision for the *BodySoul Rhythms* work. She formulated it as follows:

> Our planet is at a crucial point of transition. Humankind will either co-operate with Earth's ecosystem or destroy it. *BodySoul Rhythms* is doing what it can to contribute to a new consciousness for this planet. We recognize the embodied soul as a reality and the image as the connector between psyche and soma. Two energies—Yin/Yang, Shakti/Shiva, immanent/transcendent, soul/spirit – yearn for balance in both men and women, and we hope to integrate them in this experience. We presently have connections in Mexico, Brazil and several countries in Europe (as well as Canada and the United States) and hope to establish three branches: a leadership program, a university research program—quantum physics, microbiology, medical sciences—connecting psyche and soma, and a program for men and women who want to learn to live their own authenticity.

◆

Meeting a New Masculine

… it is only the conscious mind, in a man, that has the masculine sign, while the unconscious is by nature feminine. The reverse is true in the case of a woman. — C. G. Jung

The relationship between the masculine and the feminine is a major aspect of Jungian theory and practice. To embark on this study, my analyst asked me what were the positive traits I valued in a man. "Kindness, courtesy, strength, gentleness," I replied, also confessing that I longed to be held safe in someone's arms. Nevertheless, I thought I would be too weak in an actual relationship, probably carrying the attitude that:

"whatever you'd like to do, I'll do it," rather than risk displeasure or attack. I wanted to be loved, cared for, appreciated by someone who saw *me*, and saw that I had value.

My therapist's aim, I finally realized, was to get me to awaken in myself those attributes I valued in a man. Could I care for myself? Didn't I feel I had no value, was not worth much? I certainly didn't appreciate me! We went on to discuss my major life experiences with men, which hadn't been especially positive, and which, according to Jung, play an important role in the development of the inner masculine of a woman, which he referred to as the *Animus*, like the inner feminine (*Anima*) in a man. This major archetype surfaced more often now that some of my Shadow figures had become familiar and even relatively acceptable.

As I reexamined the important men in my life, I remembered how my brother, only a year older than I but slightly shorter in our childhood, took his resentment of this fact out on me. I would be delighted when we were taken for twins; it seemed so romantic, but he hated it, although he finally grew to a height of 6'2". It didn't help that I was also a "victim type," that is, my feelings would get hurt and I would feel bad instead of fighting back. Now he and I have a warm relationship, but the old scars may have remained on an unconscious level.

I had two fathers who were very different from each other yet both were stern, commanding, demanding and highly intelligent. I despised my biological father, who deserted my mother when I was only six months old and reappeared infrequently. He was the essence of the "bad guy" in our family—irascible, profligate (four wives, many mistresses), irresponsible (four children, all of whom he deserted when they were very young and only sporadically supported), and full of pretension, always telling stories of famous people as if he knew them intimately, to show how important he was.

I only began to make a new relationship with him in the last years of his life, finally able to forgive or ignore his total self-centeredness and parental inadequacies.

My stepfather, who entered our family life when I was two or three, was quite the opposite. He was responsible and put himself on the line to support us through difficult years of relative poverty while he himself was training to become a compassionate and gifted doctor. He was the one who truly brought us up, but I later learned that he himself was scarred by a father so tyrannical that his mother found nothing to laugh at when invited by my stepfather to see the supposed comedy, *Life with Father*. She hated it!

The last years of our relationship were full of unhappy friction, and his death came after several years of daily contact during incredibly difficult times as we both cared for my mother, who had lost most of her memory and some of her brilliant intelligence—a tragedy for the whole family. I didn't hold his depression against him, except for the fact that he seemed to take it out on me, making me the butt of his recurrent anger at life.

Doing my best to help, making breakfast, taking my mother for walks, finding a caretaker for a few hours a week—all was an uphill battle against his powerful opposition. He seemed to refuse any relief of his agony. A great lover of life, his anguish and depression increased as Mother got worse, his sight began to fail from macular degeneration and he gradually lost most of the use of his legs. Though this was largely hidden from the rest of the world, he would sometimes lash out at me, and I, suffering for both of them, didn't know how to defend myself.

My husband was quite another type, from the dyed-in-the-macho-world of South America, but with a very gentle and self-questioning side that he didn't often allow to appear in public. He had deep understanding of the psyche, read Jung and the Taoist *Secret of the Golden Flower* long before I did, but he too was crippled by an angry, unforgiving father and unable to support successfully his wife and family. For my sake, he usually controlled a tendency to drink too much, but from time to time went on frightening binges. It was my bad luck that, like both of my fathers, he was the kind of man who waked himself up by shouting at everyone in the morning. I only later realized that this was simply how the three of them got their day started. And none of them could understand why the rest of the family was tearful at breakfast!

I left Peru after eighteen years of marriage, felled by a digestive illness that was intensified by an increasingly impossible economic situation which demanded more and more of my flesh and blood. The effort to keep ahead of galloping inflation—with the devaluation of currency sometimes doubling within a week—had forced me to add other jobs to running my school in the mornings. I taught private classes in the afternoons and T'ai Chi in the evenings and on Saturdays until my body gave out from under my determination to keep the family together.

Back in New York, I found work as managing editor of a fabric and fashion magazine, hoping to be able to return to Peru some day. However, each time the opportunity seemed to approach, I would become sick. So I buried myself in work to support the family and wrapped myself in a soft cloud of depression, rather than think of starting a new life with someone else. I told myself, "Never again will I scurry around making breakfast to please an angry man, exposing myself to early morning emotional storms!"

Nevertheless, because my mother had been the image of an old-fashioned woman who stood by her man and did everything to make him content, I grew up without any sense that there was a battle between the sexes. The Biblical phrase,

"He for God and she for God in him" seemed an appropriate relationship, since we women needed men to tell us who we were. Even when women first tried to break through the glass ceilings of corporate America and demand respect, I figured they just didn't get it!

But with my new readings in psychology, and especially with my contact with Marion Woodman, I began to sense how the imprisonment of feminine spirit in a masculine-dominated world could seriously handicap individual growth and endanger society as a whole. Something had gone wrong at the roots of human relationship. Men weren't acting like men but like demanding boys, and women were too fearful and confused to figure out how to respond positively. Had a masculine drive to *do* and *conquer* taken over the western world, undervaluing the feminine qualities that were appreciated and even worshiped in some eastern countries?

Many Jungians seemed to think so. I was reminded of the Egyptian god Osiris, dismembered by his jealous twin, Set, who scattered pieces of his brother all over the face of the earth so that he could never be put together again, even by magic. But Set hadn't taken into account the courage and constancy of his brother's sister/wife, Isis, who painstakingly journeyed the world over, gathering together all the parts of Osiris to bring him back to life.

In the same way, in the last century, our attention seemed to have been magnetized and scattered all over our outer world as we busied ourselves with "doing stuff." Furthermore, the feminine principle might be sorely needed to gather the pieces together so that each of us could become whole again. Was this also why Gurdjieff so emphasized the importance of finding a *sensation* of presence in our bodies and Marion insisted on equal time for movement and voice work when studying to understand psyche and spirit?

During this inquiry into masculine nature, both my fathers and my husband appeared often in my dreams. This shook me from my still feisty attitude about whether or not dreams made any sense. My stepfather's death had ended a long period of almost inarticulate suffering between us. Afterward, his image in my dreams began to change. At first he was often in a hospital or very sick in bed, but later he appeared dressed in clothes of muted colors—purples, beiges, pinks he never would have worn in his life. His voice also became gentler, his movements slower and quieter. My therapist explained that these changes, which mystified me, signaled the gradual development of a new relationship with my own *Animus*.

Other dream images of men changed as well. First, replacing my former cops and criminals, a young boy appeared who was often attacked, teased or treated badly by other children. Then, in one dream that seemed ridiculous afterward, he was happily mowing the lawn. Yet I couldn't deny the clear image of his radiant, forceful activity, exuding positive energy. After this, my dreams were sometimes populated by attractive young men and later, encounters with pleasant, intelligent, warm middle-aged men with a sense of humor. These were the men I wished I could meet in real life.

Clearly a change was taking place in my inner relation with the masculine, and my final active-imagination dialogue was with the main character in a strong, positive dream about a strange young man who sat down among a group of people at a restaurant. I noticed something a little remote about him, and when I looked into his eyes, I saw truth there, and I heard it in his words. Although there seemed to be a value to this exchange, I felt a strong urge to look away, deny him, pretend he wasn't real, even ignore him. But I stayed face to face with him in the restaurant, respecting him even though I wasn't sure I understood what he was saying. It was as if I had to make an effort to listen in order to keep him sitting there, because it was always clear that he might leave at any moment.

Then the restaurant dream morphed into an outdoor scene in which he and I were climbing a hill or mountain on a steep, rocky path. In my dream notes I described it as "coming up from below." Walking behind me, he put his hands on my waist and hips to steady me as I slipped and stumbled, for which I felt very grateful. The touch of his hands gave me more strength and energy to go up and I rejoiced in being helped (something I find very difficult to accept in real life). It was clear that he didn't represent a possible new love relationship at all but rather an uncomfortable truth that had to be accepted or he would disappear.

After rereading my dream notes, I sat at the computer and attempted to communicate with him:

Who are you?

You know already.

Will you stay a little longer?

Depends on you.

What must I do?

You know already. You must face truth.

But I feel as though I don't quite understand, as though I will lose contact with you if I stray at all and I really am not quite clear where I am supposed to look, or what I am supposed to accept in order to keep you near.

You know enough to follow the direction.

Can you help me to understand?

Trust truth. Let it be there at the same time that you are confused or unaccepting or resistant. It is there even when you don't know what it is. Leave space, leave room for it.

Are you saying that the truth may not be what I think it is?

Exactly.

Here was a clear message that I had trouble accepting from my therapist as well: a major part of my problem was trusting anything, whether a direction, my body, or my own decisions. How to live closer to my own presence? "The Ego is off-base," Marion had said. "It lives off power and judgment—the two killers of soul. Presence is love, divine love. It can override the power and judgment archetype in us. Presence is being able to hold the love, no matter what happens."

What if I had only a year to live? How would I want to spend it? These unresolved questions led me to risk another major life change. I decided to retire from *Fortune* and spend three years in daily pursuit of presence at the Alexander Technique teacher-training course, in a further effort to bring mind, body and psyche into a more harmonious relationship.

Consciousness is the intervening variable between nature and being. It vastly enlarges the human being's dimensions; it makes possible in him a sense of awareness, responsibility, and a margin of freedom proportionate to this responsibility. — Rollo May

Four

SCHOOL FOR PRESENCE:
THE ALEXANDER TECHNIQUE

> *My technique is based on inhibition, the inhibition of*
> *undesirable, unwanted responses to stimuli, and hence*
> *it is primarily a technique for the development of the*
> *control of human reaction.*
>
> — F. M. Alexander

When I came to the Alexander Technique straight from the hard-knocks school of journalism, where deadlines take precedence over life as we live it and above all over the way we use ourselves, I had to make a 180-degree turn. It wasn't easy. I've always driven myself to succeed, whether in my search for understanding, meeting family needs or at work. Being a solutions-oriented person, I usually knew what to do, and actually loved the adrenaline rush that came with solving problems. But when it came to improving the quality of my own life, I seldom bothered to take note of the toll my "high" was taking. Living on the edge was exciting, but I had developed a permanent state of tension, magnified by the fact that my family's survival depended on my paycheck. My Jungian studies finally helped me to accept that I wasn't Superwoman and that a continual state of fight-or-flight reaction actually took me off my "edge."

After a brutal week of writing to deadlines, my shoulders and back ached and my hips complained, but a hot bath did little to relieve them. As usual, I had worked in a state of relentless tension, my back and shoulders crunched for hours in front of the computer, my eyes straining over documents. Only when it was over did I see that I'd tortured my whole body by pushing everything "unnecessary" sternly out of my path, with little thought to the rest or exercise the "container" of all this purposefulness needed.

The next day a friend came for lunch and, on hearing of my aches and pains, offered to give me an Alexander class. I lay down on my back on the living room floor with no idea what was coming next, just happy to be horizontal. She put a couple of paperback books under my head and invited me to "let go into the floor." Then she wrapped her hands around my neck and picked up my head. It felt safe and cradled as her fingers melted into my neck. "This is going to be good!" I thought. Next she burrowed her hands palms up under my back, which seemed to sink into them. "Let your legs move away from the torso," she said as she lifted them one by one and moved them all around. They seemed to be dancing in the air and my lower back unclenched in response. Then she took my hands and extended each of my arms. They drifted away from my torso, unwinding as if they'd been tightly screwed into my body. With each touch I eased a little more into a kind of quiet, semi-emotional state that felt like letting go into the unknown.

This wasn't at all like massage or other bodywork I had experienced—no pushing, pressing or pulling but a very light touch of the hands, accompanied by a few verbal suggestions. I felt my friend's whole presence attending to me, a wordless reminder that I ought to attend more to myself. "Yes," I thought, "this should definitely happen more often!" By the time I was invited to stand up, I felt deeply relaxed but unprepared for how delightfully light I was. I later learned that one of the hallmarks of a good Alexander class is the sense of lightness and freedom at the end.

As she was leaving, my friend told me about a seminar that weekend with David Gorman, a well-known teacher who had just published *The Body Moveable*, a three-volume anatomy of "the living body" with diagrams and notes written by hand. His workshop theme was "How our beliefs have shaped our bodies into the way they are today." Fascinated, I signed up for the weekend and, after that, took classes with him for several years, whenever he came to New York from London.

That was when I fell in love with the quiet attention on physical movement that is such an important part of each Alexander class, along with the sense of spaciousness and freedom in the joints. Walking out the door with a lighter, more relaxed, more *present* sense of myself left me feeling taller and more sensitive to the currents of air on the street—a welcome intrusion on my hectic life. David even suggested that I think of the breeze blowing right through my joints as I jogged to the subway on my way back to *Fortune*.

But lessons were a luxury. I had little time for them and often rushed to a class with him and hurried back to meet a deadline, losing all the freedom I had gained. When I spoke to him about this, he looked me in the eye and said, "We all make choices on how we want to live." That stopped me cold! I'd always thought this was the way it *had* to be, but his attitude was different. He walked everywhere he had to go because walking was good, even if more time was needed to get there.

In 1987 a car ran a red light and sideswiped the car I was in, jamming my door so tightly that firemen had to pry it open with crowbars while I sat there, covered with shards of glass. Luckily I was only badly bruised, but pain continued to plague my right hip and shoulder after the bruises were gone. My physical therapist, another Alexander teacher, explained that my right side was still braced against the crash. She worked with me until the pain subsided. At the end of each class I came away with a lovely sense of lightness and freedom.

Here, again, was the same joy in movement, which seemed to be a result of letting go of "my way" of doing things. It reminded me that to focus on solving a particular difficulty could be counterproductive. I needed to free myself to act as a *whole*. While I had plenty of energy, it was haphazard, going and coming every which way. A certain organization was lacking. The Alexander Technique seemed to call up an *organizing factor*, not in "thinking about" what's best, but right in the middle of the energies of the body in action.

After years of working with Gurdjieff movements and quiet attention exercises as well as T'ai Chi meditation-in-action, I began to feel that this *organizing factor* is at the heart of the connection between the head, which directs the action, and the body, which carries it out. This relationship is called into presence at the moment I cease to "know" exactly what's coming next and dare to fall back into the unknown, while at the same time maintaining a sense of mental curiosity and alert attention.

But back to my story. What a great life these teachers have, I thought, as I rushed back to the office for a late closing. They do something that helps others and also must feel wonderful to them, because you can't bring this experience of freedom to someone else without carrying it in yourself. Did I dare throw caution to the winds and make this an intimate part of my life? For years it seemed obvious that I couldn't. But when my children were grown and my courage was at its peak, I retired from *Fortune* magazine and enrolled in the teacher-training course at the American Center for the Alexander Technique (ACAT) in New York City. It was scary but exciting to commit myself to doing this wonderful stuff three hours a day, five days a week, for the next three years. To bankroll the experience, I accepted a half-time job as communications consultant for an Internet startup.

The call to bring attention to the movements of the body wasn't new to me. A shift of focus from sedentary ten-hour days glued to my computer—interviewing, researching and writing stories—was probably inevitable, given my deep need for a more balanced sense of myself. One of Gurdjieff's primary themes is the need to awaken to our situation. T'ai Chi also called for a return to the present moment, and Jung's views included accepting all of myself right then and there, not only the parts I approved of. In the Alexander experience I was invited to become aware of where I was in space, how I was in the inner space of myself, and what I was feeling and thinking. I knew this was what I really wanted to spend my time on, but these moments had to be sandwiched into evenings and Saturday morning classes while I made a living. Now, with no dependents, I stepped forward on a new experiential path.

From the very first day, the atmosphere of the school enveloped new students in its courtesy and complete acceptance of however we chose to manifest ourselves. There was no pressure to succeed, and our teachers patiently received all our reactions, criticisms and complaints. They created an environment of attentive listening, of including everything that was going on and leaving nothing out. At the same time, we students felt an unceasing demand to engage our attention in the process of being present. During the first year of training, I was convinced that ACAT was a true esoteric school. Like the Gurdjieff Foundation and other centers where there is a deep and daily commitment to spiritual exercise, it is a place where a practical method is taught for living closer to our essential nature.

Relaxing into the timeless pace, we students spent the whole first year working on our own "use of ourselves," and when we began to put our hands on others, it was only with the intention of developing a "listening hand" to sense what was going on in another person. We worked on how to make thoughtful ordinary movements without inducing unnecessary tension or straining parts of our anatomy. In the first few weeks we discovered examples everywhere in our lives of how we could choose to move, to replace stumbling after a bus or twisting around from stove to bottom of fridge too quickly. I confessed to the class that I had actually splashed boiling spaghetti water onto my hand while hurrying to finish cooking so I could get to a concert. I missed the concert and had to soak my scalded hand in tea and ice cubes for about four hours until the pain stopped.

It's not so much that accidents shouldn't happen, but that we have a choice as to how we can move. If we remember, we can choose to exchange old, faulty habits for new and useful ways to care for body and self as we move with clarity of purpose, envisioning what's necessary. Or we can continue to throw ourselves into movement in thoughtless, habitual ways. The Alexander Technique elicits thought before action, the ongoing study of one's automatic reactions, the habit of listening attentively to others, and an attitude of nonviolence in human relationships. This encourages the growth of our true *being* and offers a way to practice presence in the midst of an active life.

◆

Awareness — Inhibition – Direction

If you stop the wrong thing from happening, the right thing will do itself. — F. M. Alexander

Growing up on a lonely post in the Australian outback in the late 19th century, F. M. Alexander was accustomed to solving problems on his own. When, as a young actor in Melbourne, he repeatedly lost his voice in the midst of declaiming on stage, he set out to discover what was wrong. Assured by doctors that there was nothing medically threatening, he decided to take several months of rest before returning to the stage. But twenty minutes into his first return performance his voice failed him again. Undaunted, he bought a three-way mirror to find out what he was doing to produce this problem.

The first thing the mirror told Alexander was that no matter how "right" he felt his position to be when he spoke, he sucked in his breath as his head moved back and down. He began to be suspicious of trusting his own "feeling" of how he was in space, a false sense of "rightness" he called *debauched kinesthesia*, reminding himself then, and later his students, that only the mirror told the truth.

Was the solution to maintain his head more "forward and up?" He thought so, but no matter how hard he tried, it automatically moved back and down whenever he began to speak. Here was a habit that was stronger than he was! Determined to master it, he experimented on a subtler level by giving up the idea of speaking at all, then engaging in each step of the activity separately (opening the mouth, making a sound, saying a word, and so on). This bypassed his usual habits, and led him to the conclusion that in order to arrive at a new way of speaking he would first have to inhibit his automatic movements and be guided by a directed intention.

Over the course of eight years of study, he evolved a technique that he first used to help speakers and actors improve their voices and free their breathing. It was later applied successfully to many other problems, both physical and emotional. The Alexander Technique today is based on three cornerstone concepts that made change possible for him and his students, *Awareness, Inhibition* and *Direction.* At school, I was learning to be aware of myself both inside and in the physical space I occupy, to inhibit the first impulse to move which would simply give rise to my usual habits, and in that pause, to direct my thought into action, allowing me to move in a new, more easeful way. The most powerful word I met in my study of the Technique was '*pause.*' It offered a choice that could change everything.

Some people think this Technique is either what is loosely called "bodywork" or posture correction, but it's really about intentional thinking. It's a method of re-educating our neuro-muscular coordination through the power of directed thought. In those three years of training to be teachers, we studied both how the body works (bio-mechanics) and how to direct our thought (bio-energetics), initiating changes in habits and patterns of tension that had probably interfered with both physical and psychological freedom most of our lives. Yet the amazing thing was that we weren't learning a new *doing* so much as *undoing* movement sequences we had learned automatically and badly. I sensed a return to the ease and freedom of movement I had had as a child.

In a typical forty-five minute Alexander class, teacher and student work one-on-one to study the mechanics of how the body is meant to move and how it can do so with less stress and tension. No matter what the student's physical problem may be, the teacher will focus first, through explanations and an informed touch, on the relationship of the head to the torso, encouraging the neck to free its tight grasp of the head, so it can balance more easily on top of the spine. A lightly poised head allows the torso to lengthen and widen and releases the joints of the usually tensed arms and legs.

Many people study the Technique to find relief from chronic pain and discomfort caused by physical disabilities, such as low back pain, spinal disk problems, scoliosis, Parkinson's disease, recent surgery or—in the case of dancers, actors and musicians—simply to become more skillful. My own fellow students included a world-class violinist, a singer, an injured dancer with a damaged disk, and others like me who felt the deep need to live and move differently. We spent our time trying to become more *aware* of our old patterns of physical tension and our fixed emotional attitudes, to avoid or *inhibit* the habitual ways we held ourselves which produced these problems, and finally to *direct* our thought toward new, more easeful patterns and a more natural posture.

Good teachers help their students understand what Alexander called "a better use of oneself," so they can make this new awareness part of their everyday life. Each day in class I turned my thought away from its habitual focus on the outside world and found myself at the threshold of a new level of presence. F. M. Alexander would have asked us at the end of the day not my usual question, "How much did you get done today?" but "How well have you used yourself today?"

◆

Awareness: Turning on the Light

We could dare just to be here, and have the courage not to know what to do. — Daniel Singer

Awareness can be compared to a global light that has been turned on in the whole being. It's not to be confused with concentration, which is more like a narrowly defined spotlight that illuminates only one thing. For example, I can become so focused on a problem, a fantasy, a book, the TV or anything else "out there" that I forget my body and its needs as well as my own self and its reality.

Often when I'm "concentrated," I'm actually incapable of being aware. I'm literally "lost" in concentration and when I "come to myself" a clear inner shift takes place. My attention returns to the larger experience of myself as a *whole*, rather than being glued to the small task I'm engaged in or preoccupied with my effect on the outside world. The habit of living in my thoughts had been so strong that it could sever me from awareness of the rest of myself all day long without knowing it. But as soon as I recovered a clear awareness of my body in movement, a new inner presence would appear as new energy flowed in.

At school we were repeatedly invited back into the present awareness of our bodies without losing the participation of an active mind. For example, we often began the three-hour sessions by discussing a concept. Here's one way we studied "awareness," which you might like to try for yourself. Ask yourself, "What am I doing right now?" The instant of becoming aware is always a question. At this moment, at any moment, you could pause and wait for an answer. My own answer was helped by T'ai Chi practice and took the form of the realization that I'm standing on the earth. The law of gravity informs me of my relation to it in the considerable weight of my body going down through me into my feet. Gradually, as I tune into this experience, my feet come alive to their function and I can feel them nestling into the ground that receives them as energy shoots back up through me.

You could ask yourself often during the day Alexander's question: "How do you use yourself?" Is the ultimate goal of your day or your life similar to what mine used to be,—to get a lot done, so that every inch of you is subservient to the tasks? What is the relative importance of how you feel and how you move? I was one of those people who are always in high gear in one way or another, which is exhausting over the long haul. Once I had pushed myself too hard, I rested by collapsing in on myself and checking out of the rest of the world. I would sometimes wonder whether there might be a middle way, a kind of awareness that could tell me when I'd had enough of too much before it was too late. But for a long time I didn't try to figure it out. So I enjoyed the adrenaline rush and paid the price for it in periodic collapse.

After examining a concept in class, we would work with it, taking turns with a teacher or pairing off with each other. Once a week we brought our homework, reading aloud, discussing the texts, often disagreeing with each other's interpretation. This was a real-life challenge, because we became so wrapped up in the points we wanted to make or even in the act of reading well out loud, that we forgot our overall quality of use. The teacher would move around the circle of students, putting her hands on each of us, especially head, neck and shoulders, to remind us that our bodies were also present. If I were reading or arguing when this happened, I would come to a confused stop. The challenge to continue the discussion while releasing the tension was so difficult that it made us laugh. We were either talking heads or silent bodies! It was quite awhile before we learned to talk and be aware at the same time.

Here's something we did in class you might like to try. Sit comfortably in a straight chair with a firm seat, your back resting against it, but not slumped. Starting with a clear sense of your sit-bones at the base of the torso (you can easily find them if you sit on your hands), think up your spine from the coccyx, moving up vertebra by vertebra to the top, while noticing that your weight is sinking into the chair. Next, open your awareness to the part of the room that's on your left, imagining what's over there without turning your head to look. Then, after a minute or two, shift the focus of your attention to the space on your right. Then become aware of the air above your head and, after that, of the space below your chair. Finally bring to your mind as clear an image as possible of what you think is behind you in the room, from floor to ceiling. Only at the very end, turn your focus on what is in front of you, which is where we live most of the time. As you finish, ask yourself: "How do I feel now?"

In our exchanges, we learned that most of us conceptualized awareness as a fixed degree. Either we're aware of ourselves, and what's around us, or not. But we discovered our awareness constantly fluctuates as our attention shifts. We learned to tune in to ourselves many times during the day, in order to know what was really going on. I was surprised to discover that *non-awareness* could also be a wake-up call. An impression of mental and physical disorganization made me ask myself "What's going on?" It would begin with a sense of confusion triggered by poor judgment, such as when you bump against furniture, or press something in your hands ten times harder than necessary or forget why you came into a room.

To live more wholly we need to be *awake*, to be *there*,

completely present to ourselves again and again. Wise men and women have been telling us that for thousands of years, but the problem, which Gurdjieff pointed out so clearly, seems to be, how can we *remember* to be more aware? We learned that asking questions of ourselves was one of the best ways. How am I right now? How tense am I and why am I tense? How am I poised on my feet, on the chair, on my bed? Am I sagging into myself or surging up out of myself? Where do I feel my weight coming down into me?

Teacher Daniel Singer suggested that we look around the room from object to object to see what's there and ask ourselves each time *what is it?* to wake ourselves up repeatedly. Like a sudden sound behind us, it startles us and orients us instantly in the present moment. He explained that according to research he had read, it calms the nervous system and decreases the stress chemicals in the body. He added that the surprise value of *what is it?* lasts only a few seconds. So we must ask it again and again.

Some images that were useful to our class could help you to explore awareness: If you are lying on your back (on a firm surface), are you unconsciously holding yourself away from where you are resting? Let your back and the back of your legs, arms and head sink further into the table or the floor, as if you were supported by a cottony-soft cloud. You may notice how your breathing expands against your spine, pressing your back into the floor as you breathe in, as well as swelling your chest in front.

Or if you are sitting, ask yourself how you are holding your head. Are the muscles of the neck tense, or could your head be poised above the spine like an egg upended on a spoon or a rock balanced at the edge of a precipice? Do your shoulders usually press forward or do they pull back tightly? Are you usually slumped or do you generally hold yourself super-straight? You can remind yourself that every part of your body works hard for you 24/7, and deserves its own moment of attentive investigation.

As class ended each day, the ultimate question would appear. A global awareness had gradually appeared in each of us. *Why would we choose to live any other way?* Awareness demands our presence, but that presence doesn't disappear when we are not aware of it. At the same time, it cannot be forced. This sense of presence can only be invited and welcomed or, on the contrary, interfered with. Once we knew we wanted this new lightness and freedom in movement and we realized we weren't experiencing it most of the time, the crucial question was: How am I interfering? Do I somehow have to create more awareness or am I, in fact, part of a larger awareness from which I separate myself all the time, as some great spiritual traditions affirm? What do I practice when I am present?

These are good questions. But how do I bring them into the body? I was still a big *Doer*, so I wondered out loud how we were ever expected to get anything done and make the decisions we have to make all day long in order to live and move in the world, if we were supposed to be so concentrated on awareness. Daniel explained that what was needed was a shift to a different way of being. We could allow our choices to come from a different part of the brain. He called it *constructive thought*, rather than the "noisy thought" we live with all the time, which has many voices that often interrupt each other. His advice heralded another major discovery in my journey toward presence—the big difference between "thinking about" something and the kind of real thought which weighs data and makes informed decisions, as applied to the body. Although I was familiar with intentional thought in making major life choices, I was unaware that it could be called on to guide my everyday movements.

Nevertheless, awareness is not some complicated effort to replace how I usually am. The central problem is that I'm unaware of how I usually am and that's exactly what I need to know! As another teacher, Brooke Lieb, told us: "We need to stay in real time, to keep seeing and hearing as we try to be more aware. What takes us out of real time? Panic, judgment and expectation." Too true!

◆

The Tyranny of Habit

I ask you to do nothing and immediately you do something to do nothing. — F. M. Alexander

What holds us back from living and moving freely in the world with awareness? Primarily our automatic habits. They can cost a lot—quite literally—in wear and tear of our organism. We develop them by imitating people we admire, or by finding the quickest solution to doing what's asked of us. Take, for example, writing, which everyone learns in first or second grade. "Grip the pencil like this, press it on the paper like that." When I became aware of my contortions as I wrote in a notebook, I—a successful journalist used to taking notes all the time—was horrified. My "use" was that of a seven-year-old!

True, all habits aren't bad, but even good habits like brushing your teeth can carry a lot of tension. Just the other day one of my students told me her dentist had asked her to use a different brush because the force of her brushing was making her gums recede. Knowing how tense and angry she felt a lot of the time, I wasn't surprised that she took it out on her teeth.

And though she could and did buy an ultra-modern brushless cleaner, it was even more important for her to understand how her inner violence affected her organism.

We are clearly creatures of habit. Think back to the last time you had a painful injury. Once you've been hurt, habits are the body/mind's solution to avoiding further pain and discomfort. I'm sure you carried yourself protectively in some way—whether by putting more weight on one leg than the other, carrying a bag on only one shoulder or in some other subtle way of holding. While it was a smart and necessary adaptation for a short time, the habits created through fear of further pain can remain long after the injury is healed and the need for defenses is gone.

Whenever we are injured, by a twisted ankle for instance, it's normal for us to move in ways that protect that ankle and minimize its pain. But after the injury heals, we tend to move in the same way. Over the years we build up unrecognized habits around many things that have happened to us. Our emotional injuries also cause us to develop hidden reactions to pain, and sustain them even when the cause of pain has disappeared. Psychotherapists approach habits from the mental and emotional perspective. By contrast, Alexander teachers begin from the physical aspect—how we react with our bodies. While the two are interconnected, the physical assessment of what's going on can be particularly helpful to many, as it was to me. In either case, we may pay a high price for poor "use" of ourselves in both energy and peace of mind.

The good news is that when harmful habits are no longer necessary, their power over us can be defused. They are simply unconscious mechanisms with which we respond as we move around and meet the events and stresses of our lives. "Why are we so unaware of how poorly we use ourselves?" I asked. The answer was that as psycho-physical beings, we lose contact with ourselves at every moment as our attention jumps toward every stimulus, whether it's another person in front of us or a chair we are about to sit in. Once again the hidden culprit was lack of awareness. Our study revealed that instead of meeting ordinary situations by making thoughtful choices, we just plunged into them. We reacted blindly rather than remaining poised inside ourselves, ready to decide what to do next.

Teachers of the Alexander Technique make it clear to their students from the beginning that until they study their habits, they can't know what's really going on. And what's the good of noticing them? I wanted to crush them forever, but that's not the solution. I needed to re-educate myself by studying my habits through the prism of a newly enhanced "non-judgmental awareness." I was invited to accept rather than push aside what I saw.

I noticed that there was a whole lot I still disapproved of in myself, even though I no longer hid the fact that it was there. How could I face my many imperfections head-on and accept them? Students were repeatedly offered a choice—either to condemn ourselves as unsatisfactory (which we usually did), or simply to notice the mechanics of how we moved. It was a lot easier to examine tense habits of sitting and standing than to look at why I was full of tension in the first place! It was up to me whether I would be self-demeaning or learn to become an objective student of my habitual ways of thinking and moving.

In my early days at the school, I was encouraged to give up judging myself for newly discovered habits. Why point the finger back at myself for being "wrong?" "Think differently about your habits," suggested anatomy teacher Judy Stern. "Rather than seeing them and blaming yourself for 'doing it again,' ask yourself how you got there in the first place.

Explore. That way your habits can become your teacher. Only by knowing the old way and awakening the process of awareness, inhibition and direction can you implement the new, conscious habits you choose to develop."

So we studied anatomy to discover how the body really works and identify the harmful habits we had acquired that interfered with our "supreme inheritance" of poise and freedom, as Alexander put it. Most of the time we only realize something's wrong when our back aches, shoulder hurts, hip or knee or ankle twinges in pain. But now we began to suspect that a hidden source of pain might be something we were doing that clashed with the way human beings are designed. Lower back pain is a prime example of this. Stiffened or slouched chest or shoulders, extreme holding in of the belly or allowing it to pouch laxly out, gripping the legs too tightly with buttock muscles, holding oneself up with the ribs—all of these could just as likely cause lower back pain as putting strain on weakened muscles. In any number of ways, without knowing it, we can compromise the ease of movement that nature endowed most of us with at birth.

Here's an example of how the mechanics of habit work: You are sitting in a chair and the minute you think about standing, a message goes from brain to body and triggers your habitual pattern, *even before you move*. The fact of it boggled my mind. You will inevitably stand up in your usual way with all your familiar tensions, pulls and pushes, because you are locked into this way of moving. Your habit has taken over as soon as you *thought* of standing up—before you could even make a move. However, if you pause before standing to access what you're doing and how you want to do it, you'll be able to let go of the amount of tension you usually engage. That's the way to put a spoke in the wheel that sets off your automatic pattern.

A new movement, like 'new moment, cannot be fixed ahead of time—it is always unknown. We never step into the same river twice, even if we've done it a hundred times. But how intentionally do we take that step? We think we know where we are in our physical space, and may chuckle at the idea that we don't know how to stand up or sit down in the best possible way. But it's not easy to stand or sit as if one were doing it for the first time. Each of us has an extraordinary kinesthetic sense that tells us where our body parts are at any given moment, but we can't trust it. Our long-term habits of misuse make our usual posture or movement "feel right." For example, we each have a personal stance. Whether we stand with our hips slightly forward of the spine, as I do, or slumped in the chest, or stiffened up with shoulders "beautifully" back as in "chest out, belly in," we feel comfortable that way because this posture belongs to us. However, it might be the cause of recurrent pain.

Life is filled with patterns, some useful, some interfering with the optimal use of oneself. Our teachers helped us become aware of them as habitual ways of doing things, but reminded us that in the long run no teacher could help us inhibit them. This would be our job. We accepted that they weren't only physical but *psycho-physical*—that a mindset went along with them. The next step was to receive, *non-judgmentally*, the information reflected in the mirror, which ran floor-to-ceiling down one side of the long room. I avoided looking in it whenever possible because I was sure I would see that I was "wrong." We saw that whenever judgment or criticism entered, it interfered with the processing of information. The search was for freedom from these well-established habits.

◆

Inhibition: The Pause That Permits Choice

No matter how many specific ends you may gain, you are worse off than before if in the process of gaining them you have destroyed the integrity of the organism. — F. M. Alexander

Alexander soon learned that even though he had discovered what he was doing wrong, and tried many times to use his voice on stage in a different way as he held his head in a different position, it didn't work. Only when he gave up any positioning at all, and concentrated simply on freeing the neck and head from muscular contraction, could a change take place. What was necessary, he decided, was to abandon the whole idea of changing his position from "wrong" to "right." Only pause and inquiry could interrupt his habitual patterns.

That very desire to "feel right" or "do it right" is the biggest barrier to ease and freedom of movement. The harder I tried, the more tangled I got in the habit I wished to escape. On the other hand, creating a pause between a stimulus and my response to it could transform the quality of my movement and the situation I was in. "It is not the degree of 'willing' or 'trying' that will make it effective," wrote Alexander, "but the way in which the energy is directed." And even when he had managed to transform the way he used his own body and helped others find the same freedom, he discovered that writing a book or telling other people how to do it wasn't enough. Both the practice of inhibiting one's immediate reaction and the guidance of a teacher's educated hands were necessary at the beginning, to learn how to reorganize faulty thinking and distorted muscular patterns.

Alexander's idea of inhibition doesn't translate into

suppression of any kind. He called it "volition," which I interpreted as a willingness to be present to the immediate experience of the moment and follow oneself into movement, in contrast to the automatic way we usually live and move. One of his first teacher-trainees, Lulie Westfeldt, summarized his first experiments with inhibition as follows: "(1) a continually renewed decision to inhibit or say 'no' to the idea of speaking; (2) continually renewed thoughts to activate the new head, neck and back pattern; (3) the breaking down of the act of speaking into its smallest steps and the focusing on each step separately as if it were the end." (*F. Matthias Alexander: The Man and his Work*).

Inhibition permits a new impression of oneself. Our teachers called it "the positive *no* of choosing." They emphasized that to inhibit, to say *no* before moving, isn't to deny, but to provide more opportunity. We restrain our habitual pattern to allow the nervous system to do its job in the best possible way. As Judy Stern put it, "We say 'hush' to what's going on in us at a given moment and return to the *being* mode as opposed to the *doing* mode. Whenever we quiet the nervous system, we return to balance."

The pause between stimulus and response also inhibits *anticipation*. When you anticipate what will happen, you're not available to the actual experience of moving. As many as four choices emerge when you inhibit your reaction to a stimulus: You can do nothing, do something different, do whatever you intended in the same old way, or do it in a new way. Unfortunately, we almost never take time to make such a choice.

Here's how inhibition is used in an Alexander class. You stand in front of a chair. The teacher asks you not to sit down in the usual way, to say "no" to moving at all while his or her hands access the connection between your head and neck to free any compression of the spine. Your inhibitory thought affects a lot more than the muscles and skeleton. The whole nervous system decompresses if you are able to disconnect yourself from what you were about to do. Then you pause and join your thought to the teacher's thought of the head moving delicately forward and up off the end of the spine before you go into movement. Your organism will respond to your intention freely, without constriction.

Next, the teacher explains the act of sitting in terms of the best body mechanics, beginning with bending the knees. If you inhibit "knowing how to do it" and just follow orders and respond to the teacher's guiding hands, you'll probably feel you no longer know how to sit. You want to do it "your way." But you go along with the request in order to see what happens. You are learning to let the nervous system alone at the moment of giving yourself the order to move, instead of pressing forward or compressing yourself.

It may sound simple but it's not easy! I felt as if I'd embarked on a three-year venture into frustration at not being able to give up "my way" of doing things. Not only did I have to learn to say "no" to getting up from the chair in my habitual way, I also had to learn to deal with the psychological reaction that followed, the feeling that I couldn't possibly get up or sit down any other way. If I said "no" to controlling the movement and let the head lead the body to a standing position, I felt I'd fall down or something terrible would happen. This revealed another aspect of our dilemma. When we try to give up a long-term habit of moving, we sometimes feel sure we'll fail. That's why we need to abandon both the automatic way we usually stand *and* sit and the conviction of failure if we try any other way. Both are habitual; both make up the walls of the prison within which we move around all day without knowing it.

Since I'm often impatient, one day I tried to notice

specifically those things I usually do with irritation, hurry, or the attitude of "not wanting to waste my time on this." Examples were easy to find: brushing my teeth, tying my shoelaces and cleaning up the kitchen blocked the path to all I wanted to do right away. How to dispense with them as quickly as possible so I could move on to more important things? That particular day, I decided to give all such tasks more time than I usually allow and carry them out attentively, whether or not they irritated me.

It was a major awakening. Again and again I saw how petty, habitual and even childish my reactions were. They used up my energy, allowed almost no attention to go to what I was actually doing, and short-circuited my whole presence-in-action. This experience convinced me that Alexander 's work on inhibition and direction called for the same effort of self-observation and attention to the present moment in all its aspects that T'ai Chi and the Gurdjieff teaching had engaged me in for many years. What was new was the simplicity of this study of psycho-physical reaction at the moment it took place, in everyday mechanical movements and gestures. I realized once again what I had learned at Gurdjieff's knee: that attention is the most precious coin I have with which to pay for inner freedom.

In the middle of my first year of training, I noticed a habit of "throwing myself" into small movements—as I hurried to get out of a chair, haul something out of the fridge or grab a glass off a high shelf. When I put on my shoes, I usually rushed to get it over with and go on to whatever was in my mind to do next. The quality of my movement often seemed rather *desperate*. When I asked myself, "Why?" I discovered that I tried to do it fast to save time. As with other areas of my life, I wanted to do two things at once and sometimes to kill not just two birds with one stone, but a whole flock.

I explained this to Diane Young when she led our class to rethink our everyday activities. She suggested that when I looked down to tie my shoes or to get something from the fridge, I could "think up." She wanted me to imagine the up direction while I bent down. Think up to bend down? Another paradox! She added that it would help if I noticed how my shoulders and hips narrowed every time I reached for something. That was the kicker. I decided from then on doing one thing at a time would be enough, but I even hoped the day would come when I wouldn't have to kill any bird at all, just fly along with it!

Did I soon become a newly transformed, habitless being? Not a chance! Even after long study, habits can and almost certainly will reappear. That's why learning to inhibit them is so important. The purpose of inhibition is not to kill off a habit, but to let behavior be informed by choice. "Inhibition isn't just about stopping and saying 'no,'" Daniel told us. "It's about stopping to ask yourself: Is what I'm doing to myself what I really want to do? If not, then why not stop it?"

The Alexander Technique became a training ground that enhanced the search for presence in the rest of my life as well as my three hours a day at school. When I caught myself in a state of tension—perhaps pushing myself in some kind of task—I returned to awareness of the body and said "no" to immediate pressure to move on. Then I'd try to ease away from an incipient judgmental attack on myself for being tense. I asked myself many questions as an incentive to keep this search at the forefront of my thought. You might try them for yourself. Am I tense? Do I use more energy than is required for the movements I make, whether washing dishes or playing tennis? While waiting in line at the bank or in the subway, do I stand with one hip thrust out and most of my weight on one foot, or am I poised on both feet and ready to move forward?

When I sit, is my body slumped, spread like jelly on the chair, or lively and erect, with my weight evenly distributed on my sit bones? When I sit at the computer, am I aware of my butt in the chair or magnetized by the bright screen in front of me so I'm almost falling into it? Where's my back? Do I even remember I have a back? And how about my legs—are they relaxed but active, or have I left them out of my kinesthetic awareness as if there were no "me" from the hips down?

Our most entertaining attempts to learn inhibition were the mind-body games we played: "Red Light, Green Light," "Simon Says" and throwing a ball. In the first, a student faced the wall at one end of the long room while the rest of us started from the other side and moved quickly across the floor toward her, hoping to be first to touch her. But each time she spun around we froze because anyone she saw moving had to go back and start over. In the second game, the person who played "Simon" told us to do this or that and we quickly imitated his positions. But if we moved without "permission," not noticing that he hadn't muttered "*Simon says* do this," we were out of the game.

The "catch" was that we had to pause and do nothing before we moved forward, obeyed commands or caught a ball. It was almost impossible to establish clear awareness of the head balancing lightly on the spine and not get thrown out of the game. Catching a ball seemed pure reaction and it was just as difficult to say "no" to reacting to the stimulus and still catch it. To think it was a "good idea" to pause didn't have enough effect. Saying "no" to habit had to be a clear commitment, an inner letting go of knowing what to do next.

◆

Direction: From Thought into Action

Direction is getting your intelligence into the pathways of your nervous system. — Lucia Walker

Better not to think of an *aim*, said Alexander, but rather of a *direction* you are going in. Yesterday's aim should be today's accomplishment, and tomorrow's goal farther away than today's. Words like *destination* and *achievement* fix the mind on one place when all life is movement. At any moment the state of your body/mind will be moving either toward contraction or toward ease. Alexander "direction" involves dedicated thought rather than a thought drifting through the head like a passing cloud in the sky. As Gothic cathedral spires make the heart soar, so the repeated invitation to think of yourself moving up lightens your image of the body and your sense of its weight.

Daily we made new discoveries in class about how we compromised our ease of movement. Our respect increased for the seemingly simple process of getting in and out of a chair, now revealed as a major neuromuscular call to the whole organism. So was just about every movement we made. We often practiced small activities collected from our daily lives to examine the mechanics of the body and figure out how our actions could be realized without the usual grunts and shrugs but in a more easeful way. We sat in a circle and watched as each of us went into the center to demonstrate a personal difficulty: taking off a backpack, bending to get a heavy melon from the bottom of the fridge, and my own number-one frustration—getting into a low-slung car and battling to buckle the seatbelt.

It was as if we had to fire up our sensory awareness while saying "no" to consciously interfering with motor function. That way, we could tune into what was going on and cease to think we knew better, while the motor system did its job free of the kind of pressure we call "making an effort." Our intention was to be present and observant while maintaining a clear vision of the direction in which we wanted to go.

We discussed each example and experimented with how to do it differently, just as Alexander had worked on his problems more than a hundred years before. We thought out the best possible way, released tension in the neck before we moved, and went into these diverse activities while inviting the spine to lengthen and the arms and legs to extend freely from the torso. Can I move into a backpack or a taxi with my head poised rather than grabbing it with my neck muscles? Can I buckle a seatbelt with an expansive back and an extended spine rather than a twisted, contracted one? Alexander's four basic self-commands or "directions" were there to remind us how to think into ease: (1) allow the neck to be free so that (2) the head can balance easily on the end of the spine (which he called *forward and up* as opposed to the back-and-down pattern that was usually our home base). When this is done (3) the torso releases into length and width and (4) the arms and legs release away from the torso. The whole body expands as you begin to move, rather than contracting with your "effort" to move.

Direction uses the conscious brain to reprogram the unconscious response. It's as simple as telling someone how to get somewhere, which is just what our teachers did. They suggested with hands and voice that we think *up* even when we were sitting *down*, so the torso could ride above the legs and the head float above the torso. They explained that every attempt at directing should start with the awareness of what's actually going on. Next we could inhibit our first impulse to go into movement by creating a critical pause during which our attention is gathered and we become present to the moment we are living. Then, having determined the direction we wanted to go, we needed a clear determination that we really wanted to go there "without counting the cost," as Walter Carrington, a British master teacher closely associated with Alexander, insisted in *Thinking Aloud*. Only after that moment of presence and clarity of thought should we begin to move.

At first, I found it hard to agree with the notion that thinking can change the quality of how our bodies move. Then, in anatomy class, Judy Stern introduced us to the instantaneous message system between the joints, the muscles and the brain. "Thinking is the most powerful thing we have," she assured us. "Every thought is an energetic experience, and has an impact on our physiology. We often interpret direction as position because what we see is the position. But we don't need to 'take a position.' According to Alexander, 'the right thing does itself,' and our challenge is how to get out of the way."

In spite of her reassurance, we tried to gauge whether our efforts at direction produced the "right" result. This was a mistake. Using sensation (how it *feels*) to evaluate whether the directions were *working* didn't help. Unless we became aware of what was going on at the moment of thinking of them, so that the directions connected with the nervous system, we could say them all day to no effect. "Don't go into the system to see if it works or not," said Barbara Kent. "Because if you are in the system you can't be outside of it, observing and directing. Just trust that the lengthening spine has some organizational influence on all your movement patterns, send the thought and trust and send it again each time you sit or stand. Think 'neck free, head forward and up, back back, legs away.' At first it helps to say it out loud, but later it will become a part of your thinking."

We became discouraged when we saw how much the effort to be right or make judgments about ourselves interfered with ease of movement. But even "unsuccessful" efforts at thinking the directions can teach a lot. When we paired up to talk to each other a few minutes, Joan Frost suggested we inhibit before speaking for just a second and observe the quality of tension in our necks. I was shocked to discover how often I interrupted or finished the other person's sentence, and how much my neck would tighten and my head pull back when I did.

Daniel invited us to inhibit both the judgment about whether we were making the appropriate effort and the idea that we were not yet "there." Correctness, right posture or any kind of rightness, are opposed to freedom, he said. It's not a question of inventing a new pattern but of using the mind correctly and getting out of the way. "If you can catch the moment before moving, the old pattern can be obviated. All patterns are created in that moment because the brain is being used by a 'non-localized awareness,' in the same way the brain uses the eyes. Catch the initiation of movement at the very beginning, invite it to cease and something new will happen. Our job isn't to create the movement. We are gardeners removing the weeds."

He paused as he looked for an image to explain the experience, and added: "Direction requires depth. Imagine you have a sun in you. The direction is where the light goes, projected along a certain trajectory by awareness and will. Light can be thrown from habit or by consciousness. Habit shuts doors. Our task is to open them. We carry light in us with portals that can be opened by attention and intention. Always direct your thought to at least two places (in your body) at a time, thinking of the light streaming out of them. Your energy, combined with this directed light, is very powerful."

A few minutes later, Daniel worked with me, chuckling at

how serious I looked as I tried to follow his suggestions. He asked me to smile, inviting me to find a lighter inner attitude, which he termed an "appreciation" of how I am. My dogged intensity melted and I immediately felt lighter and not so "dedicated" to the task of remembering the directions. A sense of kinesthetic awareness of my body as a whole gradually appeared. Here was another example of the direct connection between body, mind and emotions. In Gurdjieffian terms, I experienced a moment of harmonious relationship between the centers. "Stay in the welcoming mode rather than letting your habit of being serious take over," Daniel said. "Being serious or frowning evokes tension. Well-being, on the other hand, expresses itself in a smile."

◆

Posture and Balance

The teacher's main purpose ... is ... to unlock the deep patterns of contraction that have become built into what is popularly called 'posture', to unlock those chronic patterns of tension and thus to free the natural mechanisms of posture and balance. — John Nicholls

What's "good posture?" We talk about it, we recommend it to replace slumping, but usually come guiltily out of our slump into stiff-as-a-board, super-straight uprightness. Is posture a fixed position to which we must return as often as we remember because unless we hold ourselves up we aren't quite "right?" Do we need to hold ourselves up at all? My first teacher, David Gorman, insisted that "good" posture can be as harmful for you as bad posture. The latter is usually some kind of slouch or collapse forward which interferes with breathing.

But if you straighten up, lift the chest and pull the shoulders back, you'll pull your back down with the same muscles that hold the ribs down. As he pointed out, that's just another way of restricting breathing (*In Our Own Image*).

Gorman defined posture as how we relate ourselves to gravity. He said that instead of wondering what we need to do to stand or sit up straight, we ought to ask "What are we doing to *stop* ourselves from being freely where we are?" Let go into instability, he urged, because it's not the flaw we think it is. It's the key to freedom for former four-legged creatures who now walk upright. Instability is a natural part of being upright, and the only way to reduce it is by tightening and holding on.

It may sound strange to hear that standing "straight" is not about posture or alignment. We sometimes think the solution is to stack body parts carefully one upon another so as not to fall down, but that's not how we're built. Gorman compared the body to a river, which generates energy and is in constant movement, and to a waterfall, as if our weight pours down like water through the bones. Luckily for us, our weight is modulated by the brain via the postural reflexes. The circuits of the central nervous system are the paths through which the muscles and bones talk to the brain about the messages coming from the feet on the floor about posture. "It's a thinking system," explained Judy in anatomy class, "not just a moving system. There's always a reflexive dialogue going on between the body and the brain."

Yes, posture is important. We need to avoid straining muscles, ligaments and tendons, and we can unconsciously abuse them depending on how we stand and sit. But think of posture as part of the living flow of us. In my third term, as I sat on a chair, a teacher pointed out that I was trying to hold myself up from the middle of my back, by my ribs. Ribs weren't designed for the job, she explained. Why not let my weight flow down the spine into the sit-bones at the base of the pelvis, which would allow the chair to support me? That certainly made sense, but it wasn't till the middle of the second year that I recognized organically that I didn't have to hold myself up at all. As we stood in a circle, practicing awareness, suddenly Diane called out commandingly: "Inhibit holding yourselves up!" It surprised me into abandoning the idea that I had to "do" something in order to stand there. I was already "there," standing effortlessly.

What I had just learned struck me like a literal poke in the ribs. The moment I let myself go, I felt clearly that "up" exists as a movement in me without my having to do anything about it. Amazing! It helped me see my tendency to hold myself in and down, especially in the rib cage. Only when I let go of that habitual downward drag could the body's natural design take over—my head poised and riding lightly on the spine, and my torso expanding into length and width.

Judy Stern explained why: nerves have spindles (nerve receptors that supply important sensory information to the brain) spaced all through the muscles, and even the mere thought of lengthening fires them off, affecting the whole body and sending you a message of ease and expansion even before you move. Since the digestive and respiratory systems are suspended from the neck, it wouldn't be front-page news that constant compression in the neck or a slumped chest limits the vitality of the organ systems. But there's more to it than that. Neck muscles have many more muscle spindles than other muscles do. Professor V. Abrahams from Queens University in Kingston, Canada, a leading researcher on the subject, says "the evidence that the neck plays a critical role in posture is overwhelming." So a lengthening spine promotes better health and better communication to and from the brain. It comes with the expanded territory.

Why do trainees need to study this technique for three years before teaching it? It sounds simple once you know what you're doing wrong, but there's a good reason. The crucial question for both teachers and students will always be the same: how do we get out of our own way? As Judy Lakin told us when she saw how hard we tried, "This technique is an *undoing*, not a doing. It's about reorganizing ourselves, redirecting our energy from reaction and habit to more productive use." So how do I stop pulling myself down or holding myself in? How do I let go of "doing something" whenever I decide to take a different position?

In balance as in posture, a lot more is involved than learning how to stand without falling over. True balance is about being present to oneself right now. The head, which may want to carry us away into a reverie or hone in on a problem to be solved, needs to focus on the body which stands here in real time, poised and ready to move into the future. As Gorman pointed out, to begin to move at all you have to send yourself off balance: to walk you lose your balance forward, and to sit you lose your balance backward. If we could be as free, poised and ready for action as the "spring-loaded system" he said we are, we would be balanced. Anyone who can accept feeling precarious, constantly alert and constantly changing will feel better and have fewer aches and pains at the end of the day.

According to Gorman, holding the belly in is another misconception that adversely affects posture and balance. Conventional wisdom says the abdomen should be pulled up or held in, but if you try to flatten it and narrow the waist, you actually pull your chest down toward the pelvis. The abdominal muscles run between pelvis and chest so when you pull down in back to hold up the pulling down in front, you are forcing your body into two downward pulls. Then, by tightening the oblique abdominals, which crisscross below the ribs, you also pull the ribs down and together in front. Can anyone do this and still breathe freely?

Each of our misunderstandings about how the body works educated us to view ourselves more often as a whole, because each part influences and depends on every other part. When we exercise to strengthen ourselves, we may develop one muscle system at the expense of others. And when we want to protect ourselves from pain, we are understandably "part-oriented," but solving one problem may create another. That had happened to me a few years earlier when I visited an osteopath about a frozen right shoulder. His prescription: injections of Novocain and a series of exercises with elastic bands to build up my back and shoulder muscles. I did them faithfully for a few weeks then bailed out of his treatment with a stronger, less painful shoulder and newly awakened pain in my lower back. Another common source of pain or discomfort is to stiffen a joint to solve a movement problem. For example, many people grip their legs tightly in the hip joints in a mistaken effort at balance.

Each day we saw more clearly that when one part starts to grab, all the others join in. If, in the name of posture and balance, you hold on in your hips or belly or try to manufacture spinal rigidity so as not to tip over, all the other related muscles will join in. Gorman said it best: "The openness and expansiveness of your torso as a whole vitalizes and liberates your energy so that it rises up in you. And that, more than anything else, is what gets you up and keeps you up, not bones and muscles, or balance and posture."

◆

Leading with the Head

You've got this ongoing flow of energy that is seeking to take you up against all the downward forces, and going up is what happens when you release the neck. — Walter Carrington

Let's get moving, we often say. Well, what gets us moving? Believe it or not, it's the head. Oh, sure, you say, I tell myself to move and I move. But it's more than that. The physical movement of the head actually leads us if we allow the head to balance freely, permitting an easy flow of energy as pressure is taken off the spine. The Alexander Technique aims to free the head from the habit of being tightly held to the spine by the neck muscles into a delicately poised, dynamic relationship. Think of a rock at the top of a precipice, able to move in any direction. Watch a cat jump off a high place to see head-neck freedom in action.

In our early days at school we were taught the mechanics of the connection between head and torso. Years before, David Gorman had introduced it to me with a graphic exercise. He held out his hands palms up as we faced each other. I rested the knuckle of each first finger lightly at the center of each of his palms. He then waved his hands gently in the air while my index finger joints rode lightly on them, to show me how poised the head could be as the spine moves. Next he grasped my knuckles tightly in his fists to illustrate how we usually live, clenching the head with our neck muscles.

The skull perches with its two tiny bony "feet" on two shallow declivities on the upper surface of the atlas, the top vertebra. Oh, yes! We nodded our heads at the name. We too sometimes felt like the Greek giant who carried the world on his shoulders. But we were surprised to learn that our inner world, the brain, rests so high on the spine, at the level of the ears, rather than somewhere in plain view on our necks.

If you nod your head "yes" with a free neck, the movement takes place high up behind the eyes and between the ears, on the atlas. Shake your head to say "no" and the whole skull swivels left and right at the level of the second vertebra, appropriately named the axis. But most people move their heads from lower down, bending the spine from the middle of the neck and thus interfering with the airy freedom of movement that we all had as children. Gorman's exercise helped me visualize how the head could ride lightly poised on the spine or, on the contrary, how the neck could tense to the max as I walked around weighed down by my worries—including the imagined duty of holding up my head.

The average head weighs ten to twelve pounds, with more weight in front than in back. But that's lucky for us because, if it were completely balanced, its weight would compress the spine. Instead, the head's tendency to rotate forward creates a dynamic traction that lengthens the spine as we move around. The bad news is that habitual over-contraction of the strong muscles at the back of the neck, whose job it is to counterbalance the head's weight forward, can prevent a healthful extension of the spine.

Unnecessary tensions in the face can also interfere. A frown brings the whole body down with it, weighing down even the pelvis, while a smiling response sends the head up and invites the shoulders to widen. In less poetic terms, the jaw plays an important role in the release of head, neck and torso, a relationship which Alexander dubbed "the primary control." Relaxing the jaw releases the spine. We tried tightening and loosening our jaws, and sensed the spine change. You could try it, too.

Think of the neck, with all its nerve cells, as the Master Switch. Release it and you take the emergency brake off the whole organism, which then lets go into expansion. After all, the neck isn't separate from what we call the spine, it *is* the spine, so the effect of gripping or releasing it at the top reverberates right down to the bottom of the lumbar curve.

To illustrate, Daniel took out a double-jointed, purse-sized umbrella, pointing out what a formless mess of puffs it is when folded. But press the button and bingo! Structure appears. "This is the neck," he said, pointing to the stem of the umbrella, "the essential piece that organizes all the rest. The neck is a microcosm of the whole body. When the neck slumps, the whole body slumps, just like the folded umbrella."

One day I brought pictures of my three-year-old granddaughter to class: standing, sitting, running, pretending to be a cat. You could see her energy rising upward from her front "paws" to her head. Small children carry themselves with such natural ease and freedom it's a pleasure to watch them. They sit confidently—their upper body balanced on their pelvis—or run leaning slightly forward, as if into the wind. Why do they carry themselves with such "upness?" Where did ours go? We shared stories of our childhood, of parents or teachers telling us to "sit up straight" or "keep still" or "stop wiggling." We were all forced to sit still for hours in school, grip a pencil tensely as we learned to write, and generally lived in fear of making a mistake or displeasing our elders. By the time they grow up, most people acquire a state of constant unnecessary tension—a habitual holding that's largely the result of fear and stress.

Handwriting is a prime example of what Alexander meant by poor use of oneself. Write down a sentence right now, for example, then try again, while you think of your head floating off the end of your spine. We practiced it in class, taking all the time in the world to free our necks and allow our arms and hands to extend away from the torso, fingertips leading. Then we grasped the pen lightly as we pushed it along the paper. As a professional journalist accustomed to note taking, I was horrified to expose publicly my tendency to scrawl like a seven-year-old battling awkwardly with a pencil. I'd learned to write that way and never looked back, never examined the practical implications of what I was doing every day.

However, I comforted myself with the thought that body habits could be changed. That's why I was studying the Technique. When this primary relationship of head, neck and torso is freed of tension, neurological, chemical, and energetic changes are produced which translate in our subjective experience into ease of movement and heightened awareness. The spine decompresses when the pressure of the head is moved up and off the topmost vertebra. That releases the first unnecessary brake we keep on ourselves. Then, once the neck and newly extended spine let go, the second brake can be released at the ball-and-socket hip joints. We were asked to assist this process by thinking of the knees moving forward and away from the torso as we stand, sit or walk. The shoulders and arms, which are not part of the torso but sit like a yoke on top of it, could then also release at the joints. Shoulder tension, whether you are cooking, creating art or writing on a computer, can seriously interfere with the use of the upper body and the hands. So we visualized our hands coming out of the middle of the back, led by the fingers, as we went into various activities.

Day by day, our teachers called on us to do less, not more, to attain freedom of movement. Like the secret behind hitting the target in Zen archery, we had to let go of the determination to succeed to come nearer our goal. Alexander referred to our typical determined attitude to get the job done or hit the target at any price as "end-gaining." He asked why people put all their attention on the result and none on how they got there, which he called the "means whereby." He urged his students to "cultivate … the deliberate habit of taking up every occupation with the whole mind, with a living desire to carry each action through to a successful accomplishment, a desire which necessitates bringing into play every faculty of the attention."

◆

Expansion through Breathing

We don't have to do anything to breathe; it begins by paying attention and learning to get out of our own way. — Jessica Wolf

Awareness of how we breathe is an important element of the Technique. In his early days of teaching, Alexander was often called "the breathing man." The first published description of his new technique in 1907 was called "A New Method of Respiratory Education." Everything in the body is affected by the breathing—circulation, heart and digestive system are all stimulated by the movement of the diaphragm. And the oxygen we need to survive is the "food" we breathe in and distribute to every cell. Then the out-breath carries away the waste carbon dioxide.

Habitual holding of the ribcage limits the movements of the diaphragm and restricts our breathing. Alexander Technique work can help restore its full capacity and extend our natural exhalation without forcing. This stimulates the exchange of the residual volume of CO_2 in the lungs for fresh oxygen. It's important because high levels of carbon dioxide remaining in the lungs stress the nervous system.

I learned that faulty breathing patterns contribute to both psychic and physical stress, that my respiratory habits interfered with taking optimal advantage of oxygenated in-breaths or the stale-air disposal system. Always under stress at *Fortune*,

I had sometimes noticed how often I held my breath during an interview or even as I hurried down the hall to meet with an editor. So much of what I was doing was so important that it seemed there wasn't much time to breathe! Holding your breath limits both intake and outflow, but because it happens unconsciously, you probably don't even know you're doing it. Tune in and find out.

Dr. David Garlick, a research physiologist from the University of New South Wales who specialized in muscle and neuro-physiology, pointed out some of the effects of stress on breathing in *The Lost Sixth Sense*. The repeated contraction or stiffening of muscles to meet stressful situations produces habitual shallow, quick or irregular breathing. Chronic muscle contraction may lead to an increased heart rate and higher blood pressure. On the other hand, slow, relaxed breathing indicates the appropriate use of postural muscles without over-contraction of other muscles.

Garlick's study amazed me. It compared a group of Alexander teachers with an untrained group. He measured the use of the postural *erector spinae* muscles, the appropriate ones for standing and sitting, and simultaneously recorded everyone's rate and depth of breathing. He reported that "the Alexander teachers showed more activity in their back muscles when standing and their breathing was deeper and slower than the untrained group." His explanation for this was that "if the back muscle is not contracting enough to keep the trunk upright then the abdominal and chest muscles are stiffened or contracted to assist in stabilizing the trunk. If this happens, breathing movements are restricted and breathing become shallower and more frequent." In other words, the control group held themselves up with the wrong muscle system, which interfered with their breathing. Another study led by Dr. John Austin at the Columbia-Presbyterian Medical Center in New York City showed that "the volume of the lungs appears to increase after Alexander training in normal, healthy, young adults."

At ACAT we studied the respiratory process in action, not to learn a novel way of breathing, but simply to become aware of the various interferences to normal breathing. How to let go of them? As we practiced the Alexander "directions" to free the head, neck and torso, we saw how a deeper in-breath immediately resulted from the lengthening and widening of the framework of the body. We followed our own inhalation as it entered the torso as if to expand it all the way down to the bottom of the pelvis, then accompanied the exhalation up along the spine and out through the mouth.

"People often think they have to make some special effort to breathe normally," said Alexander Technique teacher Jessica Wolf, who has explored the relationship between the Alexander Technique and breathing over the last 25 years and created a post-graduate training program she called "The Art of Breathing." An innovator in the field, Jessica formulated a series of procedures to help people gain awareness of their breathing patterns. She has found that when they are able to relinquish the habits that interfere with ideal breathing coordination, the quality of their life improves.

"Breathing is reflexive," she explained. "It begins with paying attention." The diaphragm descends as you breathe in and rises as you breathe out. When you need more air, more negative pressure created in the chest allows more air to enter. The muscles of the thorax and abdomen also respond to the in-breath and out-breath, creating an internal massage for the torso and its contents.

Practitioners of yoga and other disciplines experiment with breathing in many different ways, using it as a link between physical and psychological states. Breathing exercises help yogis control their bodies and create psychic states, but they have usually trained their bodies and thinking capacity for many years. Such exercises are not necessarily applicable to Westerners, so it might be wise to experiment with care. They might create new habits of misuse in those who've already developed problematic breathing patterns. What's more, exercises that include holding the breath can adversely alter the cardio-respiratory system.

Simple awareness is most important. Jessica cautioned us against manipulating our breathing and told us the best way to study it is to tune in to its rhythm from time to time during the day. We saw that our breathing changed as soon as we paid attention to it. It adjusted to how we moved, as well as to what we felt or thought. Jessica characterized the diaphragm as "the main muscle of emotion, which moves in response to our joy and sorrow; and, when we feel happiness or pain, the laughter or grieving originates in the diaphragm muscle."

Changes in our breathing can inform us of what's going on in our physical and emotional life if we are alert to them. Depression has its own way of constricting breathing. The upper torso hunches over as the head moves forward and down while the spine curves back. This change of posture limits the diaphragm's excursion. Instead of moving up inside the ribs, it may press on the belly. Freeing the neck and expanding the torso can relieve such a contracted state. An anxiety attack, on the other hand, may produce short, shallow upper chest breathing and a feeling of tingling, lightheadedness and nausea from hyperventilation. Slower, deeper breathing will restore calm.

Jessica led us through several exercises. We lay on the floor on our backs with knees up and feet flat on the floor, and focused our attention on the upper chest, then the ribs and belly. We put one hand on the ribs and the other on the belly below the navel. She asked us: "What do you notice? Does everything move gently with your breath or does one part move more than another?" It's an experiment I now ask all my own students to try, to become more familiar with the container of torso and the breath that moves it.

Once we tuned into the rhythm of our breathing and saw how it changed, deepened and expanded with our awareness, Jessica invited us to a visualize ourselves lying on the beach, watching the waves roll in. You could try this for yourself, lying on the floor with a couple of soft-cover books under your head to prevent it from arching back, and your hands resting on your chest and belly. Imagine you are there, watching the waves wash up on the shore, organized by forces deep within the ocean or on the moon. Then notice how the waves recede after they roll up the beach as far as they can go. Each wave is different, just like every breath. Breathing is as natural as that if it's not interfered with. And when it has completed its cycle there is a natural pause like the sudden quiet between waves. After that, it follows its own laws like the next wave rolling into the shore. Air pours in through the nose without needing your help in any way. You are present to the experience without trying to make it happen.

◆

Stress & Debauched Kinesthesia

… The teacher's task is to help people overcome the tendency to approach every situation by contracting themselves and teach them how to approach every situation by expanding themselves. — John Nicholls

We are thinking beings but we are also animals. To be good thinking animals, we need an accurate kinesthetic sense, a presence of ourselves in the body, a knowing of the body as it moves. Most of us aren't accustomed to such awareness because we almost always live under pressure. Our nervous system spends a lot more time firing away in excitation as the adrenaline flows than in reflection about what we're doing. That means our body gets accustomed to the "startle pattern," and we mostly inhabit varying degrees of a state known as the fight-or-flight reaction. When we learned this, we began to notice on streets and subways and anywhere else how any unexpected stimulus provokes an immediate startle reaction.

Danger is near, we feel, but it's not a lion in the jungle we have to defend ourselves from. It may be a deadline or an exam or an unpleasant appointment. In my case, it was often the fear that I wouldn't get where I was going on time or finish the job soon enough or well enough to please someone in authority. The Judge that my Jungian studies had uncovered kept an eye on me all day long, offering comments on each activity: "This is more important, so get it done first," or "That's less important, so hurry through it." My classmates described similar experiences, and we agreed that continual self-criticism added to our stress. Any time I worry that "I need more time to finish," stress is present.

Hurry expresses a wish to be in the future because I think I'm late. It speeds me away from the present moment I'm living through. We tried to give up that kind of pressure as often as we became aware of it, in favor of the mantra Walter Carrington repeats to himself and his students: "I *have* time." It calls on an alternative mode of the nervous system: inhibition. Instead of forcing ourselves ahead under the neuro-physical command to "do it now!" at whatever cost, we can send a message to wait, to delay action.

We all agreed it's important to relieve stress, and some of us dedicated a lot of time to exercise as a way to combat it. But while many forms of exercise aim to stretch, strengthen and tone the body, spending a stressful day at work followed by a demanding workout or a three-mile run may put unnecessary strain on the organism. On the other hand, crumpling into a couch-potato weekend or a do-nothing vacation may not help either. The folks who try this to recover from a long period of constant stimulation may vacate themselves as well. Whether they rest or act, their habitual state of excitation may continue to wreak havoc on their nervous system below the level of awareness. Many of us prefer to stay in the fight-or-flight mode, honing our "edge" and paying the price for it in physical fatigue and mental strain.

You may well ask, as I did: "How can I be expected to feel the joy of the moment when I have to stay and finish a job I no longer want to continue?" When you *have* to get something done and have no choice, it helps to acknowledge first how you really feel. Then it's well worth looking for freedom in the only remaining area—within yourself. You can experiment, as I did, with attending to parts of your body as you work. Explore the back of your neck as you sit at the computer. Let your thought move whenever and wherever the body moves, and interrupt what you're doing from time to time to get up or at least stretch out in the sitting position you are in.

If you work on a computer all day, move around frequently! Since everything's connected in the mind-body continuum, you might be surprised to what extent you can relieve your stressed-out system when you get up for a brief, non-essential walk down the hall, a peek out the window, or even a seriously deep sigh that engages you right down to the toes. Do *anything* to interrupt the deadening bond that glues all your attention to what you're writing, reading, cooking, chopping, building. Truly, the body possesses wisdom that thought doesn't understand. We can practice listening to it and expand into present reality.

Unfortunately our kinesthetic sense, which tells us where we are in space and how we are using ourselves, can be untrustworthy. Most of us suffer from the *debauched kinesthesia* Alexander identified when he looked into his three-angled mirror. In spite of his own conviction, he realized he was not positioned the way he thought he was. That's hard to accept. During an Alexander class I often think the teacher has guided me to a place where I'm bending slightly back or angled forward because it doesn't feel "quite right." But a look in the mirror tells me I'm beautifully upright. On the one hand, without sensory feedback, we wouldn't even be able to stand up, let alone up straight. But on the other hand, our belief that we are in this or that position or that we need to grip at the hips or use the shoulders to stand and sit is an illusion.

One day I discovered how trusting what I "feel" creates a vicious circle. I noticed I was achy and a little depressed. I asked my body how it felt, but the only message it returned to me was that I ached and felt low, which reinforced the state I was in and reaffirmed my conviction of the hopelessness of my situation. I experimented with an alternative approach, deciding to trust the living and constantly moving energy in the body, which has the capacity to displace upward whether or not I feel low at any given moment. As soon as I tried to think my way out of the state I was stuck in, a fresh impression of myself appeared. The "down" turned into an "up."

Once we accepted that our kinesthesia was untrustworthy, I and my fellow students developed a new habit: "going inside" to check things out and see if our Alexander thinking had changed anything. But going inward to monitor or sense the experience took us away from home base—ourselves. We were told to keep our eyes alive and focused on what was in the room. Understandably, we might want to revisit a novel sensation produced by a teacher's hands or our own moment of clear thinking, but whenever we tried to repeat it rather than reaffirm the direction, we went right back into the old habit. So we turned instead to our new *mantra: neck free to allow the head to balance lightly on the spine,* then *torso lengthening and widening,* then *legs and arms coming away.* Then gradually, like a cameraman moving backward and panning out, we would visualize our whole body in expansion. Finally we invited our inner cameraman to widen the scope of the scene we were in to include the whole room.

♦

Tension, Relaxation, Release

We are looking for a state of balanced, dynamic tension, not relaxation. It is an experience greater than the words; but sometimes all you can take away is the words. — Pearl Ausubel

What is relaxation for? A completely relaxed body can't move. Some muscular tension is necessary in order to maintain posture or initiate movement. Then what is the optimal tension that keeps us active, engaged and using but not abusing ourselves? Perhaps we could replace the word relaxation with efficiency of tone. Alexander himself preferred the word release or release-in-activity.

The usual idea of relaxation is "letting go" into a slump onto a nearby couch, settling into a comfortable position for a good break and expecting to feel rested afterward. But we often feel worse than before because a slump deadens our energy. Brooke told us that, "When you are functionally unbalanced, it's like plucking a string on a musical instrument and not allowing the vibration to take place."

Her suggestion was to bring thought to muscular action and replace "doing" with giving consent. "It's a right and left brain coordination," she explained. "The static from my judgmental head, my emotional flack, even my physical distress, all interfere with my sensitivity to what's going on and my responsiveness to it."

There has to be another way to deal with pressure while an emergency lasts, but the aftereffects of our usual solution end in collapse or some drastic form of recovery. Elizabeth Walker, a master teacher visiting our class from England, was a living example of a different way of living. Vibrating with energy at age 86, she was emphatic. "You are coming here to learn to *think*, not *do!*" she said. "Although the activities of the day may call for all kinds of movements and tensions, you don't have to *stay* like that. You can return to your optimum state of rest, your state of balance."

How to substitute some way of thinking into release for my tendency to hold on tight in a crisis? How could I "think" into release? When I'm faced with an emergency I cling to a concept, almost like a prayer, to oppose the pressure that rigidifies me. When I discover I've pressed down on the freeze-frame button, I remind myself that everything living is in movement, inner or outer or both, that everything vibrates in the dance of atoms and molecules. Blood courses through me at tremendous speed. My bones themselves vibrate.

While it's natural to feel down-in-the-mouth sometimes (note the physiology of the expression), every cell has an *up* along with its *down*. In trying to think up as we worked with each other and on our own thinking, we felt the movement of our energy go up. At the same time, as our teachers reminded us, you can't *stay* in a released state. Our *up* might last for a tenth of a second as we directed our thought. But although we couldn't stay there, we could return again and again, allowing ourselves to open into expansion. In other words, we could practice returning to our own presence.

By the end of my second year, I finally accepted that no matter how hard I tried, I couldn't hold onto a state of release. It's a contradiction in terms. The important thing was to return repeatedly to awareness of what I was doing, to inhibit the first coarse reaction (usually accompanied by a tightening in the neck), and give a clear direction to my thought. That way I prepared the ground for a new release to take place. As Judy Stern put it: "The startle response—with the head pushed back and down—is part of being human. So it's OK. But it shouldn't dominate the scene." Knowing that, we accepted to *practice* rather than hope to change everything and stay in a new place. We returned to the present moment again and again to free ourselves from unnecessary tension.

◆

Emotions and Reactions

Here is a technique for control over the reactions that prevent the human response of the organism. Your freedom is here now, and only your conviction stands in the way of it. — Daniel Singer

Ever since David Gorman first presented me with his theory that our belief system has shaped our bodies over time into the way they look and function now, the connection between physical and emotional states has fascinated me. The Alexander Technique confirmed what I'd accepted in my heart long before from personal experiences. As psychologist Karlfried von Durckheim stated in *The Way of Transformation*: "Body and psyche are not two separate entities: rather, they are the two modes by which man, with his rational, divided vision, perceives himself."

Anyone engaged in body/mind studies, from the ancient practices of T'ai Chi and Qi Gong to modern methods of release and relief of physical pain and distortion, knows that thought and emotions exert a powerful influence on the body. Some experts say body and mind are related; others, like Carl Jung and von Durckheim, insist they are two ends of the very same stick. How can knowing this help us understand ourselves better? For one thing, we need to accept that emotions interfere more with the state of poise we seek than our physical tensions do. They are invariably expressed in and through the body by grippings and holdings.

The study of mind, body and emotions offers a double feedback. Tuning into our muscles and joints offers a window into mental and emotional habits and the opportunity to let go of unnecessary physical tensions. Observation of emotions and their effect on the body tells us where we need to "let go" of our psychic hold on things. As we gain increased awareness of our muscular tensions and release them, our attention turns to the quality of our emotional state. Consciousness of an emotional reaction can trigger an inquiry into where and why the body is tense.

It's crucial information because when either muscular or emotional tensions persist over a long time, they can lead to physical problems. As the body gradually becomes programmed to live in a constant state of unnecessary tension, fatigued muscles will help perpetuate the emotional state. But when we bring awareness, inhibition and direction to relearn the movements we made with exaggerated tension, we can undo the patterns that interfere with natural coordination. We then become centered in a more balanced psycho-physical state, a state of readiness for action, of presence to the moment.

One morning as I walked to the subway on my way to the Alexander school, I found myself muttering: "Boy, am I tired!" As I became aware of my fatigued body, I queried: "*Where* are you tired?" The minute I asked, there was a physical response of increased tension in my solar plexis. The rest of the body let go in relief. Was I suffering from a poorly digested breakfast or an emotional reaction? I couldn't pinpoint that, but whatever it was, it was suddenly localized in one small part of me, rather than holding all of me hostage in a general vise of fatigue.

Fear is the number one emotion to elicit instant physical response, especially the neck-tightening, fight-or-flight reaction. There can be fear of being hurt, fear of commitment, fear of failure, fear of being exposed as the inadequate person one suspects oneself to be, fear of being wrong, and many others. All of them interfere with how one holds oneself and the clarity of one's movements. Yet according to *Weight Watchers Handbook*, "there's no such thing as failure. There's only feedback." And feedback is exactly what we need.

One day our class experimented with how we could respond differently to a familiar fear. One by one we entered the room while everyone else sat in a row of chairs staring at the door. The first time we each felt judged as well as embarrassed and didn't know where to look. The second time our teacher, Kim Jessor, stood out in the hall with each of us before we entered. When it was my turn, she reminded me that "we always have a choice if we come back to the process." She suggested that I stay centered in myself and expand my awareness to include the whole room as soon as I entered it, rather than focus on the row of watching "judges." With her hands and voice, she invited me to inhabit my back consciously, as well as the front of my body, and to observe people without focusing all my attention on them.

We all felt greater freedom the second time we walked in,

a lesson in the power of preparation and the practice of presence. The word "process" was key: to believe in the process and give it our best attention, rather than stay in the fearful part of ourselves. Self-aware, we were ready to confront others and able to maintain a strong intention to remain rooted in our bodies. We came into the space without diminishing or defending ourselves, fully occupying the small space of our bodies within the larger space of the room. "Even the room felt friendlier," said one of my classmates.

That experiment helped us discover other fixed emotional attitudes about ourselves. What frame of mind were we in when we observed our body? What anxieties did we have about how we "looked" to other people? The mirror that ran the length of the classroom invited a choice every day. We could either see ourselves as too fat or too thin, with a back that's too curved or not curved enough, or simply observe our habits as we moved.

Although I'd always suspected there were emotional elements in my tendency to slump, I was surprised by subtler habitual attitudes that went along with it. For example, a lot of the time I looked slightly down, which I discovered made me "feel down." I also noticed the mixed message I gave when I placed my hands on fellow students. As I told them to free their neck so that their head could move easily on the spine, I realized I only half believed it would "work." The doubt in my mind came just at the moment I was trying to help them initiate change. Another emotional habit surfaced when I sat down with a student to give and receive feedback. As I listened eagerly to what she thought of my teaching skills, I opened towards her, but then I pulled back, ready to close my mind to what I didn't want to hear. I was both going forward in space and pulling back at the same time!

This tendency to short circuit my efforts became more

visible when, halfway through training, I realized that every time I put hands on a teacher (our most daunting assignment), a plaintive voice in me would say "I can't do this!" Once, I "taught" the director, who patiently sat and stood while I tried unsuccessfully to keep my sense of direction up rather than worry about whether or not I was giving her the right message with my hands. She stopped me to ask what I was thinking at that very moment. With a shock I realized I had been thinking, "I'm not good enough for this." She smiled and said, "That's your deep habit. Try to see it each time it appears."

This habit reappeared whenever I played the role of teacher. I was anxious to "help" classmates to a new balance, while at the same time wondering whether I was "doing them any good." Whenever the helpless feeling that my message wasn't going to work emerged, my commitment to clear thinking disappeared. This led me to ask myself how often in my life my emotions went in two directions at once.

By the beginning of my third year I became more confident. I no longer worried about whether I was "good" or "bad" at teaching as I began to trust not my *feelings* about what I was doing but the reliability of the Alexander process itself. If I was doing my job properly, both with myself and with the student, there was no time for worry about how either of us "felt" about it. Our attention was elsewhere as we either moved toward better use of ourselves or not. As Walter Carrington likes to say, "It's simple. You are either moving up or down."

The powerful effect of fear on the functioning of the body can't be overestimated. It applies to both sides of the teacher/student relationship. Just as the teacher wants to succeed with the student, it's the most natural thing in the world for the student to want to please the teacher and be a "good" student. We hate to be wrong, and want to do what we're supposed to, which means we're in danger of putting our success in the teacher's hands. When we recognize the power of this fear of not pleasing we are in a better place to let go of it and acknowledge that it's hard to learn anything without sometimes being "wrong."

◆

Changes in the Use of Oneself

Put freeing yourself at the top of your to-do list and keep it there.
— Judy Stern

Charles Darwin said, "It is not the strongest of the species that survive, nor the most intelligent, but the ones most responsive to change." The Alexander Technique can effect powerful changes over time in our ability to respond to—or inhibit—the stimuli coming at us every waking minute from all sides. It certainly helped me allow more time for everything and enjoy more what I chose to engage in. During the three-year training many changes took place in my body and in my ability to pay attention. In the first two years the slumped chest and curved shoulders I'd expected to carry to my grave underwent major reconstruction, as did my tendency to stand with my hips a little forward of my legs. If you decide to study the Technique, remember to return again and again, as I did, to enliven your intentional thought and to keep the structure of the living body in your mind's eye. If you do, real changes will take place.

They may come in the form of less hunch in the shoulders, diminished pain in the lower back, a belly that no longer thrusts forward from the hips or, quite simply, ease of movement. New students may not notice early differences until a teacher points them out or may rejoice in a dramatic shift right from the start. A student with sciatica who complained that she couldn't walk two city blocks without pain, strolled a painless eleven blocks after her first lesson with me. A student with Parkinson's disease exclaimed at the end of her first lesson, "It's as if the lights have been turned on everywhere in me!"

The next thing students usually want to know is "How can I keep this 'new body'?" And the answer is, "You can't." You discover that your thought can bring about a change; thought can connect you more intimately to how you are in the present moment, but it's never once-and-for-all. We live in a world that bombards us all day long with stimuli that demand our reaction or response. So we work along a continuum, not towards being perfect or perfectly "up" but remembering, as Alexander once said, that no matter what you do or how subtle your perception becomes, you'll still encounter all the habits of your life. "Nobody gets to stay there," Judy Stern told us. "All 'ups' must come down. We're not trying to capture something but to return to an expanded field of attention."

Alexander teacher trainees want to hold on to feeling good just like anyone else, so we were often mired in internal concentration on performance. Sometimes we tried so hard to move slowly with direction that we seemed like zombies and, when this was pointed out to us, we'd move so quickly we lost our sense of self. At other times we wanted to be "right" and became fixed, so intent on the forward-and-up direction of the head that we walked around stretching our necks like giraffes. Often we forgot that inhibition is exploratory, the pause of not knowing, as we tried to "correct" ourselves.

One helpful exercise was to find appropriate adjectives to fit whatever state we were in at any moment of the day. *Static, rigid, fixed, stagnant* were obvious downers, while *dynamic, energetic, fluid, changing, adaptable* went in the direction of freedom. We became more accurate instruments, sensitive to aches and fatigues, able to listen more attentively to what was going on in mind, body and emotions. This increased awareness made us feel more responsible for our state of being, inviting us to become more careful and attentive. When you teach, you truly have to put any reactions to one side and focus all your attention on your own inner balance and that of your students. Without engaging in the practice of your own presence, you can't help their find theirs.

As we noticed changes in our levels of tension, we developed a "listening hand." When we touched our fellow students we could perceive this same *letting go* in them. In the third year we provided "aha!" experiences for each other, and saw that this communication of release depended largely on the teacher's depth of presence at the moment of touch. It no longer seemed as though we were transmitting some magical energy, but simply directing our thought with clarity while centered in our own being, as we guided another student.

In the middle of winter break in my third year I was overwhelmed by a strong resistance to returning to school. After several days of battling with it, I made the agonized decision not to pressure myself to go back. To my surprise, as soon as I did, an intolerable burden lifted. I realized that my resistance was a sign of progress. My life felt like a meat-grinder and I was the meat! I had forged ahead with Alexander school every morning, worked halftime and spent evenings at the Gurdjieff Foundation. Now I was forced to listen to the real message, which I had been refusing for months, perhaps years: "*I need time!*"

As soon as I allowed myself time off and let go of any stigma of "weakness" due to my need for a break, the Alexander directions appeared spontaneously, whether I was sitting or walking or bending to throw something into the wastebasket. Now that

I had given myself permission to take time, I became free of the pressure to succeed. "I need time" had become a blessing, rather than a curse. The old, habitual way of living—stuffing too many activities into each day—was no longer acceptable to the developing person I was and to my changing nervous system. My whole pace slowed down.

After ten days' vacation in Florida, I returned quietly to Alexander school, accepting that time was needed to digest this extraordinary new life aborning in me. I had to find a way to live more in accord with my nature and the reality of life. Three years of study had led me to a second key question that serves the ageless human cry: "Who am I?" Now, wherever I go, I'm called from within, sometimes when I least expect it, to answer the query: "Where am I?" Or in Alexander terms: "How am I using myself right now?"

To answer honestly calls for a total commitment, a disengaging of my thought from its usual half-hearted meanderings, or even its wholehearted identifications. A usually dormant faculty is called into play, which generates a major change in my psychophysical state. These days I continue to remind myself to pause and let go of the need to succeed as the world defines success, to cherish a more authentic relation with myself and with others and to return, with the help of Alexander's insights, to the experience of my own presence.

As a journalist, I've spent a lot of time and energy trying to find out the whys and wherefores that cause things to happen as they do, but now I know that an ardent search for answers, while valuable, doesn't lead me where I want to go. The wish to know has been replaced by pausing and opening to what's going on in me and in the world right now. It redirects the same wish-energy from ferreting out answers to finding freedom in this moment. To the practice of presence.

If you are interested in learning more about the Alexander

Technique in the U.S. and Canada, you can contact the *American Society for the Alexander Technique* at PO Box 60008, Florence, MA 01062, or 800-473-0620 or alexandertech@earthlink.net. They also have a list of certified practitioners around the world. In Europe, you can get in touch with the *Society of Teachers of the Alexander Technique*, 129 Camden Mews, London NW1 9AH, England, call 020-7284-3338, e-mail www.stat.org.uk. I studied at the *American Center for the Alexander Technique*, 39 West 14th Street, New York, NY, 10011, 212-633-2229. Its e-mail address is acat@acatnyc.org.

The most valuable knowledge we can possess is that of the use and functioning of the self. — F. M. Alexander

Five

THE PATH OF
PRAYER AND MEDITATION

Nearer to us than breathing.

— Shankara

✺

Prayer has been part of my daily practice since childhood and, along with meditation, has come to represent the essence of *being* rather than *doing*. The busyness of all my "doing" in life seemed to take me away from myself, and my contemplative practice provided a welcome return journey toward centeredness.

My tendency to hurry out of the present and into the future was one of the first things I noticed in Gurdjieff exercises, and it was confirmed again later as I practiced T'ai Chi and the Alexander Technique. Or I might be mired in reactions to some past event or perceived misunderstanding. However, each time I pray or meditate, I get a lesson in letting go, for a few treasured moments, of all my life aims and intentions, wounds, fears, worries and calculations. Quite simply, I attempt to sit, stand, walk and work in the light of who I am, rather than feel driven forward or held back.

It's hard to see through the windshield of the mortal car I'm driving to find out where I'm going. If I'm lucky, I'll bump against the edge of a boulder and wake up before I crash. Hopefully, I won't hit a pedestrian, though I often hurt someone accidentally. Wounding other people shows me how blind I've been and forces me to try to see more clearly where I am and where I'm going. Relieved not to have done more damage to myself and to others, I may then (literally or figuratively) sink to my knees in gratitude, filled with remorse for my actions. This gesture reorients my whole inner world.

In my experience, the grace we all hope will descend on us from time to time depends on such a remorseful awakening. The minute I discover, often painfully, that once again I am not "appropriate," not corresponding to the full stature of a human being, a new contact with myself appears. If in such a moment I can acknowledge my lack of awareness, I come closer to myself. It is also a reminder that two need to be present at the same time, and I'll borrow from the title of Martin Buber's great book to call them *I and Thou*. Until I can acknowledge that I'm related to an "other"—a name isn't necessary—I dwell in a very small corner of myself. I may feel good or bad or embarrassed or angry—the whole gamut of reactions is always available—but in every case I am disconnected from a higher possibility in myself. Perhaps it would be more accurate to say that unless 'Thou' is present to some extent, I *am* my reactions, rather than the person I wish to be.

When I acknowledge that there's a witness to all my actions present in me, who provides a larger context within which my life is lived, I feel relief, even if I'm unhappy. Not that I can call up this "other" at will, but the reminder that somewhere there is another, larger presence, creates hope, combined with a sense of loss. I've been missing something important to me.

We have all experienced that "other" at some level of intensity, although it has many different names. Some call it simply "Spirit." Others call it God, Brahma, Allah, Jehovah and many other names in different parts of the world. Those who live on the slopes of Peru's highest mountain call it *Gollanagapac*— He Who Calls from Eternity. Whatever the name, the power behind it can carry a mighty clout. A higher power by any name, or even without one, is what it is.

The possibility of hearing this call exists in each of us, but in the midst of the busy lives we lead, we often lose the capacity to listen. We forget Jesus' advice that "He who has ears to hear let him hear." Our inner ear needs refining so that when the vibration of truth is heard, we are ready to tune ourselves to it and follow where it leads. This quality of attentive listening for the call opens the way to understanding ourselves and to finding our place in the universe. It is the path of prayer and meditation.

◆

The Search for Meaning

What am I? I am myself a word spoken by God. Can God speak a word that does not have any meaning? — Thomas Merton

The search we are engaged in is a search for what makes life, any life, worth living. It is a search for meaning. Although inevitably individual and personal, it can be supported by organized religious forms. However, our true spiritual life may have nothing to do with the religious beliefs we profess or deny, possibly imposed on us in childhood. The Spirit can never be imposed. It can only be discovered—it can only appear. For it's been there all along.

Nevertheless, we want to play an active part in its appearance by seeking out the appropriate conditions. So those who feel that their path might best be followed through religious observance, that an organization would help support their search, may want to investigate several alternative ways of worship, to help connect them to a larger world than the limited horizon within which they usually live. If a form feels authentic, embrace it. Although there's no single way to pray or meditate and no one religion superior to others, it's best to avoid too much shopping around or "spiritual tourism." Sri Ramakrishna compared this to digging a lot of wells without ever going deep enough to find water.

If you don't know where to dig, don't get discouraged. Finding one's own path is never easy and may take a lifetime. Along the way, you'll probably meet others who feel saved from confusion and doubt by their religion and want you to join it. They may even insist that theirs is the only true path. But keep on exploring until your inner guide seems ready to drop anchor, because there are many paths that could lead you to your authentic *being*. Some seekers find solace in the ritual of communion in a Catholic Church. Others light candles for the Jewish Shabbat, chant in a Hindu or Moslem temple, or count breaths in a Zen sitting. Some set up their own private altar or sacred place. Many paths lead "home." But where *is* home? And how do we get there?

Since childhood, we've had hints from fairy tales and parables. We learned about the "hero"—often a simple person like us—whose heart's desire awaits him if only he or she could wake up and undertake the Great Adventure. Perhaps we didn't absorb or appreciate the depth of the message then, but now, in the middle of the journey of our lives, we begin to suspect that there could indeed be a precious treasure somewhere, buried deep.

I remember it was usually guarded by a *force majeure* like a monster, a ferocious dragon, a terrifying witch or a powerful wizard. The former two could devour you; the latter two could make you disappear—possibly an accurate analogy for how life energy drains away while daily cares distract us from searching more deeply. Or perhaps we were fearful of the consequences of stopping our activity to look more carefully at what's going on.

Through all the intervening years since childhood, a longing for centeredness has been walled up inside us like the princess who slept for a hundred years in her castle, while thorn bushes grew up around it to keep intruders and princes away. We have a strong wish for freedom from slavery to everything "out there" so that we might be more alive right here inside ourselves, but those monster guardians do their job well and keep us walled up by fear or drugged by hypnotic sleep.

What can awaken the sleeping prince or princess born to rule our personal inner kingdom? Many of us had some kind of religious education or parental training to live a virtuous life and respect our fellows. Whether or not we continue to practice its forms, a ground-work has been established, a sense that there is a larger purpose to human existence. I was profoundly affected by sporadic early childhood visits to a little country church in Connecticut. Sunday School infused me with a vague idea of Christ as an elder brother and intermediary with the divine, located somewhere very high up in the sky.

In one of the few early dreams I clearly remember, after having done something "terrible," I sped downward on an elevator to Hell accompanied by the devil. I started to cry out in terror to God to save me. Immediately I heard thunder, the structure trembled with earthquake force and began to crack open as we plunged through black space. When I realized my call for help might destroy me, I quickly redirected my prayer to Jesus. Suddenly He stood beside me in the elevator, looking toward the door as if waiting for the next floor. The elevator stopped, the doors opened, and I got off with Him, though we never exchanged either a word or a glance, because He never turned toward me or acknowledged me in any way. I've never forgotten that vivid early impression that help exists, but the tremendous power of the divine can shatter on an earthly level without a mediator.

Divine energy can touch and even transform our lives if we can find a way to open ourselves to it, and many teachings and spiritual practices are available to help us learn how. My studies and experiences over the years led me to agree with what I first heard proposed by a Mexican archaeologist many years ago in Lima: that all the religions and sacred rituals that have come down to us since man's time on earth began stem from one Great Tradition. Like the source of the longest river that comes down from the highest mountain, it long ago branched into smaller streams of higher knowledge, which spread all over the earth. In each local region, this knowledge was interpreted in many ways and on many levels. Some traces of this Great Tradition have degenerated into belief systems; others continue to be living containers of the Great Truth.

Taoist, Egyptian, Hindu, Hebrew and Buddhist thought were clear early manifestations of this Great Tradition. Christian, Moslem, Sufi and many other large and small religions, and disciplines too numerous to name, also flowed forth in their time from the same original source. Gurdjieff said he gleaned his teaching from remote monasteries where that tradition was kept alive. He often referred to it as "esoteric

Christianity," but it also has much in common with Taoism and Zen.

As this mountain stream flows down and spreads out, it brings nourishment to many fields in the valleys below. Some of them are nameless, but no less valuable. Others are clearly identified and influence many people. Among the latter, I have written here about Jung, who with a prescient inner openness was led by his fearless taste for truth and informed scientist's mind to explore the depths of the psyche; and Alexander, who investigated the body's own truth and developed his Technique out of an unrelenting study of his own habits and reactions.

Wherever we dig at a vein of truth, we are mining from the one great Mother Lode. What is important to each of us, for our own growth, is not the name or form but the path itself, which teaches us how to live in a way that can transform our own daily life. It behooves us to be deeply grateful to those representatives of a higher level, irrespective of the faith they pursued, who awaken us to the call of our own inner guide.

◆

Is Happiness Possible?

When a man finds no peace with himself, it is useless to seek it elsewhere. — Goethe

Do you know anyone who doesn't wish to be happy? We all look for happiness, which we sometimes sum up in the word *peace* or the phrase *peace of mind*. The Bible speaks of "the peace that passeth understanding," which is a peace of the heart. In it, the heart comes to rest. Anxiety has disappeared and our tendency to react to whatever's happening has subsided. The mind quiets too, and the body relaxes. This is the peace we all long for, when the problems of yesterday and tomorrow cease to burden us, when our memories and preoccupations no longer disturb our digestive, respiratory or circulatory systems and we can engage (perhaps gently) in doing what we really wish to do.

Can such peace only be found in churches, on mountaintops or at the feet of gurus? The *Taittiriya Upanishad*, one of the world's oldest sacred texts, states that "… Happiness is Brahman; from Happiness, indeed, all these creatures are born; when born they live through Happiness; when they depart they enter into Happiness." The Buddha told his monks that the source of all suffering is the hankering and the dejection which seem to rule the ebb and flow of human inner life. Pantanjali affirmed that "there is no cure for the misery of longing but to fix the heart on the eternal." Akbar advised: "the world is a bridge. Build no house on it."

If misery arises primarily from fears and unsatisfied yearnings, what can change all that? And what can those of us do who haven't been endowed with such deep religious dedication that we want to leave the world behind? We want to find happiness in our present lives and wonder, as we muddle through life's trials and tribulations, why we seldom can. What's more, many spiritual and religious leaders have assured us that happiness is right here under our noses as a possibility all the time, and we don't have to *do* anything to *get* it. In fact, they invite us to stop some of our *doing* and give up a large helping of our self-preoccupation.

After leaving college, I worked as a reporter at *Time* magazine, and later, when I lived in Peru, I scrambled to find jobs to help support my family. During all that time, I often wondered uncomfortably whether my spiritual aspirations were drowning in my busyness. Then one day, heartsick about this, I read the words of the Persian mystic, Rumi, which gave sense to my suffering: "There is in man a passion, an agony, an itch, an importunity such that though a hundred thousand worlds were his to own, yet he would not rest nor find repose. These creatures dabble successively in every trade and craft and office; they study astronomy and medicine and the rest, and take no repose; for they have not attained the object of their quest. Men call the Beloved 'Heart's Ease' because the heart finds ease in the Beloved. How then should it find ease and rest in any other?"

I recognized that I had set aside my inner world, my most private space, to put all my energy into solving life's ceaseless demands. Often my days were exciting and stimulating. My Gurdjieff training had bred in me a love of challenges, which I met with all my energy. But I became so absorbed in the battle I was waging that I no longer noticed the absence of a whole other life in me. As I tried to solve endless problems and raise a family, I often felt like Superwoman, a conqueror of any difficulties in my path. I'm sure, as I look back now, that I was riding on the wings of psychic *inflation*, inordinately pleased with myself at doing so much for so many.

But why didn't I turn more frequently to seek the Beloved? If something was missing from my against-all-odds success story, which it seemed to be, what did I need to *do* about it? When I read Thomas Merton's gentle comment in *No Man Is an Island,* my attitude changed. His chapter, "Doing and Being," two words at the center of my conflict, assured me that: "It is … a very great thing to be little, which is to say: to be ourselves."

Clearly, my "doing" side had blown up out of all proportion to the rest of me, yet in all fairness to myself, life demanded action from me all day long. Although I usually thought I knew what to do and where I was going, it was time to face the truth that I really *didn't know much*! It was a relief to absorb that realization. Once you get over the need to appear omniscient, admitting you don't know brings great inner freedom and even joy—freedom from the *oughts* that bind us, and escape from the weight of pretension that bolsters up our pseudo self-assurance.

At that time my children often asked me to read a favorite story about a very savvy cat who saved a poor young man from starvation, then step by step won for him a job, a girl and a kingdom. Every time the boy stuttered his thanks, amazed, repeating out loud what he just learned as if to remind himself of it, the cat replied: "Well, you don't know much, but now at least you know that much!" I began to mutter this phrase myself when shocked out of complacency by inescapable proof of my level of ignorance. "Patty, you don't know much, but at least you know *that* much!" became my mantra. So as we undertake a study of the religious and spiritual dimensions of the search for *presence* where high passions run deep, perhaps it would be useful to acknowledge that we, like the boy, don't know much. In order to identify a true path to a happier life, we need first to know ourselves better.

◆

The Scent of Reality

Who knows himself knows his Lord. — Eastern saying

What does it mean to know oneself? We know a lot of things *about* ourselves, not only weight, height, eye and hair color, but what we like to eat, our likes and dislikes and how many cups of tea or coffee we need to keep going. We may also know how a walk in the woods or a few minutes of thoughtful reflection can open us to wider horizons, and how helpful it is to return home, to sit quietly and experience how this body that contains the rest of us feels. But my *self*? That's a mystery, an unknown element that perhaps will never be known. Who am I really? Where did this person I feel myself to be come from and where is he or she headed? What purpose does my life serve? Are there other dimensions of Self?

The contemporary Hindu teacher Jean Klein said we can never know what we are, but we *can* know what we are not. In his book, *The Ease of Being*, he spoke about the stages of self-knowledge that unfold from self-questioning. Even at the beginning it can kindle an "intimation of reality," awakening a feeling of emptiness which may send us off to hunt in many directions for something to fill our sense of lack. Then, each time we think we've got what we were looking for, there may be a moment of peace. But soon we'll be off again, "like a hunting dog who cannot find the scent," in frantic search for what we think we can't do without.

Although nothing might satisfy us for long, Klein pointed out that such experiences gradually educate us. As we understand ourselves, and the repetitive lure of 'wanting,' better, we become attracted to what he called "the scent of reality." It begins to center us, creating a sense of valuation for the spiritual search, as well as quieting our habitual agitation. Gurdjieff referred to this process as the development of 'magnetic center,' a place within our psychic makeup that resonates to the sound or presence of truth.

In spite of the fact that awakening to presence begins with questioning, my reasoning mind found it difficult to accept that spending time pondering questions could help me. I wanted answers, not more questions. Like many people, I wanted safety in a secure truth, without having to work at it.

We all share this wish for security, but it's important to allow the difficult queries for which we have no answers to settle deep into our flesh and bones, to see them as the poet Rainer Maria Rilke did, like locked rooms containing something precious but to which we have no key. In this way, they may lead us to deeper questions and expose the fact that the stock answers we stash in the closet of our minds are of little value. In moments of great loss or suffering, or even of great joy, such formulations don't tell us much that's useful. It took a long time for me to accept that true self-knowledge isn't owning an answer. It's knowledge of my own nature.

What seemed underdeveloped in my search for presence was the indispensable faculty of attention so often emphasized by Gurdjieff. Most of us lack the capacity to attend for long to any one thing. Those who can are good athletes, good listeners, good thinkers, good workers at anything they do. In *Waiting for God*, Simone Weil insisted that the whole purpose of school studies was to develop a child's attention, and that the quality of a student's effort to attend was even more important than whether or not a problem was correctly solved.

But as long as movies and television fire images at us like bullets, our ability to attend to one thing with awareness will get little encouragement. Training for the Olympics, which demands years of daily discipline and practice, is a highly worthwhile ideal for young people. Money is spent, coaches are hired to animate flagging enthusiasm and hone athletic talent. Yet most of us resist undertaking daily work to develop our attention for a spiritual purpose. Surely finding our heart's desire is a form of bringing home the gold!

Wherever our attention is, there our energy goes. Whatever we dwell on, whether past or future, is fed by our present energy. At any moment, I'm turning my attention towards something or someone, giving away this precious energy or letting it trickle out of me into all kinds of unnecessary distractions or reactions to the world around me. For example, my energy goes into making inner assumptions and judgments about people I see for a moment on bus or subway. Or I'm disconnected from myself as I walk along the street, concentrated on hypnotizing the green light so it won't turn red before I can cross at the corner. Energy hemorrhages from me in a multitude of similar ways. Everything around me seems to call me to act or react, to pay attention to what's going on *out there*.

What's the alternative? No matter what I'm doing or looking at, if I value this extraordinary capacity to be present to my life, I can open up to an impression of what's *in here*. It's a reaffirmation that I am here, myself, standing, sitting, walking or lying down, in the middle of the world. *I am needed!* But I must be present to acknowledge it. Can there be a sense of presence without attention to one's own existence at this very moment? Gurdjieff considered it a prerequisite for "man without quotation marks" to bring one's best attention to everything one does, minutely, carefully, at the same time seeking the sensation of the body both in movement and at rest. Zen masters make the same demand: "when you eat, eat; when you sit, sit." On the battlefield in the *Bhagavad Gita*, Krishna advised Arjuna to give himself wholly to the task at hand without holding back.

In my experience, I either push forward against all odds or resist the pressures of life by holding on or holding back. Whenever I catch myself dissatisfied, I have to ask myself: Is it possible to accept life as it comes, experiencing it flowing through my hands and in my mind as I live it, rather than rushing through whatever I do in search of something else, something better? What could be better than to bring every inch of myself into my daily life?

While it may not be at the top of everybody's wish-list, the knowledge we need most is how to bring our own attention to the process of being here now. We can follow instructions to learn how something works, but to make it work we need first-hand experience of ourselves as we struggle to master it. Riding a bicycle or driving a car are impossible without mind and senses involved. We didn't learn to do either by reading the manuals. We practiced bit by bit with the help of a teacher until we were able to do it ourselves. We could approach the experience of learning to live more fully in the same way.

Our senses are a good place to start. A few questions to ask: I can taste and smell, but do I invoke these powers when I eat or do I bolt the meal down to get on to the next thing? Do I really listen when people speak to me, to their tone of voice and the message their words carry, and even to what's behind their words? Or have I already formulated my reply before they finish speaking? Am I aware of the constant touch of air or clothing on my skin? Am I alive to the kinesthetic sense of where I am in space, of my feet pressed into the floor or my butt poised on the chair? And what do my eyes see? A clear example of non-attention is the fact that I often don't even see what I'm looking at. I'm drawn too deeply into inner needs, desires, dreams, arguments, fears.

Then, beyond the five senses and the inquiring mind, lies another level of experience. The great Hindu yoga teacher, Patanjali, considered it "incomprehensible to ordinary knowledge." He and many others affirmed that beyond our immediate sensory experience, and beyond the intellectual world of agreement and disagreement where people debate, among other things, whether or not there is a God, a mystery beckons us—the voiceless perception of what is.

◆

Prayer as Petition

There is no God but God! — Muslim prayer

No one knows all about prayer—not even a priest or rabbi. Although the path of prayer requires daily dedication, following a belief system doesn't guarantee progress on the way. Everyone who begins to explore our relation to higher forces starts out on an adventure filled with uncertainty—whether stumbling into hidden potholes or soaring ahead on wings of feeling.

Cutting through the tangled vines of your intentions and reactions in this virgin forest may not be easy if your *machete* of discrimination proves as rusty as mine. I always hated to make choices. But I had to sharpen it when I discovered that going with the flow was only an option if I didn't care where I was going. There was a luxuriant growth of excuses to slice through if I wanted to stay with an intention, rather than following whatever current of thought or emotion pushed me along. As one pundit said, "Just because you don't know where you are going doesn't mean that any road will get you there." Even if I'm really confused about what will happen next, I've found that resting on the present moment and watching what's going on relieves some of the uncertainty. Confusion may prompt me to ask if I'm where I wish to be right now. And if not, what do I have to do to get there?

How do I pray? How do I return to contact with myself, calling my attention back from life's pressures and distractions to center in my deepest wish? It's not easy in the heat of an active day to say a momentary "no" to what automatically attracts my thoughts. Nor is it easy to quiet all the desires and fears that channel and dissipate my energy as they rule my life.

That's why the Muslim practice of sounding the call to prayer at intervals during the day seems so appropriate. Upon hearing the call, Muslims turn away from whatever they are engaged in to kneel and prostrate themselves anywhere they are, in an active physical gesture of surrendering personal autonomy to a higher authority.

This repeated act of immediate, unquestioned obedience is one of several kinds of prayer that attempts to connect with the higher energy some call God. Most of us pray automatically for safety when we, or our loved ones, are in real danger. Our prayer is a cry for help against impossible odds or even against the consequences of our own acts. In such moments of crisis we bargain however we can, offering to pay any price. Perhaps that's what prompted Gurdjieff to say that most prayer consists in asking the Lord to grant "that two and two be not four." A Hindu friend calls it "the Great Petition, or the art of sitting down to be very quiet, saying, 'God, give me a break!'"

Prayer can be used to ask that our "cup" be taken from us or invoke help for courage to face what's to come. It can also be thought of as inner work, a cleansing of our usual mental and emotional clutter. A state of prayer can even appear spontaneously as if we are sought out by a force that silences our interest in other things. A peaceful interior focus can come while we are looking at a flower, pondering a poem or remembering a friend.

Those with a disposition to inner openness may be gifted frequently with this kind of inner intensity of feeling. They often find a state of grace in the present moment. But most of us only connect with such an experience in extraordinary situations like the threat of serious danger or death to ourselves or loved ones. We can also find it in the presence of a tremendous affirmation of nature—on a mountaintop, by a waterfall, or in the power of a great storm. As ecologist Michael Viney says, at such a time the landscape "takes on … an almost metaphysical power of silence and solitude." All the inner voices that usually beckon and nag at us become still, and we are available to hear the call of another level. Such deeply felt experience fills our hearts with a sense of gratitude that we are alive. When I was a child I called it "being touched by the finger of God."

These moments are likely to become more frequent on the way of prayer, as we set aside daily times to listen for this call. It's as if my wish connects to a reminding factor that brings me more often to a sense of my own presence. A series of such spontaneous experiences may lead to religious conversion, as in the case of C. S. Lewis, who described this gradual process in his book, *Surprised by Joy*. In *The Seven Storey Mountain*, Thomas Merton told us what led to his decision to abandon a lively, even dissipated way of life in his twenties to enter a strict monastic order.

In my own case, prayer has been a petition that I may find the strength to live my life more often from the center of myself rather than the periphery. My wish flowers from a seed of longing to remember my own organic need to be present as well as to honor a deep wish that "Thy will," not my own little preferences, be carried out in full-bodied affirmation of a presence larger than my own. Often this kind of prayer becomes the essence of silence, of listening to and allowing myself to be seen by that larger presence.

But presence is sometimes hard to attain. They even say, "You can't get there from here." The difficult concept of non-doing is supposed to help us cross that metaphysical bridge. I often try to submit to it but find myself tensing on some subtle psychic level. To encourage the letting-go I sometimes think of the time of prayer as a chance to enter a garden or a beautiful room. Gurdjieff said the "fourth room" was only attainable through a balanced relationship among body, mind and feeling. Since any pressure to "get there" would reverberate in the body and interfere, I'd imagine I was standing at the door to this room, waiting for it to open, but accepting that I seem to have lost the key.

Waiting patiently for a possible connection to take place is a necessary talent in prayer. So the question becomes, "How do I wait?" "Like a hunter," said Gurdjieffian leader Henri Tracol. There, in front of the door, I gather my scattered attention through conscious awareness of head, heart and every aspect of the body, visiting them one by one to invite their cooperation. Gradually, in the process of doing this, I become quieter and more deeply relaxed until I'm very aware of myself in front of the door. At that point it's necessary to accept whatever happens. I hope someone behind the door will open it, but maybe it will remain closed. Or maybe it will open just a little, enough for the perfume of that place to reach me but not enough space for me to pass through. Perhaps it will even open wide but I won't be invited in. And, then again, I may even discover I've been inside all the time without knowing it!

This inner quiet is like sun energy entering me. It kindles my own light and provides a fresh impression of the source of spiritual energy. Then the "earth of me" seeks to be porous to the subtler substance of the sun, to absorb it in all my cells. For, as many religious and spiritual traditions tell us, and as we often tell our children (to silence the questions we don't know how to answer), we come from a level beyond the planet Earth, energized by the sun and stars. Sun energy radiates in us as well as "out there." Our bodies are the temporary dwellings of this life, and this coming into consciousness of our true source is what Gurdjieff called *remembering oneself*. Taoists described it as the appearance of The True Man, and Jung referred to it as the process of individuation.

◆

Prayer of the Heart

Purity of heart is to will one thing. — Kierkegaard

Conscious dedication to prayer requires purity of intention. We must realize how little we know and how deep is our need to understand more. When I pray with all my being, I move toward an uncertain encounter with the unknown. Do I really want to pass through my own defenses, my castle wall, to glimpse the awful face of the deity or, as Thomas Merton said, to go "naked and defenseless into the center of that dread where we stand alone before God"?

Merton's *Contemplative Prayer*, published after his tragic early death, is a practical guide to serious prayer. It examines the heart of *metanoia*, the transformation or deep inner change that can result from daily dedication to a spiritual life. Merton also points out the false dreams of sanctity the seeker may experience—spiritual warts and pimples that can flourish even in a life dedicated to God.

The contemplative life is not a retreat from suffering, as Merton makes clear. Not even the monk escapes "man's ordinary anguish, his self-searching, his moments of nausea at his own vanity, falsity and capacity for betrayal." None of us is free from existential doubt, which sooner or later brings us to question the ultimate meaning of life. Thomas Keating's *Open Mind, Open Heart* offers us another well-polished window into the mystery of contemplative prayer, which he refers to as "the purification, healing, and sanctification of the substance of the soul and its faculties."

When I was a teenager, my mother gave me the Russian book, *Philokalia*, writings of the early Christian Fathers about

Prayer of the Heart. These recluses lived alone or in secluded monasteries for years and developed practices that were both simple and unimaginably difficult. Among these was the perpetual invocation of the name of God "in the mind, in the heart and on the lips." It introduced me to a new way of practice during the day, quietly speaking words of prayer when I was out in the world as a reminder of my own presence.

There is no true prayer that doesn't include the heart. As those on the path of prayer soon discover, without the cooperation of the attention from directed thought, the moment of opening quickly vanishes. I am immediately attracted to the next external stimulus. Or I begin to "think about" praying or about what I'll be doing when I finish. Inner work is necessary. A friend of mine recently visited several monasteries on Mt. Athos, a secluded island with twenty Eastern Orthodox monasteries and several thousand monks, a central source of the writings of the *Philokalia*. He asked about grace, and one of the monks told him, quite simply, "When I practice, grace may come. If I don't practice, grace will not come."

The real work in prayer is a kind of listening—bringing both the head and the heart together into one inner question. However, if I can focus on one simple thought or action, as the monks perpetually invoked God's name, I may stay closer to the present moment or return to it more often.

According to Merton, the Christian church recognizes three levels of prayer, all of which invite the combined attention of head and heart. The first level is *meditatio*, reading the word of God and reflecting upon it. The second level is *oratio*, heartfelt prayer which supplicants hoped would develop into a final state of *contemplatio*, in which they could rest in God, in deep inner peace and quiet. Merton described this last state as a " wordless and total surrender of the heart in silence … the essence of monastic meditation … a way of keeping oneself in the presence of God and of reality, rooted in one's own inner truth." He added, "This silence, this listening, this questioning, this humble and courageous exposure to ... both good and evil (is) the monk's chief service to the world."

Such is life totally dedicated to prayer. But we live in the secular world. Our emotional machinery constantly churns out reactions while our thinking machine spews out comments, thoughts and judgments all day long. And they are not going to stop. These two are essential parts of us—in perpetual motion as long as we live. We want to live more roundly, more completely, and less like a mouse in a maze. The essential question is, how can we find and maintain connection with a more centered part of ourselves from which we can seek our place in a larger context?

I've found the primary interference to centering comes from my ego, which tries to control everything and pretends to be what it's not. My ego likes to be the boss, so prayer and meditation threaten its very life. Whenever I ask: Who am I? a great enigma rises to consciousness. The prayer that says not my will but Thy will be done, not I in charge but Thou in me, is a slap in the face of the ego.

That doesn't mean it has no place at all in my inner temple—just not the place it thinks it should have! There is a person engaged in this search—me. I am someone who lived her life as best she could and who, at the moment of prayer, seeks a clear path toward a deeper connection with Spirit. While the ego's job is to interface with the world, it may lead me to these first moments of prayer—usually under the illusion that praying was its own idea and one more thing it knows how to do well! So it's called on to help begin the task, but soon I need to pause and listen and wait until its clamoring for attention dies down, so I can open to another possibility.

Which brings us back to the central question: how to pray?

How do I include my busy head in the effort, without believing in all its commentaries? How do I open to the world of feeling, while observing all that's going on? How do I receive the sensation of my body, the servant of my life? Various religions address this mysterious connection of the lower with the higher Self in different ways. Some suggest we need to empty ourselves completely for God to enter.

My experience of the mystery at the heart of prayer passed through several stages. For a long time I thought there was no "I am," but only "Thou art." After all, I wasn't worth much, was I? Whenever a sense of "Thou" was present, I could both trust myself and follow that authority wherever it led, sometimes gripped by an emotion so strong I wanted to fall on my knees. But when that powerful feeling was absent I felt lost. There was nobody here but a very small "i," as Gurdjieff might say, in my usual confusion and doubt, doing my best, but disapproving of all my shortcomings.

I tried to let go of anything that seemed to be my superficial self and open myself to what I thought was another level of being, striving to turn myself over to a "Thou" in order to make myself worthwhile. And if I couldn't find "Thou," it seemed nobody was there at all. This accentuated my sense of unworthiness, which mixed into many parts of my life and left me vulnerable to other people's criticism. They must be right since I, in fact, didn't know who I was!

However, self-denial is dangerous. It can lead to negative states of dependency or passivity and illnesses like bulimia, depression and high blood pressure. As children we all have a wish to obey a higher authority, whether God or parent or simply whatever's "right." But if that authority remains external when we grow up, we may be in trouble. This is particularly true if we think availability to a higher authority in prayer exacts the price of becoming an empty shell to be filled by a

"Thou." How, I asked, could it ever be appropriate to annihilate myself?

When I discussed this with my mother, she said firmly, "Nobody should ever turn themselves over to somebody else." That surprised me. "Not even to God?" She paused a while to reflect, then quietly affirmed: "God isn't somebody else!" Her pronouncement opened me to a new point of view, which has proved very fruitful. For whatever it's worth, when I pray, I acknowledge that "Here I am: contingent, confused or arrogant and full of myself." Instead of trying to make myself disappear so that Something Else can fill me, I seek to discover what in me, at any moment, stands in the path of the light.

◆

From Concentration to Contemplation

Meditation is evolution in reverse. ... Beginning at the surface of life, the meditative mind goes inward, seeking always the cause behind the appearance, and then the cause behind the cause, until the innermost Reality is reached. — Patanjali

Among Eastern religions, meditation has long been practiced using a number of techniques. Patanjali's Yoga Sutras (literally *threads*) had a powerful influence on my understanding, with its step-by-step description of the process of centering, from the wish to find inner illumination to the actual experiencing of it. The first word of his first sutra is *atha yoganusanam,* and *atha,* usually translated by the English word "now," invites or connotes a deep sense of presence.

Patanjali said that those who wish to meditate must acknowledge that the mind should separate itself from the distraction of thoughts, desires, judgments and commentaries of every kind, on everything in our inner and outer world, which constantly flow through us, cluttering up our mental equipment. Then they should practice focusing on one larger thought, a sensation of the body, or an image or phrase that can interrupt the distracting inner chatter. The purpose of this is to drown out all other thoughts as the mind is purified in the fire of *concentration.*

Anyone who's tried this knows it's not easy. At first the attention wanders; irrelevant thoughts take over even before you are aware of them. You may wake up with a start, feeling guilty. You'll want to know how you can be so easily distracted from something you wanted so much to do. Nevertheless it's important to leapfrog over any sense of guilt and continue trying to meditate for short periods, because daily practice increases the ability to concentrate. By counting breaths, repeating a prayer or fixing the mind on an image (both Krishna and Christ invited their worshipers to fix attention on them), you can gradually remain present for longer intervals.

An alternative to this ancient path of focusing the powerful searchlight of the mind on a god-figure or sacred text is to invite your thought to dwell on your deepest wish. I tried this, although I often wasn't clear just what it was. What I did know was that it was truly my own, not someone else's need or formulation. Bringing both heart and mind to this wish briefly in the morning could transform the rest of my day. Later in the day, I'd remind myself from time to time in the midst of my activities how much this sense of presence had meant to me earlier. Although my busyness often overpowered my wish to remember, in the long run these attempts provided increased reminders. I knew that each time I turned toward my wish I could honor what was of greatest value to me.

Patanjali called the second stage *meditation,* "an unbroken flow of thought toward the object of concentration." You are no longer thinking *about* something or doing battle with continually wandering thoughts. Now that mental chatter ceases to distract your attention, meditation begins to fill your whole mind.

The third stage is ***absorption***, also called *samadhi* or enlightenment, in which the meditator becomes completely absorbed in the centering itself, without distraction from imagination, thoughts or objects. *Samadhi* is considered direct knowledge of the Self. "Just as the pure chrystal (sic) takes color from the object which is nearest to it, so the mind, when cleared of thought-waves, achieves *Samadhi*," Patanjali explained. He presented the mind as divided into three parts: *manas*, which records impressions; *buddhi*, which discriminates and classifies them; and *ahamkar*, which reacts to them and stores them up in memory. *Purusha*, the true self, literally the Godhead within the body, is pure consciousness or intelligence itself, reflected in the individual mind.

Meditators may wonder which level they have reached. An Indian formula goes like this: if you can keep the mind from jumping away from its focus on one thing for 12 seconds, you've arrived at an accepted level of concentration. If you can do it for 12 X 12 seconds or two minutes and 24 seconds, you are meditating. And with 12 X 12 more seconds of investment in "onepointedness" you may claim to have entered *samadhi*. But better not to count on packaged formulas! What's really important is regular practice.

The mind, like the body, is an instrument of a Higher Self that can experience, know and perceive what's going on at many levels, but something always interferes with our connection to it, usually the ego or small self. The mind identifies with everything from a pain in the tooth to what Patanjali called thought-waves, such as "I feel, I think, I know, I experience" or

"I am happy, I am sad." This identification is the source of our misery, and he recommended that we learn to control these thought-waves—not in order to stop them or do violence to the mind, but to learn how to avoid distraction.

It's because the ego is such a great do-er that meditation calls for non-doing, or ceasing to identify with the small self, the little 'i' which is usually so pleased with itself or so discouraged. While every perception produces the sense *I know this*, it's just the ego identifying itself with the Higher Self. This prevents us from knowing our real nature, the real self that lives beyond thought-waves, in a state of unchanging happiness. "It is as if a little electric light bulb would declare: 'I am the electric current,'" explained Patanjali's translators, Swami Prabhavananda and Christopher Isherwood.

If we could develop the awareness and discrimination to recognize how distracted we are, we could choose to live in greater contact with that Higher Self. But when the ego identifies consciousness with what reflects it, by denying or forgetting what is higher in ourselves, we deny or forget it everywhere else. We still seek happiness, but outside ourselves, unable to differentiate levels of consciousness from our ordinary mind and functions.

These various levels of consciousness are often difficult to decipher in the practical experience of those who seek understanding and being. Patanjali's translators compared the Higher Self to the sun, "the light-giver," and the ordinary mind to the moon, which illuminates only by reflection. Krishna provided another helpful analogy in the *Bhagavad Gita*, when he differentiated the field, the knower of the field and he who knows both the field and its knower. Krishna himself represented the highest level of all—the Knower of the field in all fields.

The Hindu religion has developed several schools of yoga (paths to union with God) that correspond to different types of people. *Bhakti*, based on loving devotion, is most suitable for those who are passionate and contemplative. Its many rituals and prayers help the practitioner develop an intense personal relationship with God, comparable to the life of prayer of the dedicated Christian monk or nun. *Karma Yoga* practices active selflessness, dedication of one's acts to God in the midst of society. It's a life of duty and service similar to the Christian path of good works in service to God and to one another, and brings a sense of peace through disinterested action. *Jnana Yoga* is the way of the mind, of learning to discriminate between the real and the unreal, rejecting the latter with "*neti, neti*" (not this, not that). Adepts gradually separate themselves from constant domination by the ego or small self. Finally there is *Raja Yoga*—the Royal Yoga—comparable to Gurdjieff's *Fourth Way* in that it combines the practices of the three other paths into a discipline that includes action, contemplation and ritual as well as a detailed study of how body and mind function.

◆

Mindfulness and Sitting Still

Zazen started even before Buddha, and will continue forever. — Suzuki

Mindfulness is another word for a meditative state in which mind and body come together as one's attention follows the sensation of the body and the energy moving through it. Mindfulness meditation can be practiced amid the demands of a busy day and the distractions of the world.

How can I be present in movement when my attention is automatically attracted away from the core of myself? First I need to practice sitting meditation every day in a tranquil setting and experiment with going into movement from there. Settled in a quiet state, with a clear intention to stay in contact with my presence, I can take on the challenge of going to the phone and calling a friend, or preparing breakfast at a slow pace.

Subtle reactions enter into play both before I move and as soon as I move. For example, as I sit I may notice that a new feeling or sensation begins to rise. My body becomes more vibrant. But as soon as I entertain a feeling of satisfaction at "reaching this level," it disappears. While I long for what Buddhists call a "quiet mind," it may not appear. Resistances appear even as changes occur and the body becomes more relaxed. In such a situation, I need patience to accept this subtle interference, even though it's a barrier to where I want to be. Then, no matter how deeply I centered myself earlier, as I go into movement my sense of presence sooner or later disappears. I need to revive my wish again and again. In *To Live Within*, Sri Anirvan counseled that unless one could maintain at least 55% of one's attention on oneself one would quickly be lost.

The Buddha's *Fourfold Setting up of Mindfulness* is a fine guide. He gathered his monks around him five centuries before Christ and summoned them back from the tendency to drift away from awareness of the body into thought alone. He told them, with endless repetitions, how to focus their attention on themselves as they sat, stood, walked and moved through the small tasks of life.

After he died, the Buddha's teaching was interpreted by his followers in different ways. Each group developed its own structure and methods. The traditionalist *Theravada*, or the Way of the Elders, grew into eighteen different schools in India and Southeast Asia and now flourishes in Sri Lanka. The more liberal *Mahayana* teachings speak of the Middle Way, in which everything is relative and interdependent; and *Yogachara* postulates that all that exists is pure consciousness—material things are projections of the mind.

Another offshoot, Tantric Buddhism, introduced the study of *mandalas*, circular designs used for one-pointed meditation; *mantras* or words for the same purpose; *mudras*, which are hand positions expressing certain qualities; and *vidams*, images of gods or spirits. Around the turn of the millennium when Buddhism moved into China, several schools developed there, including Zen, with its meditation on emptiness. Five hundred years later Buddhism spread to Korea and Japan, and a few hundred years after that, so the story goes, a Tantric master from India went to conquer demons in Tibet.

With so many different schools, it's not surprising that Buddhists have developed many ways of working at mindfulness. They range from special emphasis on focusing attention and concentrating thought to the practice of a state of simple presence in which every thought, emotion or sensation enters into a space of open awareness. Some Buddhists work primarily for their own inner development, but many choose to work in the secular world, engaging every day in the cultivation of compassion as well as mindfulness. They practice special exercises to transform negative reactions into positive energy, with the vow that no matter how high and far their own meditation may take them, they will not retire from the world until every other sentient being finds peace.

Zen Buddhists teach by example and focus on living in the present moment. One of their methods to silence the mind is the *koan*, or unanswerable question ("What is the sound of one hand clapping?"). The disciple turns such a question over in his mind for months or years until a resolution is found, then returns to the master to receive a new enigma.

Zen stories convey this work on awareness in the same indirect way. Consider the tale of the master who refused to speak to his new disciple beyond ordering him to cut wood, fetch water, etc. for years. While his pupil worked, the master would sneak up on him from any angle at any moment to hit him with a stick. Gradually the disciple learned to maintain constant awareness, alert in a 360-degree radius around himself, no matter what he did. Or the story of the two monks, one young, one elderly, who came upon a woman unable to cross a stream. The old man picked her up and carried her across while the young one watched in amazement. Hours later he asked, "You know we aren't supposed to touch women. How could you pick her up?" The old monk smiled and said: "I put her down as soon as we crossed the stream, but I see you've been carrying her for hours!"

Shunryu Suzuki's *Zen Mind, Beginner's Mind* expresses the utter simplicity of mindfulness. Sitting is a part of life, he told his students: "We just come and sit. After communicating with each other we go home and resume our own everyday activity as a continuity of our pure practice." He insisted in his gentle voice that experience is more important than philosophy, a message heard many times in these pages. Words, even great ideas, are not enough. Work is necessary. We must take action and affirm the direction in which we wish to go, seeking to be present in our daily lives.

Major Christian thinkers, such as the 13th-century mystic, Meister Eckhart, agree that there can be as great a power in sitting still as in the words of prayer. Or perhaps they mean that sitting still and being attentive is in itself a prayerful act. The body's usual restlessness needs to quiet, to let go of its automatic pursuit of doing something. In meditation, I seek to go beyond surface reality, beyond resolving superficial conflicts, to connect with my essential being or larger Self, or with God. Through awareness of my state and the sensation of the body, the present moment links inner and outer reality.

Then, if the discursive mind can finally become quiet, I may be able to access a timeless inner state of immense quiescent energy, centered in deep silence.

In *Raja-Yoga, or Conquering the Internal Nature*, Swami Vivekananda explained that the universe is made up of two materials, undifferentiated matter (*akasa*) or "omnipresent, all-penetrating existence," and the latent energy (*prana*), which shapes it. Although we usually translate *prana* as breath, he says breath is only one aspect of this "infinite, omnipresent manifesting power," which includes motion, gravity, magnetism, and "the vital force in every being." Behind *akasa* and *prana* lies the silence, the wholeness called Brahman or Ultimate Reality. Whenever we practice concentration, meditation or prayer to arrive at illumination (*samadhi, satori, nirvana*, Buddha mind, true contemplation of the Godhead, or whatever we choose to call it), we are seeking to pass through the stages or states between ordinary life and this ultimate reality.

Jean Klein called illumination "a listening which demands letting go of all that you think you know, all conditioning, all patterns." Even though questions and perceptions arise, the meditator continues to concentrate on listening until stillness itself becomes the background of everything that appears. "Your body, senses, mind, and all states come and go," Klein said. "But you are this timeless presence. ... At this moment you are at the threshold of your real being, but no amount of willing can take you across. You are seized by being itself."

Such an experience is at the edge of the known world, pushing the envelope of physics and mysticism, where the question has been asked: are we in the world or is the world in us? Quantum physicists tell us that fields of energy exist before forms come into being. Some spiritual guides state categorically that the body is in the mind and not vice versa, because the experience at that level of meditation is truly a return to the larger quiet in which we live and move and have our being. Our ignorance of the existence of these worlds within worlds can be compared to our looking up at a multitude of stars in the night sky without understanding that some of them form groups of planets around suns and that all of them are gathered within a wholeness called the Milky Way.

◆

The Temple of the Living God

The contact and mutual attraction between body and soul creates a ... unique situation, generating the human self, which is neither body nor soul but a merging of the two. — Adin Steinsaltz

All of our parts are there to serve us and whomever we serve. The mind is only an instrument of that which is "Lord" in each of us even though it assumes command all the time. We claim to be "of one mind" about many things, even as our states change, and our attitudes change with them. Everything's moving inside us, but until we can slow down our busyness to find a quiet interior space, we remain unaware of the swift shifts in our minds and moods.

It's lucky for us that our body is blessed with a permanent limitation. While our thoughts can soar like birds and our emotions can roar like lions, our feet have no choice but to stay on the ground. They will walk us everywhere we want to go, just as our hands will cook dinner or build a house or accomplish the feats our mind proposes. But they can only do one thing at a time.

We can count on this body to do its best, to be true to itself in its responses, and since time immemorial, with all its limitations and its built-in honesty, it has played a key role in worship. Both in primitive tribes and sophisticated societies, sacred dance and sacred gesture have been our response to the rising of the sun and to many of life's milestones that call for hallowing. Whether to propitiate or thank the gods, to ward off evil or cry out with joy, whenever we need to express deep, non-verbal feeling, sacred movement begins. Every body longs to move, to express the feelings that rise from our depths.

What makes a movement sacred? In my understanding, it's the intention, the wish, the need to communicate and receive from a level above and beyond our usual state. When we anchor ourselves in the body to meditate, we seek a conscious sensation of our physical parts. We become aware of the rise and fall of the chest as we count breaths or describe them to ourselves ("breathing in, breathing out"), or fix our attention on one member (butt on the chair, feet on the floor, hands touching each other), which connects our inner presence directly to our vehicle and the energies coursing through it.

Sacred drama or ritual may have the power to bridge a connection with higher energy when we are unable to make the passage by ourselves. Unfortunately, ritual has a tarnished image—hypnotized adepts performing blood sacrifices or, on the contrary, meaningless repetitive movements carried out by the credulous and naïve. But the Japanese tea ceremony, in which all of the participant's attention is gathered around the act of making tea, or the Zen form of archery in which, after years of preparation, the archer hits the target with his eyes closed, are linked to the practice of presence.

All those who perform ritual, from the learner to the initiate, play a part in this practice, although they have differing degrees of commitment, which controls the depth of their experience. For example, in the Christian ceremony of "washing the disciples' feet," some may wash the feet of the poor full of inner superiority, while others desire to serve in spite of their distaste. Only a few can do it with a true awareness that this beggar is my brother or sister.

Jews rock back and forth in prayer. Sufis sway and step sideways in an interlaced circle with arms on each other's shoulders. Dervishes whirl while maintaining awareness of the central axis of the spine. Flowing hand gestures in Hindu dance speak a language of their own. These movements and those of Qi Gong, T'ai Chi and Yoga aim to bring the higher and lower energies of the world and ourselves into a state of harmony. From vestal virgins to Shakers, from tribal dances that call down the rain to the drinking of Christ's blood and the eating of His body in the Christian Mass, ritual movement and sacred gesture are central to the act of worship.

In some communities, whether primitive or sophisticated, prayer in dance and gesture has been restricted to consecrated performers, while in others everyone participates. In either case, the relation of the soul to the body and the possibility of a conscious union between the two has preoccupied spiritual thinkers for centuries. In *The Thirteen Petalled Rose*, Jewish mystic Adin Steinsaltz called it the "descent of the soul into matter," insisting that this connection is an exchange that works in both directions: "Just as the union of body and soul gives life to the body, so does it wrap the soul in material substance, providing it with the powers of the physical body."

The symbolic drama of the crucified Christ and that of the pre-Columbian god, Quetzalcoatl, who dives down into the darkness each night in order to rise again as the morning star, represent our possibility of dying to life as we have known it, in order to rise up again with new, spiritual energy. And it is the coming to a new consciousness that leads to this rebirth. "Consciousness ... is the way of man's ascent to perfection," said Steinsaltz, and must include the body.

Any act can carry a quality of ritual depending on how it is performed, and thus can "become a direct link between man and his Maker," according to Steinsaltz. The ritual act may center the mind and engage the heart in service to the Self, to the master or to God. It may provide a glimpse of the spiritual journey to come, as the body leads the distractible mind to a sacred space where they can unite to awaken feeling. If the right gesture is made, the result will be inevitable, as Meister Eckhart made clear in one of his sermons: "Do not imagine that God is like a carpenter who works or not, just as he pleases," he said. "When he finds you ready he must act, and pour into you, just as when the air is clear and pure the sun must pour into it and may not hold back."

But for centuries we have relegated the body to a separate, lower level than soul or spirit, so it's easy to forget that the soul depends on it. Many people view their body with fear, disdain or downright disrespect. In fact, some treat the body like a stubborn donkey, to be pushed to the utmost and beaten when it comes to a stop. One friend who dedicated most of her life to find out how to live on a higher spiritual plane, told me to "treat the body like a wound." Shocked, I wondered what relationship such an attitude might create.

When we characterize the body as "mere flesh and blood," we forget that it's a vessel containing all that is precious in us. In Martin Buber's view: "The soul is not really united, unless all bodily energies, all the limbs of the body, are united." Steinsaltz agreed. He deplored the separation of body and soul so prevalent in Western thought: "The principal action of the soul … lies not in its … remoteness from the physical world, but precisely in the world of living creatures," he explained. "In its contact with matter … especially relations with its own body—the soul is able to reach far higher levels than it can in its abstract state of separate essence." In other words, whether we follow the way of the East Indian meditating for three days under a banyan tree or the American Indian gesturing at dawn to make the sun rise, all of our parts must come to the altar if we wish to bathe in the light of our own presence.

Sometimes, in the confusion of our own dark wood, we realize how seldom mind and body connect and function in concord. But are we aware that we almost always lack contact with real feeling, another word for *soul*? Mostly we are caught in the "hankering and the dejection" roused in us by the Ten Thousand Things. We are invaded by reactions to stimuli and present only to a small corner of ourselves, if at all. Like the horse in Gurdjieff's analogy, our emotions pull the carriage of the body any which way, while the driver-mind sits helplessly on top, shouting and cracking his whip. And often the poor broken-down carriage, never properly oiled or cared for, stands at the curb for hours with the hungry horse. Meanwhile the driver sits in his favorite pub, buying beer with his master's feed money and entertaining fantastic dreams of the wonderful places he might go.

Left alone, the body functions in the name of physical survival and that's its job. Seeking spiritual advantage by ravaging or destroying it through flagellation or other forms of self-torture (drugs or intentional starvation, for example) is as futile as trying to kill the ego to further our need for wholeness. Jean Klein recommended that we study the body as a field of tensions, knowing that the ego lives in the same field. "The traditional approach is through listening to the body, not mastering it," he said. "Dominating the body is violence."

It's our spiritual nature that raises the experience of human conflict and human suffering to a new level of *being*, called in the East *Higher Mind*. It could just as well be called *Higher Feeling*. In support of this awakening, nothing is more powerful than connecting our thought with our five senses. To taste each mouthful of food, to sense whatever we touch, truly to perceive what we look at or to listen with an active engagement that precludes mind-wandering, all these are royal roads to the discovery of my presence in the moment.

While the idea of connecting with our senses isn't new and certainly sounds right, it's not as easy to achieve as one might think. In listening to others, for example, I almost always assume I know what they're saying, perhaps even before they finish. And when I try to listen to what's going on inside me, I get sidetracked by thoughts and associations, including judgments about how well or badly I'm making the effort! So I need an anchor. The body can provide that anchor.

◆

Sacrifice and Discipline

All that we are is the result of what we have thought. — Dhammapada

Integral to prayer is sacrifice in the true sense of the word's meaning—to make sacred. When I pray I choose between a "sacred" and a profane action, whether or not to honor my new intention or direction. If I waver, I can ask myself: "What do I really wish to make sacred?"

Perhaps I'll turn away from my new aim. This brings a moment of suffering in which I'm caught, as Gurdjieff would say, between two stools—unable to be comfortable where I am but not convinced I want to abandon the haven of my armchair. Suffering has several meanings, one of which is *allowing*. Do I dare to experience confusion, to accept not knowing what to do or which way to go? It's a sacrifice of safety, of needing to have an answer, needing to know instantly what to do. But if I can permit myself that sacrifice, my reward is an impression of reality, which brings me closer to the present moment.

Sacrifice is related to discipline, another word whose sound none of us likes, although we'd probably all agree we need more of it! Its origin is the word *disciple*. When I think of it that way, I accept discipline to become my own disciple or that of the person or principles I choose to follow. Although a form of self-control, it's related to a specific aim: I give up all the possible other things I could do so as to make time for what I've chosen above everything else.

Sacrifice and discipline must include freedom. Mom and Dad and the police didn't make us say "yes" to an effort at presence, or to commit to a new direction in our lives, even if they might think it's a good idea. Nothing should force us to conform; we choose to engage ourselves in this enterprise. From that point of view, self-denial isn't denial of the Self but refusal of satisfaction on one level in order to satisfy oneself on a higher level. Just as we gave up a party to get some work done or stay home with a sick child, we deny ourselves one satisfaction in the name of something more valuable to us. We leave the door to one room closed for the moment, in order to open another and step inside.

Admittedly, such a choice can turn into a tug of war. When I've lost contact with the wish that set me on fire, I'm often left with nothing but a dry sense of duty or a promise made. Even then, accepting to go ahead without that total commitment keeps me honest. But if I yield to temptation and give it up, I must learn to forgive myself my human flaws—treating the defection as I would a child caught stealing cookies.

What should my new discipline be for the practice of presence? In the *Gita*, Krishna asked his followers, apart from their daily practice, to revere their teachers, observe harmlessness and truthfulness toward their fellow human beings, and maintain physical cleanliness and purity. That's not a whole lot of grief. So what interferes with spiritual discipline when the rubber of my intention hits the reality road? I often "just don't feel like it." In that case, whenever I renege on daily work to develop attention for a spiritual purpose, I try to look it right in the eye. If training for the Olympics demands years of daily discipline and practice, why should finding my heart's desire cost less?

Long ago the Katha Upanishad called the senses horses and the roads on which they travel "mazes of desire." Gurdjieff also portrayed emotional reaction as a horse, which along with the mind as the driver of the carriage, our body, makes up our equipage. You may decide to do this or that, he pointed out, but "when the horse kicks" you are carried away from your avowed intention.

Patanjali affirmed that ignorance creates all other obstacles to enlightenment. He called them *tendencies*, habits developed over time that pull us away from our intention. They drive us to what Swami Prabhavananda named "obstacle building." That's a helpful, non-judgmental way to look at our situation. Through self-observation we can gather information on each obstacle or tendency, discovering how deeply we believe in it and acknowledging how it blocks the physical or mental action we need to take. Then it's up to us to choose.

Like our habits, these obstacles don't disappear. The *Talmud* says that a bad habit enters as a guest, then joins the family, and finally takes control. But if we are no longer fooled into believing in them and at the same time accept that they will always impede our path, we can recognize them, re-commit to our task and move on. They won't go away, but they may evolve from stumbling blocks to milestones on our path as we dedicate ourselves to the daily practice of presence.

◆

Love and Transformation

The task of every man, according to Hasidic teaching, is to affirm for God's sake the world and himself and by this very means to transform both. — Martin Buber

We often speak of love as a transformer, but there are many kinds. Love may be based on attraction, whether physical, emotional or mental. The first, if it's mutual, can lead to very satisfactory sexual relationships. The second may be a sentimental quagmire or a source of wordless suffering. Trust the French to get to the heart of the matter: "In love there is always one who loves more and the other who gets bored." Selfless devotion can wear the disguise of love, as can self-satisfaction. Both may seek a subtle power over another or abandonment of one's own individuality.

It took a lot of living and loving for me to understand that it was not just someone else, my lover, my children, my parents, who called this love out of me. I bring my own deep well of possibility to each encounter, with all my holding back and neediness attached, and all my stipulations. Those who think they know all about love should think again. They should ponder, savor and understand better the force of love, both as a bridge to relationship with others and as part of one's own nature.

Shakespeare said, "Love is not love that alters when it alteration finds." Are we capable of being true, not to ourselves or to the other, but to love itself? I doubt it. We live on this side of love as we live on this side of a connection with something larger than ourselves. It may enter our lives as a sweet fragrance wafted on a gentle breeze from time to time, but we can't count on its presence lasting. Is it sensible to focus all our energy in hot pursuit of a dream of love when there's a real possibility worth working for right here and now?

Does love conquer all? Martin Buber invoked searing honesty when he wrote:

> Do not protest: 'Let love alone rule!'
> Can you prove it true?
> But resolve: every morning I shall concern myself anew
> About the boundary between the love-deed-Yes
> And the power-deed-No, And pressing forward honor reality.

When I press forward to honor reality and bring my resolve to it every morning, I approach the practice of presence, even though I may feel bereft of love on the human level. We have all experienced loss, emptiness, the paucity that St. Paul spoke of when he said, "If I have not love I am become as sounding brass and clanging cymbal." But one can still live in love, even without an intimate personal relationship with another. Or perhaps all relationships become intimate when we connect with our own depths in the present moment.

Why can't we let loose the river of love within us? The love we might feel often seems dammed up into a stagnant pool of indifference, resentment or self-pity. Patanjali offered the image of a reservoir of water, ready to irrigate the field of the soul if only we could break down the barriers so that the water of life "flows through by its own nature." To allow life energy—which is also love energy—to flow through me rather than cutting it off by creating barriers, is the process of letting love out as I let it in.

It would seem that by accessing a higher level of being-experience, even for a short time, what has become fixed on a lower level can be dissolved. While that's important information for everyone, it's especially crucial for older people. As the boundless energy I used to feel has proved more limited in the last few years, I've often asked myself: "If this energy isn't mine (and I don't believe it is), then whose is it and what has it been given to me for?" And if my ordinary self is always darting off to engage in attitudes and reactions to the world, isn't it time to rethink the importance of anger, irritation, and depression? Surrendering myself to these states may not be "expressing myself" at all, as psychology would have us believe. Instead, I waste my limited substance on a barren exercise. For is this not the energy given to me for transformation?

Myriad teachings in the many streams that have come down to us from the highest mountain concern a process of transformation, of incarnation in this earthly body of another level of life. Surely the aim of our small lives is to bring to birth in this earth that I am, again and again, the sacred presence of another level of life that can transform us into lovers and servants of another master, the master within.

◆

The Guru is Within Us

Follow yourself and you will find me. Follow me and you will lose both me and yourself. — Eastern saying

My mother often quoted this Eastern aphorism to me. She emphasized that sooner or later we must each set out on our own path and leave behind the wise words and centering presence of the teacher. We all need help and companionship on the path of our choice, so it's natural and appropriate to revere the person who brings it. However, we must be careful not to confuse the copper wire with the electric current or the moon with the finger that points at it. No one should place his or her inmost soul in someone else's hands.

Yet what a temptation it is! Let's say I've searched for years and at last find someone who can guide me, who knows so much more than I do that I want to lay down my own search at his or her feet. But I'd better not give up my individuality as well! There's a danger in the habit of never thinking things out for oneself, not weighing values and meanings or coming to one's own conclusions. It's also perilous to worship another human being as if he or she were a god, because it threatens the balance of both guru and disciple.

Nevertheless, it's natural to identify with spiritual teachers, to do what they do and like what they like. In India, it's common practice for disciples to give up everything in order to live near a master or guru for many years—serving, listening to and modeling themselves after the teacher. This devotion helps them sacrifice many things they once thought valuable, and let go of their old habits as they begin to live in a new way, under new principles. Gradually the wish to serve acquires a new intensity of meaning in the devotee when compared to his or her former life, which may have been dominated by self-gratification.

Some psychologists tell us that religious devotion is only *projection*, that we project a spiritual part of ourselves onto the guru. Even if they are right, it can be an important developmental phase. The seeker who has given up one way of life may be a child to the new one, needing guidance to confront its complexities with intelligence and intention. The teacher represents a living example of our possibility, and students feel that if they can imitate him in every aspect, they may someday achieve his level of realization. The dedicated disciple, while serving the master in every conceivable way, develops gradually from a perception of separateness—"I" and the guru, one attempting to follow the other—to a sense that "I" and the guru are one, sourced by the same divine energy.

Teachers offer us, by their very lives, a reminder of our own potential, of what a life of dedication, patience, effort and clear intention can bring about. Yet the greatest of saints is still mortal and therefore only a mediator, a representative of the divine that dwells in all of us. What he or she can provide is a precious example of the process of growth from the level of a less-developed human being to that of a more realized individual—someone more closely in touch with the divine in us all. We respect what they say, observe how they live, listen to their words and try to imitate them, because they are living proof that it's possible to find truth, clarity and joy of living. However, someday the time will come to "kill the Buddha," to give up imitation and worship of an outer authority to follow an inner guide, grown from a seed or an intuition to become the voice of the master within.

◆

Keeping the Connection Alive

God must be brought to birth in the soul again and again. — Meister Eckhart

The disciples of any spiritual path have one burning question in common, central to the practice of presence: How do I keep the connection alive? No matter how deeply I may approach a relationship to a larger reality during prayer or meditation, why is it that when I go back out into my daily life, that golden thread is so easily cut? How quickly we are lost! The sense of presence evaporates no matter how intensely connected I was to it only moments before. This is one of the hardest truths to swallow.

Seekers and sages throughout the ages have instructed us on how to direct some part of our attention towards that intimate relationship as we go about our chores. "Remember who you are," commands Gurdjieff. "Keep your thought on your energy in movement," orders the T'ai Chi master. "When you sit, sit; when you cook, cook," says the Zen roshi. "Take no thought of tomorrow," says the Christ. In the Hindu tradition, Karma Yoga calls on those who lead a busy life to dedicate each act to Krishna.

But how do you stay in touch with presence and, at the same time, abandon hope of profiting from your actions in the world? I suppose we weren't meant to succeed at the first attempt or even the first hundred. Perhaps we're engaged in a training exercise and our whole lives are a training ground. Certainly every honest attempt at remembering one's deeper nature brings a direct experience of the power of one's ego. It also illuminates the quality of what I'm doing and continually raises questions: Am I wholly engaged? Am I sincere in my effort? Is my action beneficial or detrimental to me or to the rest of the world? Gradually those who practice *presence* become more interested in understanding the quality of what goes on in and around them. They develop a certain detachment from the results of what they are doing.

The most impassioned seekers become our guides. Some live in the longing, and others in the acceptance of living at a distance from what they most desire. A few have dared to live their deepest questions by wandering the world in dissatisfaction: the "madman" with the burning eyes and tortured soul who refuses to sleep in the same bed twice, the restless nomad walking for decades in search of someone to teach him how to pray, or the hermit perched on a rock and staring for hours at the sun. Like seekers before and after them, they discovered their own practice after years of suffering. Their need called them back from every distraction and refocused them again and again.

Others have found serenity by living within a deep acceptance of the division of body, mind and questing spirit. Such was the case of the author(s) of *The Cloud of Unknowing*, and such was the way described by Brother Lawrence, the humble 16th-century lay monk who never made it into the inner circle of the monastery. His letters to an aspiring young monk (*The Practice of the Presence of God*) offer unparalleled insight into the work on daily presence. Whether sweeping the refectory floor or scrubbing out the great cooking pots, Brother Lawrence kept his connection alive by offering up to God each movement of his body, each thought of mind and outpouring of heart. Also inspiring are the works and example of Hildegard of Bingen, who endured great physical pain to give birth to her visions.

Like them and myriad others, each of us must struggle to find our own way if we want to maintain that connection or frequently return to it. Why are we so lost in the world, that we rarely return to experience the truth of ourselves? Our dedication may not be so complete, but the distractions are much more invasive than they were in previous centuries. It helps to think of our response to the call as a repetitive process like breathing. I am close to myself, I move away, and then I return once again. It's important to examine honestly whether our spiritual in-breath comes once an hour, once a week or only once a year.

Another way to stay in touch with the present moment is to maintain the physical sense of one's own place. When I meditate as the day begins, I may sense clearly that I am in the presence of something larger than myself to which I am related. Then, as I go into my daily routines, I try to maintain this connection by reminding myself repeatedly that my place is within something greater, whether it be God or the starry universe. It is the source of my energy. When I wake up with dismay in the midst of the day's activities, lost again in what I'm trying to accomplish, I'm reminded to return to the essential, the larger "body of life."

I've also found it helpful to imagine that I'm accompanied by a companion who goes with me everywhere and who is a little truer to my ideals and intentions than I may be at any given moment. I'm trying to keep up with him or her, to follow, to listen for the voice in me that's sometimes very faint. Whenever I hear it, I'm reminded of what my real wish is.

Every contact with nature can center me. Animals, plants, trees speak to me of my own nature and of the natural cycle of birth, flowering, decay and death. When I walk in the park, I awaken to the living presence of trees and can almost hear them grow. Flower arranging is a rewarding practice. Beautiful flowers open a door inside me, though at their fullest they sometimes make me want to weep, for what will be left of them tomorrow? I breathe in their scent with conscious intention to receive it—perhaps even to invite it to replace the negative thoughts I was thinking a moment before.

My cat, Gatsby, is another reminder. His instinctive intelligence, his independence or, on the contrary, his sudden need to be petted and, above all, his own presence as a living being, calls my attention away from personal preoccupations and anxieties. Relieved by the new focus, I ask him to sit by me with the pat of my hand. He looks me over for a moment to decide if the move is worthwhile, then comes to a nearby spot, but *never* exactly where I indicated. Best of all is when I forget him entirely, leaving him gloriously stretched out asleep in a sun-patch on the living room floor as I go to check my email at the far end of my apartment. When I finally close the computer and swivel on my stool, there he is, inches away from me, deeply asleep on the nearest chair! The joyful surprise of finding him there so close, so determined to be near me, reminds me through his loving presence of my own. Sometimes "the other" is nearer than we think.

T'ai Chi taught me the importance of "following" in order to stay in touch with myself. I can study how my energy is used throughout the day by tuning in to how I move and what I do, starting from that early morning moment when I sit quietly and feel myself being *filled up*. When I think about it, I'm amazed at how many states I live through every single day! The gamut of emotions I feel in the body ranges from exhilaration to boredom to deep physical fatigue and resistance to what I'm engaged in. My anxiety and tense identification with what I'm doing comes to my attention from a clenched hand on the doorknob or from the grim purposefulness of my quick march down the street, determined to be where I want to go before my body could possibly get me there.

If we were able to tie our awareness to our emotional states consciously even for one day, we would see what a roller coaster ride we are on most of the time! As I watch my emotions pull me into busyness, excitement, elation, fatigue or depression, I can ask myself: What happens when I become disconnected? It seems as though someone with the intention of staying present gives up. Who gives me up? What little 'i' takes over?

Human relationship to the divine is open to many interpretations. Some, like the Gnostics, the Quakers and Hasidic Jews, see our task as orienting daily life toward the essentials and toward God. "Meditation has no point and no reality unless it is rooted in life," said Thomas Merton. There's a spark of the divine in everything living. We aren't on earth to fit into a mold or to repeat what someone else has accomplished but to find our own unique way, to bring to fruition our own potential, to practice our own presence. In fact, as the Lord Krishna told the warrior Arjuna in the *Bhagavad Gita*, it would be a grievous error to try to accomplish someone else's *dharma* (duty). One must find one's own.

The Jewish view differs from the Christian paradigm of sin and redemption with which I was brought up, although it also sees the world as a battleground between God and Satan. One of God's names is Shekhinah, defined in the *Encyclopedia Judaica* as "the Divine Presence … the numinous immanence of God in the world." Rooted in the Hebrew word for *dwelling, resting*, it also means "the battleground between the divine powers of good and evil, the first and the main target of Satan."

If there's a perpetual battle between the presence of God in the world and Satan, perhaps it's up to us to choose consciously under which banner we wish to enlist. The decision isn't a once-and-for-all mental act. That would be easy. It's a daily commitment to living within the tension of that choice. Does it lie between *sin* and *virtue* as in the Christian paradigm? I prefer the Greek translation of sin—*missing the mark*—because it offers an active reorientation to try again. Jewish theologian Adin Steinsaltz said the essential punishment for sin or violence is alienation from one's own true Self. Martin Buber invited us to what he called "the way of reversal." Repentance is "an incentive to … active reversal," he said. But it's the "turning" away from sin, not the attack on oneself, that's important.

Buber's "way of reversal" calls on us to withdraw the energy and attention we invest in continual reactions to life's stresses and entrust it to the act of being present to ourselves. That could be our path to discover the particular task in life we were born for. "It is the things that happen to me day after day, the things that claim me day after day—these contain my essential task," he affirmed. "… The soil we till, the materials we shape, the tools we use … all contain a mysterious spiritual substance which depends on us for helping it towards its pure form. … Man was created for the purpose of unifying the two worlds. … God's grace consists precisely in this, that he wants to let himself be won by man, that he places himself … into man's hands." Through the practice of our own presence we seek to return the gesture and open ourselves to the experience of that grace. Each time we practice presence, we learn anew the meaning of *trust*. Each time we practice presence we take a step forward on our own unique path.

This Self is the honey of all beings, and all beings are the honey of this Self. — Upanishads

Six

Finding Your Own
Unique Path

*Our treasure is hidden beneath the hearth of our
own home.*

— Martin Buber

As I come to the end of writing this book, I see it has taken a
lifetime to receive and respond to the truths I first met as a child.
Yet, as Gurdjieff told his followers, "No effort is made in vain." He
also said that every attempt we make toward developing a sense
of presence deposits a needed substance within us. Throughout
my life, his words encouraged me to try again each time I fell
short of my intentions. Guided by the practices I've described
here, I've tried to live life fully, rather than "be lived" by it.

Many roads lead to the top of the mountain. Each of these
five paths brought me closer to my heart's desire. And although
they differ in some ways, each educated me in the practice of
presence as it opened a new door to experiencing daily life as

a spiritual encounter. However, we each have to find our own path. What may be powerfully orienting to you or me may be difficult for someone else.

How to begin? Pondering the difficult questions can bring one's own direction into focus. When I was young, my mother often asked me, "What is your real wish? What do you desire above all else?" Asking myself that question reoriented me again and again. Or the question inspired by Christ's admonition to Martha, who complained that her sister Mary sat idly at His feet: "What is *the one thing necessary*?"

Others further along the various paths than I might give you more concrete guidance as to what the "one thing necessary" is for you. But remember, it's *your* life and belongs to no one else. Your body, mind and heart have a unique configuration in which only you can intervene to develop your attention, courage and humility.

Don't be afraid to experiment. Although each of us wants to be "right" and to find the "right way," no "expert" can know *you* as well as you can learn to know yourself, if you work at it. Here are some insights from my daily practice in the paths you've read about here that might be useful to you.

◆

Beggars on a Golden Bench

Remember that what pulls the strings is the force hidden within, there lies the power to persuade, there the life ... there ... the real man.
— Marcus Aurelius

How many people do you know who think they lead miserable lives? Whether they have money or a job or friends or a lover is immaterial. Everything that happens to them seems to provide grounds for complaint and suffering, and they never seem to put a positive interpretation on their circumstances. Instead, they feel victimized by life, that everyone's out to get them and no one understands them.

Gurdjieff often said that to find our heart's desire we must give up our suffering. That's not easy. Our plaintive tale weighs us down, and learning how to digest what happens to us is a necessary stage in the drama of our own becoming. Most people are faced with real suffering, serious illness or injury, their own imminent death or the death of a loved one. They must find a way through a state of helplessness to confront reality as best they can.

However, reality can teach us hope as well as despair. My stepfather had a blind Princeton professor as a patient, who had played Russian roulette as a young man in a moment of desperation. The bullet destroyed his eyesight without killing him, and from the moment he woke up in the hospital he was flooded with enormous gratitude that he was still alive. His friends might have understood and been generous to his moods if he had sulked in a corner or insisted on constant care. But he quickly learned to move around independently, later married, had children, and even learned how to ski downhill again, along with his wife, who told him when to turn.

The experience of Jacques Lusseyran, who wrote *And There Was Light*, provides another example. Blinded by an accident at school when he was eight, he discovered at that early age that the light of the world was not lost to him but, quite to his own surprise, was contained inside him. Not only was he a truly happy man until his accidental death at the age of 46, but he was also a survivor of 18 months at Buchenwald, where he became the spiritual and psychological mainstay of hundreds of people who daily faced hunger and death at the Nazi internment camp. Recently we were amazed by the gritty courage and positive attitude of Aron Ralston. This young Colorado mountain climber described how he was pinned by a rock and forced to cut off his own arm with a pocketknife in order to escape certain death (*Between a Rock and a Hard Place*). What did these three people learn from their horrendous experiences that the rest of us complainers have overlooked? Each of them had to connect forcibly with reality—a stark, brutal reality that the rest of us perhaps deny. In any case, they met their challenges with an attitude very different than ours.

The window to a new view of life appeared to me many years ago in Peru when I was translating into Spanish *To Live Within*, Lizelle Reymond's book about Sri Anirvan. He told her that "Man is at the same time the cat that eats the mouse and the mouse devoured by the cat, for these are the two ways in which life comes toward us." What if we deliberately placed that truth at the center of our lives, rather than bemoaning the irritating or threatening difficulties poking up like weeds through our chosen path? Isn't it our attitude that makes the difference? The Dalai Lama, when asked by reporters in what way he was better than ordinary people, replied that he was not. The only difference, he told them, was that "every morning when I wake up I adjust my attitude."

Gurdjieff's student and chronicler, P. D. Ouspensky, often said that there might not be much we could change about our lives, but we could always change our attitude. I found that the best way for me to change my attitude is what Gurdjieff called acting "as if." Here's how it works: when you don't feel like doing a task, but have to do it anyway, or you must meet and talk with someone you don't like, instead of dwelling on your distaste and internal complaint, you determine to act *as if* you wanted to do the job or talk to the person. You may discover quite early in your pretending that the negative burden of your former attitude has disappeared. Though we often suffer greatly, we seldom suspect that the power to shift our state and circumstance often lies *within* rather than *outside* us.

◆

Getting Started

Between the idea and the reality falls the shadow. — T. S. Eliot

It's not always easy to get going when you're standing still. It's even harder to get up when you're sitting down, unless the body's dying to get into action or you know exactly what you want (a cup of coffee?) and how to get it. So when you decide to make a fresh start, to undertake a new approach to living, don't underestimate the resistance of your mindset and your organism, not to mention the "I-don't-feel-like-it" reaction. Even with all your good intentions to help someone else or improve yourself, you will still have to say "no" to a multitude of habits and mini-comforts. Prepare yourself for stumbling blocks that trip you up, along with large and small demons of doubt and irritation.

In spite of our determination to set a new course for ourselves, passive forces resist change. How we begin is crucial. The first step of our new direction can influence the whole endeavor, and even a small step can raise us to a new possibility. But no matter how determined we are, whenever we are inspired to take action in favor of the new life we wish to lead, we will be challenged by the gulf between the idea and the reality of our desired goal.

The first step is to admit that the gap between where we

are and where we want to be really exists. That way we can take its measure and prepare to shift from thought to action. It's never easy. Even the smoker whose doctor tells him he's killing himself with each cigarette and needs to quit must make a real effort to change that habit.

Clear visualization of the obstacles ahead is essential. One big one is discouragement, literally "loss of heart." You think something's wrong because you seem to be beginning again and again. But don't let that get you down because, in fact, that's precisely what you are doing! And beginning again is the only way I know of keeping an intention alive.

You'll be less discouraged if you recognize the fluctuations in your ability to keep to an intention at different times of day. While we may begin each day with wonderful new energy, it can disappear after lunch as we go into a psychic slump. To deal with the daily afternoon letdown while working at *Fortune*, I used to flood myself with sugar or strong cups of tea. But that quick fix seldom helped. However, if I curled over on the desk with my head on my hands or, better still, lay down on my back on the floor, I would find myself newly energized and ready to go on with my job in around fifteen minutes.

Intentional yielding to fatigue can be an effective way to shift gears. For example, I mastered the art of snoozing while looking wide-awake at boring afternoon meetings. It always surprised me that such short breaks from pressing on the same productivity "nerve" helped so much, but I needed them to work on a story late into the night.

I felt I'd passed another milestone when I learned how to keep to my own inner schedule rather than live according to someone else's. Before I realized the importance of this, I spent a lot of my life forcing myself to adapt to other people's rhythms. It's important to be visible to oneself, rather than blend in to please other people or live in the hope of not being noticed. "Remember yourself always and everywhere," said Gurdjieff. Even small acts of remembering point us in the right direction. Keep your wish to practice presence alive inside, even when you are working for someone else.

◆

Accept Division

In man are many things. There is mouse and there is bird. The bird carries the cage upwards while the mouse drags it downwards.
— Rumi

I often ponder, "Why is it so hard for me to stay in touch with my aim?" How many times do I make a new resolution, understand something in a very deep way, and feel that a major change is inevitable? The "light" dawns and the way I want to live becomes very clear. But despite such *ahah!* moments, my clarity of purpose fluctuates, and so does my firm intention to live differently.

It's been difficult to accept that I'm often a battleground for several sides of myself, which seem to act in opposition to one another. Is there any solution to feeling so divided? Krishnamurti said, "… in division there is insecurity, there is war, there is uncertainty. But when the mind sees the danger of division very clearly—not intellectually, not emotionally, but actually *sees* it—then there is a totally different kind of action."

That new action lies at a level above the yes-and-no level on which we live, and a new attitude can help us find the way to it. The Jungian concept so often mentioned by Marion Woodman suggests we can approach it by "holding the tension of the opposites." If we can resist the magnetic attraction of one side of any situation long enough to acknowledge both sides, however painful that may be, we rise above division, rather than imprisoning ourselves in it.

The other day I woke up feeling tired and semi-depressed. A slight headache accompanied me through the morning as I went about my duties. At about noon, I suddenly remembered I had made the commitment the night before to go to the park right after breakfast. "No time," I thought, "and besides, I don't feel like it." How many times have I heard myself say that before! But in spite of my resistance, just before lunch I gave up writing and, grumbling that a Tylenol would probably serve me better, I plodded to the park, promising myself it would be a quickie of a walk.

Once out the door, to my surprise, I felt better right away, and by the time I reached the park my headache had disappeared. Soon I was sitting on a bench in the springtime cool, surrounded by trees, bathed in sun and bird song. I heard a kind of singing in my soul. Amazed at the change, I asked myself: *Why* was it so hard to get here? *Who* in me thought it was more important to feel depressed or spend hours writing at my computer? *What* in me opposes what another part of me obviously wants and needs? Are the interests of my head demanding control over my heart and body?

A similar division appears in me whenever I feel stuck in a disgruntled, irritated or depressed state, unable to let it go. Why do I hold on to those miserable emotions? If I wake up to the state I'm in, I can sometimes expose myself to helpful conditions. A walk in the park is one example of that; hugging my cat, Gatsby, is another. When I hold him in my arms and feel his warm, pulsating body in contact with mine, I often experience a major shift in state.

Another way to escape the prison of these negative states is to explore the questions they raise. I'd only been in the park five minutes when the weight on my chest began to lift, the ache in my tired eyes disappeared and the slight feeling of depression (what I call my "There's no way out" syndrome) was gone. Why had I resisted going? Disruption of the status quo brings discomfort and uncertainty. What's unknown can't be guarded against. On the other hand, as many have discovered before me, the state of "not knowing" can forge a path to inner freedom.

The next time I resisted a walk in the park I began to dialogue with this "stuck-in-the-mud" part of me. "Why such obstinate refusal? What's the problem?" I asked myself. An inner voice responded with a sigh: "Is it really worth it?" "Worth what?" I queried. Then, from deep in another part of my inner landscape a new voice interrupted this plaintive exchange, exclaiming, "*Worth all the time it takes!*" Somebody besides the writer and problem-solver in me needs my time and isn't getting enough. That little interior dialogue helped me see that with all I tried to accomplish, I was allowing no time for my deeper self, for my own expansion into awareness of the present moment.

Such divided states occur in me every day, mostly under my radar. So to find out how I feel, to know what's really going on, I must take the time to become consciously aware of how I feel and what I need. When I got to the park, I asked myself to sum up in one word what I felt, surrounded by trees, grass and fresh air. The answer shouted back at me was: "*RELIEF!* Relief from oppression." Something had oppressed me and I finally realized that it was I, myself. I've put pressure on myself all my life to deal with the "oughts" and "shoulds" that fill my day. The question is, *Who* am I taking with me wherever I go? And who am I in this new mode, this state of relief? Surely I'm not diminished from the person I was, hunched over my computer fifteen minutes ago?

Does such an experience change everything? No, but it can make an enormous difference in my sense of myself. When I came home from the park I still felt tired, I still had work to do, but I was more open, more relaxed, less demanding. My headache was gone and I was no longer depressed. All parts of me were more present. I had entered the big *Now*.

This return to presence gives me the opportunity to appreciate what we usually ignore because we're too busy: the present tense of our life, which provides fresh perceptions of ourselves and the rest of the world. If we refuse it, we are cut off, sadly unaware of what we've lost. When we choose to be quiet and listen attentively to our own inner voices, we create space for something else to fill us besides that "know-it-all" ego. But, mired in duties, we don't always welcome the new possibility. Like the biblical Jacob, we often wrestle with our angels and try to defeat them.

◆

Experiment with Becoming Present

If not now, when? If not here, where? — Sufi saying

A wise man told his adventuring son to "Beware of the surface of things!" in René Daumal's *Mount Analogue*—an essential text for any seeker undertaking the journey. To enter the present moment, we often need to slow down because we usually skim along the surface of our lives at breakneck speed. Slowing down may create discomfort or irritate us, but altering one's usual pace is a master key to the door of living in the present. We must go head-to-head with the relentless pressure that pushes us forward into the future or drags our thoughts and emotions back to replay past events and try to "solve" them differently.

Only when we free ourselves from pressure, judgment and calculation can we experience our life anew. First we need to notice how insistently our habitual thoughts grasp at us. Then we can confront two important truths: first, life doesn't need to be as mechanized as it usually is and, second, presence must be practiced.

Next, it helps to watch out for the automatic impulse to want to "do it right," to "be right." This inner control freak disguised as a virtue is the authority we are attempting to go beyond. How can we know what's "right" then and there, except by letting go of the strictures and pressures we were under a moment before? "Out beyond wrongdoing and right-doing there is a field," said Rumi. "I'll meet you there." That's the field we're looking for. That's where presence can be practiced.

On my way to work through the park one day, I picked up a fallen apple blossom, perfect in every way but very delicate. I placed it in the center of my cluttered desk. All day, as I worked around it, sometimes annoyed, sometimes filled with emotion, I felt it call me into present awareness. The blossom reminded me of exquisite delicacy, a quality my job had no room for, and yet it also represented the impermanence of beauty, nature and myself. After that poignant experience, I often put something fragile or beautiful at the center of my desk.

We sometimes cling to the discouraging belief that we are stuck where we are—that no change is possible. But once we've been able to shift in our state through reasoning, we know change can happen. How to bring it about? We try to become more receptive to the present moment, practicing awareness, remembering more often to question, "What's going on?" One can start by saying: "Here I am." Then comes acceptance. "I see this is how things are and how I truly am, whether I like it or not." Next one tries not to react to what is seen, refusing to yield to the attitude: "Oh well, that's life, it's inevitable and nothing can be done about it" or the judgment: "I'm so awful, I'm not worth anything."

Another way to return to the present moment is through acceptance of "not-knowing." *The Cloud of Unknowing* describes the uncertainty that one must embrace to find God. We can also embrace uncertainty to find ourselves. But it's hard to say "yes" to the unknown, even when uncertainty has previously led to new experiences. I prefer certainty. I want to be either lost or found. It's difficult to acknowledge that the way out of my dark corner may be to accept "not-knowing" again and again. There really is no "beyond" where I am now, so why not give up hope that I'll get through the fog of uncertainty to some place where All Is Clear. The *present moment* in all its aspects can be ours. Nothing more.

When I feel disconnected or out of sorts, I recall special moments of self-remembering to change my inner landscape. I think about when I last felt most alive—that mountain landscape, that sunset of all sunsets, that tree of all trees, that narrow escape from danger. Those are moments of true remembering, of presence to my life. Each time I revisit those memories, I am present to them all over again, in every detail.

For example, one summer day fifty years ago is as clear to me right now as when it happened. I climbed a steep cliff in Switzerland with my brother, foolishly unaware that the rock was brittle shale. By the time we got halfway up the crevice, we saw that our footholds had crumbled into a river of fragments. My athletic brother climbed up over an outcropping above us, far beyond my courage or ability to attempt, so my only path was back down. Or stay there, helpless. I lay trembling against the warm rock for a while, listening to his steady stream of advice: "Stay pressed against the rock. Keep at least two or three holds with hands and feet. *Never* put all your weight on just one of them."

Clearly etched in my mind is the way, in the middle of his advice, I slowly, helplessly, began to slide down. The rock and earth brushed my face as I slid down that cliff, faster and faster. I saw a tiny bushy stem come into view, growing from a crevice below and to my left. I muttered, "I'm sorry," to my brother and clutched that plant with my left hand, all my heart and all my weight. Life seemed very precious at that moment. This tiny green life that stretched out from a fold in the rock stopped my slide. That plant gave me the courage to continue inch by inch down to the bottom of the hill, grateful for each outcropping my shaking hands discovered along the way. I was alive!

◆

The Challenge of Living in the Present

Yesterday's gone. Tomorrow may never be mine ...
— Song heard in the New York subway

I know my aim is to connect as often as possible with my present reality, but this space between yesterday and tomorrow can be a very painful place. Yesterday I strove to meet others' needs and demands or satisfy my own desires. And the days ahead provide the impetus to get up and go to work. I assume I work *for* something—for some future meaningful goal.

But how about today itself? Can I become aware of the present, right now? The answer is "Yes. If I'm feeling well." If I'm happy, it's easy. I can embrace today like a lover as I look inward and become present to myself. But when body and spirit ache, when I long to understand why people suffer so much, then what can salve my wounds?

Whatever today's wounds may be, they sometimes feel like open sores which no balm can soothe. For example, caring for an aging or dying relative can plunge you into anguish. Both my parents and my stepfather were in need of my attention for years, and I confess to wishing many times I could be anywhere but where duty demanded. I spent hours every day in a place of pain—aching, sorrowful agony. "Why does the end of life have to be like this?" I would ask myself as I responded to the stressful demands at hand. "Where has it all gone, the clarion call of duty and the gentle flowering of love?"

In such a state of suffering, I welcome any dulling of sensation to escape present reality. I only hope my sense of sorrow and inadequacy will someday fade or become compost for a new and happier future. But when I'm suffering, it discolors that future, turning life into a barren desert, where the sun beats down uncaring and the unforgiving winds blow sand in my eyes. Words rarely offered comfort. At such times, what helped most was simply to "give up." I would think, "No more! I can't go on!" Relief always followed this complete surrender as I rediscovered my flesh-and-blood self in the present moment. In spite of the pain, life no longer weighed me down. I was ready to go on. That moment of yielding into presence helped me meet the truths that were so difficult to face, transforming my experience of pain to an immediate sensation of myself.

Each time I become present, I experience the state of my body, mind and emotions all at once. My body is a container of all that I am, and within it I'm teeming with jumping thoughts, popping emotions, pulling tensions. When I wish to rest on the present moment, I need to empty a lot of that "stuff" out to make room for my own awareness. Until I do, I have no listening space. I'm all reaction.

Past pain is often experienced in the body. It can give me indigestion. When I become aware of it, I visualize flushing the past down through my body and out the bottom. I assume the relevant knowledge gained from past experiences has been digested and deposited deep in my brain, blood and bones so the detritus has no more value. As for the future, like most of us, I experience anxiety about the unknown, wishing for or fearing things that haven't yet happened, holding anxiety in my body. I feel it most in the upper torso—tensed rib cage, a vibration that clutches at my heart. When I loosen up a little, it will often travel to my jaw. So whenever I notice that my ribs are tight, my heart hurts or my jaw is tense, I'll ask myself, "What am I holding onto?" "What do I fear?" Then my state of tension may become lighter and I can invite these future threats to float out of the top of my head.

Notice what parts of your body are tightly held and try to discover what helps you release them. What opens you up to sensing more of yourself? What returns your presence in each moment you live through? Perhaps it's music; maybe it's nature or silence. Stretch from time to time as cats and dogs do; take a walk around the block; place a flower in the middle of your desk; spend your lunch hour exercising in a health club; lie down for ten minutes in the afternoon, or all of the above. When I turn my attention to my inner world, the experience often amazes me. As Ouspensky put it: "I. Here. And in this place!" It's a wonderful place to be. But rather than glorying in the immediate sense of wonder, I can open myself to the new *now* that follows on its heels.

◆

Take Time

*No one ever sees a flower—really—it is so small—we haven't time—
and to see takes time.* — Georgia O'Keefe

To practice staying in the present, I need to value taking time. This suggests, quite rightly, that we have to do something active to alter the situation, rather than just hope it will change. Nobody has been more dedicated than I to cutting corners, killing three birds with one stone as I telescoped a three-hour assignment into one pressured hour. But everything I decide to do not only deserves my best effort, it also deserves a legitimate amount of time.

We slow down by readjusting our way of thinking and acting. If it's your habit to fit too many activities into a small time frame, as I usually do, then you already know the advantages of working that way. Much more gets done! But we goal-oriented people forget to add in the price of mistakes or the aches and pains we will have to pay for in the future. And, because we fail to realize how much we stress ourselves in order to succeed, our aches and tensions increase exponentially as we age. Body, mind, soul, and spirit all shrink when we're in a hurry, and long-term contractions build into permanent holding patterns.

Even after three years of intensive daily training to become an Alexander teacher, I've only begun to plumb the depths of physical tension buried in my system from years of living under pressure. I often catch myself moving on to the next thing in my mind before I finish what I'm doing, rushing through its final stages with little care or thought. I used to ignore the consequences because, at that point, it always seemed much more important to hurry, finish and go on.

In *Thinking Aloud*, Walter Carrington, a senior statesman of the Alexander Technique, spoke of his visit to the Imperial Riding Academy in Berlin, where the instructor took the cadets out in formation and said, "Now, gentlemen, when I give the order 'ride canter,' what do you say?" And the answer he expected was not "Yes, Sir!" but simply "*I have time.*" If everyone had hurried into a canter, the exercise would have ended in chaos. Instead, they took the time to move smoothly into the new pace.

My sincere wish to *take time* produced a remarkable change in me. Very gradually, because I was a big "end-gainer," I learned to allow a little more space in the day for each thing that needs to be done. That meant postponing some that were less urgent for another day, and questioning the automatic assumption that there won't be enough time, so I'd better hurry. Nowadays I often find myself saying aloud, to allay my anxiety: "I have time!"

Another challenge surfaces when I'm faced with a task that I just don't want to spend time on. In response to the initial irritation, I pretend I don't even know how to do it. That way, I must focus all my attention on organizing a plan for doing it, and visualize all the physical movements necessary to accomplish it. Try it for yourself. If you want to stay connected with your own inner rhythm, but are overwhelmed by the many demands on you or confused by not knowing what to do, sing it out loud: "I have time!" Pretend you are here right now and that there's no other place to be. Tell yourself, "This is the state I am in and these are the tasks I have to accomplish." Only then, turn to meet the challenge.

Most importantly, we need to take time for a conscious quieting of our nervous system at intervals during the day, a return to what is most true in ourselves. Why true? Our ego and animal nature have many ways of limiting our efforts to return to central intelligence, some of them quite subtle. It's necessary to wait out their reactions and listen for "the voice in the wilderness." My inner life can be a wilderness when I'm lost in the outside world.

◆

Begin the Day Meaningfully

The things that happen to me day after day, the things that claim me day after day—these contain my essential task. — Martin Buber

You may have discovered how much a planned practice every morning helps center your day. Mine begins with splashing cold water on my face, then stretching, T'ai Chi or yoga, followed by meditation. My practices aren't fixed in stone. I change, add or subtract when I feel something different is necessary. But if I fail to take the time for them, my day gets off to a confused start, leaving me ungrounded. I overreact to whatever's going on and feel unconnected to my "wholer" self. (I say "wholer" first because, on any particular day my best efforts to ground myself may not succeed and, second, because I don't think I'll ever come to the end of my search for wholeness or find the final answer to the question, "Who am I?")

No matter how early you have to set the alarm, you'll soon agree that it's worth having time to center yourself in your own sense of presence before the activities of family or world close in. When I lived in Peru, my days began before six so I'd have some time to myself before orchestrating breakfast, putting my kids on the school bus and going off to run my own school at eight o'clock.

Never exercise as an unpleasant but necessary task, a habit

devoid of your attention and empty of feeling for yourself. Exercise with all of yourself. Nothing is deadlier than meaningless repetition. Perhaps before moving into what you choose to do, running, pushups, gym work, yoga, etc, you could begin by standing quietly, waiting until all of you comes together and listening for the presence of "the spirit within the heart." Accustom your mind to take interest and tune into how your body feels. Then, when the physical parts—which, after all, love to move—accede with their own "Yes!" you can to go into action.

After exercising, I sit quietly for about half an hour, trying to empty my mind of yesterday and tomorrow. I focus on the experience of myself sitting here, now. I listen to my inner world as it quiets down and melts into silence. Holding the image of a pool of water can help. At first it's opaque and turbulent, then the mud particles gradually settle downward and clarity emerges. On days when nothing can silence the mind or emotions, I try to listen to my thoughts or reactions as I link myself to the body in which they live. Before getting up to go into action, still steeped in whatever connection I established with my presence, I formulate a wish to reconnect with myself during the soon-to-be-busy day. I often set up appointment times with myself to pause and interrupt the flow of activities.

Breakfast comes next with hot cereal and herb tea. I read a few pages from a book that lights up my mind and heart like *The Ease of Being* by Jean Klein or *Zen Mind, Beginner's Mind* by Shunryu Suzuki. Many others also provide refreshment. I close the book when I feel my heart has been pierced and opened by a fresh thought or feeling, food for *being*, that I can ponder during the day, whenever I'm not engaged. Then I may go for a walk in the park, applying Alexander directions as I seek the sense of the whole of myself in movement.

Don't hesitate to commit to a new and demanding personal schedule. Just try it for a week or even a day. You may agree that how you feel the rest of the day makes the effort worthwhile. Being present—enlivened, awakened from top to toe—for even a short time at the beginning of the day can be a powerful experience. You'll soon long for it and welcome the practice into your life.

◆

Walk Sinking the 'Chi'

As nature is always in motion, so should man act to strengthen himself without interruption. — I Ching

A walk is one of the greatest pleasures in my day. When I was a reporter at *Fortune*, I often walked to work through Central Park, and sometimes returned home the same way. What a blessing after those twelve-hour workdays, even when it was dark and I had to come home along Fifth Avenue! My commitment to this particular trek began when I learned from a friend that she walked from 82nd Street and East End to her office on West 44th Street every day, after a three-mile dawn run along the East River. It helps to have a friend provide the challenge.

If you work at home, it's very important to expand into a larger world sometime in the morning. When you feel low, tired, depressed or just unable to get going, your personal mood needs the fresh air and a world with other people in it. As you say hello to the deli guy, the news vendor or someone in your neighborhood, a change in your state is almost inevitable. Too much time alone at home constricts our outlook. When we're out in the world, we expand into the space shared by all living beings.

Now that I work at home, a trip outside is indispensable to me. My mood changes and my posture revitalizes as I think Alexander thoughts while the "old bod" gets under way. If there's no good reason to go out, I look for one from the ever present list of things I have to do, something that's been postponed, like taking clothes to the cleaners, returning an unsatisfactory purchase or buying something I forgot to get last time I was out.

We embark on a mini-adventure every time we go out, for we never know what might happen or whom we might meet. It's good to let go consciously at the front door, threshold to the larger world, and acknowledge the uncertainty of what's coming. Then we step out open to new impressions both of the world and of ourselves. Otherwise we seldom see what's in front of us. Perhaps that's because we always think we know what we're seeing. I took a drawing class recently, and was amazed to discover that if I focus on only the light and dark of what I'm looking at, or only on space and mass, I'm living in a totally different universe.

Usually, by the time I get to the street, thoughts and plans for the day buzz in my head like angry bees or, if I'm still somewhat in contact with the morning quiet, they may circle slowly around me like birds searching for a perch to land on. As I walk along, my thoughts are captured by what I need to do later rather than absorb the beauty of the natural world that surrounds me. If the attraction of what's coming later is too strong, I may try one of Gurdjieff's counting exercises to fit the rhythm of my walk and free myself from turning thoughts. For example, I put my attention on my right arm and count from 1 to 4, then shift to the right leg as I return from 4 to 1. Then I sense the left leg as I start counting from one number higher (2 – 5), left arm (5 – 2) and so on. Each time I become more deeply aware of the sensation of my limbs as they swing along. I finish the exercise on the count of 9-12, 12-9.

As I give myself to the physical rhythm and the pleasurable sense of my body in movement, I can gradually feel the energy move down from my head and chest, in the same way that the *ch'i* sinks in the T'ai Chi solo exercise. As I walk with more freedom, weight centered in the belly region, my thinking apparatus slows down. My arrogant, self-important head quietens, yielding to the humility of presence. Yes, *humility*, because the knowledge of the small place I actually occupy in the world is a humbling as well as joyful experience. To be right there where I stand or walk and nowhere else in my mind, I must resist any attempt to control tomorrow or even the next moment, and refuse to fill myself up by reliving yesterday.

Here and now is three-dimensional. It's a very special place to be. To stay here is an act of following rather than leading or controlling, because the present moment is always moving on. If I grab onto a thought, feeling or sensation, even though it may be pleasant, I'm already in the immediate past. So if I want to stay open to the present, I sink my thought into my belly and just walk along, taking in the sights and sounds around and inside me, without criticism or commentary.

◆

Trees – The Alternative Cathedral

Stand still. The trees ahead and bushes beside you
Are not lost. Wherever you are is called Here,
And you must treat it as a powerful stranger,
Must ask permission to know it and be known. — David Wagoner

Contact with nature confers a gift of presence. I try to open up to it rather than pursue distracting thoughts or emotions. As an urban dweller, walking in a park fills me with a sense of my roots in the natural world. Seashore, mountains, meadows, woods and desert all invite us to discover our own nature in theirs, to meet their presence with our own. So whenever I feel too far from my deepest wish, off-balance, shaken by the blows of life or mired in the inertia of not caring, I seek contact with nature—a primary source of re-centering.

Each of us responds more deeply to one or another great natural scene, depending perhaps on where we received our earliest impressions. At this time in my life, the deepest call comes to me from trees, their triumphant *upness* as well as their deep-rootedness in the ground. When I'm under trees, I'm back where I belong. For all I know, this place is unreach-able by any conscious effort I could make. But dwarfed by great trunks and shaded by spreading branches, I no longer clutch at the past or hurry to keep up with today's duties. I am *right here.*

After a couple of hours working at my computer, I like to unleash my energy in the park. As I walk the familiar path, I may be brought to a standstill, silenced by the power of the trees towering on either side of me. In winter, my eyes follow the strength of their hefty branches, which break out into smaller and smaller branches and twigs, articulated against the sky. They remind me of the veins and stems of the myriad leaves to come and of my own veins and arteries, and my whole system is invigorated.

When I asked David Wagoner about his extraordinarily evocative poem, he told me it was inspired by a time he was lost in the woods. It's clear that the experience of the presence of the trees brought him back to his own presence and quieted his fear. Such an adventure puts our fear of the unknown into a different perspective. We, also, are unknown.

In the park, I'm reminded that all of life is in movement. Squirrels jump, bees and butterflies explore the flowers. Trees pour their energy upward into swaying branches and grip deep down into the earth. I hear a bird call. I'm all too often unaware of all that lives around me until I'm in a transformative place where I can become one with nature and my own inner nature—without fear, without pressure. Something deep within me relaxes. Bending down to pull unwanted weeds from a neglected garden on the esplanade by the river, I feel whatever clutches me let go.

Even on grimy city streets, which I walk a lot, scruffy trees send a delicate message. They remind me both of my nature and their great gift to our planet, purifying the air we breathe. I climb up the subway stairs on my way home, tired and hungry, my mind still wrapped around my day's activities. Then I focus on a tree I'm walking toward, consciously breathing in its freshness and exhaling my anxieties and fatigue.

◆

Food for Thought

Sweet food of sweetly uttered knowledge. — Sir Philip Sidney

Each meal tastes better to me when it has a beginning, a middle and an end. Some of my friends swoop into the kitchen at lunchtime, grab this or that from the fridge, nibble and crunch before their plate even hits the table. And they may pop up every few minutes for a forgotten something. But how much more peaceful and satisfying it is to prepare a plate of lunch carefully and lovingly, set it on the table with the necessary paraphernalia, and then sit down to eat, focusing entirely on the food and the expanding moment.

Meals can become an important daily ritual. My stepfather had a very clear idea of their importance, perhaps influenced by sitting at Gurdjieff's table. Every mealtime in our household was a fiesta, a time of sharing excellent food, which he insisted on and sometimes criticized to the point of rudeness. It was also an opportunity for various members of the household to exchange their thoughts, plans or adventures.

Now that my family is gone, I often eat alone. But alone or with others, mealtime represents to me a moment when all the hubbub of "doing" recedes. It's a time and place to sit and contemplate and let go of any chore-related tension. Whatever I was previously engaged in can be examined with a longer view as my plans change or clarify. Reading a short passage from a good book can refocus the mind. Then, at the meal's end, when the conversation languishes or one comes to the end of a chapter, there's a clear moment of closure as one rises, wipes the tray, mat or table and begins to wash the dishes.

If I wish to experience each moment fully, this intentional

attitude can apply to many daily activities. Before beginning anything, I can center my thoughts on what I'm going to do and the order in which I'll do it. Then I'm able to gather the necessary equipment and move into the task, without holding back. Each job constitutes a challenge, not as a bore or a burden, but as something that needs my full attention. When I approach my tasks grounded in my presence, there's no need to hurry to get on to "other things." The present activity is its own food for *being*.

Unfortunately it's taken almost all my life to learn that rushing through what I *have* to do to move on to what I *want* to do simply "tastes" bad. I'm too familiar with a slew of reactions and excuses such as "I don't *want* to right now," "Why should I?" or "Why bother?" But now, if I remember to choose, I can evoke past experience. Tasks often begin in inertia, because whatever is standing still prefers not to spend energy revving up into voluntary movement, including me.

◆

Work from the Ground Up

Give me a place to stand on and I can move the world. — Archimedes

When I feel I just can't get underway, scrubbing pots is one of the best ways to get myself moving. One day as I scrubbed, I suddenly realized that my jaw was locked tight and my neck stiff. Why? Soon I discovered that just about every time I scrubbed or hauled or pushed something heavy, I tensed my jaw and did the work with my neck and shoulders. Alexander studies made me suspicious of such tensions and the poor use of my muscles. Now, when faced with such tasks, I try to remember to sink my attention down into my feet and scrub, haul or push from the ground up.

The challenge is to get those pots really clean. Since it takes physical effort, I root myself into the floor while my torso and arms go into action. This also works nicely for carrying or moving objects. When I bring the whole weight of the object down into my feet, there's less strain and I no longer rely on a few inadequate muscles to get the job done. Even when I work at my computer, where I'm usually hopelessly unaware of my legs and feet, it helps to sense that they are there. I add the thought that my fingertips on the keys are an extension of my arms, coming out of a strong back. Then suddenly *all of me* is present working at my computer and not just my head and hands.

Sensing your feet on the ground is a significant path to awareness. The trunks of trees aren't strong because of their thickness, but because their roots go deep into the soil and spread wide. When I first tried to be consciously aware of my weight on my feet as I worked, I was amazed to feel my jaw release. My body suddenly functioned as an organized whole. My strong back was engaged, from which my hard-working arms sprang out like branches. I discovered I had no need to rely on my head, jaw and shoulders to attempt what they weren't meant to do!

While we want to be strong to face life's difficulties, that inner strength, like the tree's, comes from the rooting, not the holding on. I used to dream that I was in a lifeboat in a wild, stormy sea. I clung to the dock with my hands, digging my fingernails into it, although the boat was tied up to it and anchored to the bottom of the harbor. Thinking about that dream one morning, I finally got the message. It was time to stop holding on "for dear life" and allow myself to move within the push-pull rhythm of the waves, trusting to psychic-rope and body-anchor to keep me near shore. The dream never returned.

Fear is the most powerful rigidifier. Rigidity prevents me from having contact with my body and its sense perceptions. I've noticed that when I'm most afraid, I'm most fixed. When I hold onto a permanent position, no matter how straight or strong my body seems, it's stiffened. To hold on tight because of fear is natural because we never know where the next "blow" may come from. But if we hold on most of the time, just in case, that seriously interferes with the practice of presence.

How can one let go or get rid of fear? I find that to acknowledge its physical presence in my body helps a lot. I try to register the whole impression as my attention travels through every part of me from tensed jaw to tightened toes, without denying the facts or fears in any way. Such an organic connection with my psychic state can sometimes flip me out of the frying pan of fear and into the fire of transformation.

◆

Trust What You Need Rather Than What You "Feel" Like

Feelings dwell in man, but man dwells in his love. — Martin Buber

When I was growing up, I was taught to do blindly what had to be done, without inner or outer argument. I then learned from Jungian studies that I was behaving like a donkey beaten by its master, the superego. Younger generations than mine adopted an opposite approach, postponing an unpleasant task or even just an effortful one because "I don't FEEEEL like it!" This puts the human being at the mercy of Newton's Law of Inertia: What is at rest will remain at rest until acted on by a force. If we want to get things done, some kind of intermediate activation is necessary, somewhere between kicking oneself in the butt and spinelessly giving up.

Gurdjieff, Taoism and the Alexander Technique send useful messages to anyone who tends to wait to "feel like it" before taking action. Resistance is a necessary element of creativity and can be passive or active depending on the demand. As a passive force it rises to meet and oppose an active intention to accomplish something. Therefore, whenever resistance appears, it's worth reminding ourselves that it's inevitable. Whether encountered on our own small road to balance or on the level of the universe, resistance is indispensable to a new happening. But if I just sink into it, nothing will happen.

One day I ate too much for breakfast at my friend's groaning table in Maine. I didn't feel like hauling my heavy body into the customary three-mile morning walk, which started up a long, steep hill. Maybe I should turn left and just take a short stroll down the dead-end road? But instead of veering onto it, I stopped at the turnoff and took time to look both ways. I relived how energized I had felt coming home the two previous mornings. I could recall the sensation of it: how the whole of me felt nourished and stimulated by the sweet-smelling pine woods. This memory propelled me, only half convinced, back onto the longer road. Gradually my sense of heaviness receded and a joyous awareness reappeared. I recognized, once again, that I'm part machine, ruled by inertia. The other part needs to be reminded of the joy of moving to bring the whole *shebang* into action!

When we're stuck, in order to avoid what Gurdjieff called "an endless hesitation in the same place," we need a change of attitude to activate the "Third Force" or the Reconciling Force. Many religions call it the Holy Spirit. It's an invisible energy connected with another level of feeling and being which never aligns itself with either *Yes* or *No*, active or passive. This invisible redeeming factor opens doors usually closed to us. It's the source of miracles. Linked to our authentic presence, it can bring active and passive forces into a fruitful relationship, to help us over the barrier of inertia.

The Third Force can take many forms. Presence to reality is one of them. The sacred act of forgiving is another. When we admit we don't know and open into the unknown, we feel its existence like a blessing. It can shift our values at any moment, in the midst of ordinary life.

◆

Discover Which Part Rules Your Roost

Man is a citizen of three worlds, in all of which, even now, he has his being. — Krishna Prem

Gurdjieff's division of the human being into three centers—head, heart and body—which behave like three people who live in three separate worlds and seldom communicate with each other, offers a clear baseline from which to search for balance. But in order to study the relationship among them, we need to find out which of them usually runs the show. People differ. Some are cerebral; some are body-oriented sports, yoga or dance enthusiasts. Still others react first emotionally. At any specific moment, we tend to respond to life's demands with habitual one-centered preferences as one of these three parts subjugates our whole field.

To find which center dominates your responses to life, and how much authority you automatically give it, ask yourself:

• Is my body on the back burner in life, or does it
always take precedence?

•   Am I a thinking person who believes the rest of me
is only there to serve the life of the mind?

• Does my emotional reaction come first in any
situation, rocking my life as if it were a small boat on
a rough sea?

Consider whether you are starving segments of yourself, which ought to be valued as much as your favorite parts. Being present to all of yourself might bring you to an overall sense of balance. How do churning thoughts interfere with a real experience of myself? I remember walking home through the woods to the house where I stayed in Maine. As soon as the roof came into view, I found I was mentally sitting down at the computer to write the thoughts formulated on my walk, dead to the beautiful world I passed through. On another occasion I recall standing in the doorway of a long, cold room, feeling my arms clench as if I were closing the window twenty feet away.

I've always had difficulty giving up the strident demands of my organizing mind which, like *Mrs. Rigid*, decides in advance how everything ought to unfold and what's "needed" for any given day. *Mrs. R.* always wants to turn her opinion into a "religion." She's a mind-driven, disconnected piece of me that interferes with the possibility of making a fresh connection with the needs of each moment.

When my repetitive thoughts insist and my body or feelings object, I've learned simply to stop for a moment. To pause. This allows me time to make a choice or renew an intention. Only after I've reviewed the situation can I consciously select what to do next and act on it. I may well decide to continue concentrating, but only after a drink of water, a call to a friend or a walk to the store. Or perhaps I'll notice I have an upset stomach or an ache in my body. Then I remember that these pains may be a direct result of my head's greediness for all my attention.

A running monologue in our heads guides most of us much of the time. This automatic thinking machine keeps us in its thrall with churning associations. Our energy seems to rise to our head and shoulders as we carry life like a burden and mull over our problems. We've all been caught in this kind of meandering flow of thought. We also know that when we've been very anxious or concentrated on some assignment to the point of getting a headache, we can often bring ourselves down to earth by exercising or engaging in physical labor. It's important to send our roots consciously down into the earth or our thoughts into body awareness—to stay on the ground rather than fly up in anxieties, dreams or imagination.

◆

Make Use of the Power of Thought

Learn to separate the fine from the coarse. — Hermes Trismegistus

This is our paradox: we must give up being led by our head's automatic associations, which drive us unconsciously all day long, in order to follow another leader. But the mind—our reasoned, conscious thought—is just such a guide. Our conscious mind can help us develop a new level of awareness and recognize where our attention is needed at any given moment. Given a chance, it will teach us how to choose our path through the strident cacophony of inner and outer demands and reactions. It will lead us to the practice of presence.

The Alexander Technique showed me how powerfully directed thought can influence the body. I had already learned from relaxation techniques, my Jungian readings and my own digestive problems how the body carries psychic pain. New experiences of how thought can read the body came to me at school, where teachers were able to inform me where the flow of my energy was blocked. For example, one teacher put hands on my head and neck and said: "You are holding on to your right hip and most of your weight is on your left leg. Think of your energy going down the right side." Another pointed out that "the middle of your back can never support the weight of your head. Let go of it." After working for a year and a half I noticed that when I put my hands on a classmate and sent a clear thought to free my own head, neck and torso from unnecessary tension, there was an immediate release in her body.

If the touch of a teacher can release unnecessary tension, there's no reason why we can't help ourselves in the same way. Perhaps my thought alone isn't as quick or as powerful when it's not combined with the trained hands of a teacher, but it can have a very positive effect on my contracted state. Make the experiment by concentrating your thought on one part of your body that feels tight. First take the time needed to become deeply aware of its state of tension—you could call that "listening" to it—and then consciously invite whatever "holding" has been noticed to let go.

Such messages to various parts of your body are a "wish" rather than a peremptory order. You invite relaxation because you cannot force it. You may sense that you gradually fill with energy as you move your attention from one part of your body to another with this conscious wish to recognize and release tension, until you have visited your whole self. This is *you*. Your energized whole. We all block the flow of energy or *ch'i* with our fears and tensions. We can learn to let go, step by step, and allow the energy to flow through us. Organized by thought-power, we can work with the body rather than against it.

◆

Embrace the Whole of Yourself

As a spark, a part containing something of the whole, the soul's essential wholeness cannot be achieved except through effort, through work with the greater whole. — Adin Steinsaltz

We hear a lot of talk about wholeness these days, the wish to be more whole, by which we usually mean "all of a piece," or perhaps "of one mind." But were we to access the whole of ourselves right now, we might find there are more pieces to us than we had ever dreamed of. And we may not like some of those pieces at all! True wholeness must include what Jung called our shadow side, the parts of us we hide from ourselves and from others, and whose existence we deny and even scorn. "*I'm* not like *that!*" we sometimes say or think proudly, when we notice something about someone else we don't like. Well, maybe we are! Gurdjieff said that if we could ever see all of our attitudes at once—all of the many "i's" that take turns dominating our carriage—if we were to realize how we hate what we love and love what we despise—we would go mad.

Refusing to accept the attitudes we don't like in ourselves, we often scorn or condemn them in others. We forget that all humans are brothers and sisters in the dark underworld of the psyche. We are each unique, but we all share the same tendencies. Only through self-knowledge can the path to resolving our conflicting desires become apparent. Through the careful observation of a scientist who isn't interested in whether something is right or wrong but only in what actually occurs, we can gradually see and accept our flaws and limitations.

Those of us whose response to the world skews toward criticism or disapproval may be led, through self-knowledge, to accept human frailty in ourselves and in others. However, if we intend to bring our deep longing for wholeness into daily life, we must learn to hear the primary wish that surges from our depths. It's why listening is so important. As we seek the source of that faint, seldom-heeded vibration, we respond to a call that invites us to be attentive to ourselves in the midst of all the excitement of life, connected to a larger whole. To paraphrase St. Paul, although we think in parts and feel in parts, when that which is whole calls us, our fascination with parts will fade away.

◆

Live More Simply

Living with the limits that make my life my own. — Marion Woodman

You may find it necessary to accept the fact that you'll get fewer things done each day. That's a harsh statement for over-achievers like me. Although the laundry list of obligations, duties and even delights seems endless, the length of our lives is limited. As Ravi Ravindra so aptly put it in *Pilgrim Without Boundaries*, "The limitation is in the vessel."

So if you tend to over-schedule yourself as I do, consider pacing yourself differently. Think of the day as an accordion, expanding steadily, moment by moment, into the present, rather than a narrow railroad track of duties you must faithfully follow to the end. Learn to recognize how quickly the head commits itself and you to a lot of obligations, and how full it is of ideas, some of them quite good. But if you always follow its orders, when will the rest of you receive its share of attention?

While it's one thing to recognize the need to change such a one-sided, unbalanced situation, it's quite another to practice presence. I was amazed at how determined I was to get all my duties out of the way, in spite of a deep wish for a new life. As the wish became increasingly insistent, I tried to squeeze space for my new practice into my tightly packed day. This only produced more pressure! So to help myself, I reformulated my priorities. I wrote my wish down on a brightly colored paper and stuck it on my bedroom mirror. Then, every time I looked at myself in the mirror, the note reminded me of my intention. If I then paid no attention to it, at least I wasn't fooling myself!

I had to learn the art of the possible. As I fought to oppose my lifetime habit of saying "yes" to every demand, I redis-covered the importance of *choosing*. I must learn to wait and listen attentively, to be ready to put aside a plan or go against the tendency to compress several things into a small space of time. At any moment of the day I might be called on to give something up, and there was no way of knowing ahead of time what I'd need to sacrifice.

Whenever I didn't know what to do, I'd try to stay in contact with the present moment by asking the following question: "Which choice will bring me closer to the 'self' that I want to spend more of my time on earth with?" Alexander teacher Judith Leibowitz used to challenge students who tended to crunch their bodies in their hurry to get tasks done, by asking them the unexpected question: "Is it worth losing your front length for?" A forward slump compromises our breathing as well as the spine and musculature of the torso. We can't be "whole" when we aren't wholly available.

I also learned the importance of alternating work and rest. To survive each day, I had to include "time-outs." That was clear. But taking a whole day off in a wish to be present to myself was a luxury I thought I couldn't afford. Try to avoid my mistake. Think of it as a necessity. Without a day of leisure in the work-week, the intensity of life, with all its urgency, produces a debilitating 24/7 lifestyle. When is there any time to recharge our batteries? After all, even the Creator rested on the seventh day! Scriptures recommend one day a week to rest for a very good reason. We would be wise to honor that wisdom.

That special one-day-a-week unhooks the central axis of my being from all that normally engages me. I become quiet as I limit my physical and mental activity. When I do that, speaking can turn into listening; action can become contemplation. For those with a full work week, it's difficult to separate quiet time from weekend shopping, cleaning and errands, but it can be done. I think of it as an essential rhythm, an organic form of breathing my life *in* when most of the week I've been breathing it *out*.

You may feel that setting aside a whole day to center yourself is impossible, given all you have to accomplish. But before dismissing it as impractical, you might attend to the deeper message, because it isn't just about *physical* rest. As Peter de Celles, a 12th-century Benedictine abbot, said, "God works in us while we rest in Him." Perhaps only when we become truly quiet are we able to receive the spiritual grace and refreshment we seek.

◆

Repeat Yourself

To love life through labor is to be intimate with life's inmost secret.
— Khalil Gibran

Every time you repeat an action, every time you even think of it, you deepen your psycho-neuro-physical connection to it. You also produce a chemical change in yourself. The obvious downside of this is that when you repeat a bad habit you allow it more autonomous authority over you. But the upside is that with conscious attention, by waiting until the automatic resistance that rises with each intended effort subsides, you can create a deeper channel in your system for the actions and responses you prefer to express. Among these, you can develop the habit of making more room for the practice of presence as you connect it with the many small acts you perform every day.

Ritual intends to accomplish this, although it doesn't always succeed. People may pride themselves on going through the motions of T'ai Chi or a religious or personal ritual, but if their thoughts are on what's for dinner or what they should have told someone this morning, they won't benefit as they might. To carve a decent channel in the direction you want to go, you need to bring your best capacity for thought or attention as well as awareness of your body and a heartful reminder of why you care about this at all.

Some settings may be more conducive than others. In the case of T'ai Chi, I found it easier to elicit that magical state of awareness in the park or on the beach. However, while my living room may not provide the same sublime setting, any space in which I've chosen to practice presence is enhanced.

The most difficult moment often comes at the beginning. Gathering mind, heart and body together is an uphill effort, which is why it may be hard to get started. Reason or sense of duty or memory may bring me to the starting point, but is met with resistance from a lazy body or mind that just doesn't want to be bothered. To take into account my initial resistance, I remind myself that when I have to interrupt other activities to fulfill an intention, my first response is often: "Okay, but not *now*. Later." It can also help to recall that many others are undertaking these same movements at this very moment, somewhere in the world. Whoever and wherever they may be, they share the same wish to serve a larger purpose, to rise above the self-affirming ego, to understand the meaning and aim of their existence. Or perhaps they long, as I do, to create a space in themselves for an unknown energy to enter.

Gradually, with attentive repetition, ritual gestures take on deeper meaning. As you begin once more to honor your intention, the memory of previous times calls the scattered parts of you to join the experience. Once they are gathered, you become open to the magical power of presence, which can turn an ordinary moment into an extraordinary one. By ritual repetition, answers to the question "Why am I doing this?" become less confused, and the experience of these precious moments of joyful presence clarifies our path.

When to try? Daily is better than weekly, because the practice of presence will reorient you toward the present moment and away from fragmentation. Better yet, do it whenever you hear the faint but seldom-insistent call. Any moment can flower into self-awareness. Even your daily tasks and activities could take on a similar quality of conscious presence. Making the bed, vacuuming the room or cleaning up any disorder can serve to rouse the sleeper in us, or phoning an elderly parent or a sick friend. The spirit behind the action transforms it and makes it sacred.

One of my favorite rituals is washing the dishes. It took a long time to overcome my childhood resistance to this unwelcome chore my brother and I took turns at every evening. But after intensive weeks of work with others in the Gurdjieff community, I developed a new taste for the experience. In that special milieu five or six people washed dishes after meals for a hundred people, a task that took about an hour. Whether somewhere in South America, on a back porch overlooking the sea in Nova Scotia, or in a dilapidated barn on a farm near Toronto, the enlivening sense of participation in a ritual was the same. The work was accompanied by songs in two or three parts or experiments with attention exercises, to help us move both quickly and carefully. One day, to my surprise, I discovered that washing dishes at home lifted me right up into that same state of joy. The hot soapy water, the feel of the dish or glass in one hand passed over to the other to set in the rack, reactivated the community experience. Since then I've never wanted a dishwasher—I wouldn't sacrifice the kitchen wash-up for anything!

◆

Welcome Interruptions

Lord, lead me from the unreal to the real. — Upanishads

Without our being aware of it, our attention is focused either on one small corner inside ourselves or on the outside world. And we often become annoyed when called away from the book we're reading, the movie we're submerged in or the cabinet we're trying to fix. If we could see at that moment how narrow our world has become, we might develop a more positive attitude toward interruptions. As long as the irritation isn't stoked until it becomes active resentment, any interruption can awaken a new impression, a new feeling and a new level of contact with ourselves.

Every interruption offers an opportunity to embrace the present moment. We've been stopped. This allows us to begin again from a new place, just as Gurdjieff's shouted command did, with his order that we freeze our physical position to observe how scattered we were inside. When I'm totally immersed in writing, my cat gently nibbles at my ankle; then, if I don't respond, he sinks his teeth in a little further. I'm forced to take action. A few years ago, I would have been tempted to swat or scold him, but now I'm more likely to welcome his insistence, turn from where I'm glued to my computer and roll on the floor with him.

True, one-pointedness is necessary to get a job done well or to select the precise words to express a thought, but after an hour or so of such concentration, I'm totally lost to the rest of me, to a sense of all that I am. Better to jump up, get a glass of water or even go for a quick walk around the block! Within a few minutes another, fresher person has emerged in me who can continue the important work I was doing.

In the Moslem world the call to interrupt whatever you're fixated on comes five times a day, when the cry of the *muezzin* summons the world to prayer. Similar daily interruptions occur in monasteries, where the monks commit to leave their duties at prescribed times to "keep the hours" of worship. To turn from one's identification with whatever is at hand and put one's head on the ground in the deepest of all bows is truly a momentary sacrifice of the small self. First the interruption, then the deep bow, and finally the relinquishing of the busyness of the mind as it turns, cleansed, to praising

God. It may be strange to our worldly, western culture, this practice of obedient response to a call wherever you are, without argument. Yet it provides an opportunity to reconnect with presence.

Such interruptions can be created intentionally. If you put a pebble in your shoe or on your path, you may feel pain or stumble over it if life puts you to sleep. Gurdjieff used to recommend that we invent "alarm clocks," so as not to sleep our life away. He put his students into many difficult situations precisely for that reason.

When I have a lot of work to do at the computer, I set an egg timer. When it goes off, I commit myself to get up and walk away for a moment, or at least to turn away from the screen and stretch. As the kinks loosen and I begin to walk around, I'm newly cognizant of how delicious body awareness can be. What a relief to go into movement! I investigate the differences in various parts of my body as I move around. Whenever I become aware of feeling heavy or light, tall or stooped, tight or loose, I learn something about my entire inner state, not just my physical condition.

Like a child, an animal is a perfect interrupter; they often demand your attention when you are totally engaged in something else and they refuse to take "not now" for an answer. I scarcely need my egg timer since Gatsby's been around. A few moments of petting, feeding, brushing or just playing with him offer big benefits. Of course it's natural to be annoyed if the interference seems less important than what you were doing. But an interruption is often a demand for love that offers love in return. Refuse love at your peril! Receive the gift, hug the child, play with the cat or dog, and then return to work with new energy.

◆

Be Sensuous

Nature needs man for what no angel can perform on it, namely, its hallowing. — Martin Buber

We can also call ourselves back from our usual problem-solving mindset or a tendency to daydream when we engage in conscious participation with one or more of our five senses. Both concentrating and daydreaming are automatic modes that take us away from reality and from awareness of ourselves in space. The return to where we live—in our bodies and in the present moment—activates our faculties. We become more alive to the world and more sensitive to ourselves.

For example, to touch another person is an intimate and extraordinary sensory experience. It can trigger a kind of awakening, whether I connect with the softness of a baby's cheek, a firm handshake, a comforting hug or a loving sexual encounter. Some people are very sensitive to what they touch while others never notice. The latter would do well to find out what they've been missing and why.

And how about listening? Whenever I have a problem, my immediate solution is to do something about it right away. But sometimes what I really need to do is listen to all its aspects before taking action. It could be the pause that both refreshes and reorganizes my original intention. As for listening to others, I ask myself, "What do I have to 'do' to hear what you are saying?" We often narrow and compress our bodies when we listen or express ourselves to other people. Our bodies may reach forward or shrink back unconsciously, rather than giving or receiving the message in the space we occupy. It's a rich and difficult experience to stay rooted in my own presence in front of another person as I speak or listen, taking in their message or communicating mine.

And then there's singing or humming. What a great way to release tension and become aware of myself! I experience the vitality of my own vibrations while putting them out there in the world. When we sing a song from the heart we access and link more parts of ourselves than are usually in contact with each other. Whether noble themes in church, battle cries in action, anguished love songs that rend the heart or joyous arpeggios in the shower, singing awakens a part of us that searches to express what we feel. And even when I'm unaware of what I feel, whatever song I'm humming is frequently a message from the unconscious.

A primary receptive activity is *seeing*. We see more whenever we look consciously at the world or someone in it or even at ourselves. When I see with awareness, I become more connected with my whole being. I am here with my seat on the chair or my feet on the ground, viewing the world with my eyes inside my head. I let what's out there come to me, reminding my eyes that they don't need to pop out to grab what's in front and bring it back to me (my frequent habit).

To find the balance I seek, body awareness is essential. When I explore through my senses, I expand. The quality of my movements changes dramatically. Manifestations of imbalance also carry a useful message. Whenever I trip or stumble, I receive it as a call from "Central Intelligence" to stop for a moment. Maybe I was deep in thought and cut off from my meat and bones, flying through the stratosphere on mental wings. Since I tend to lose contact with one direction or the other, I vow to come down into my feet, reminding myself that the function of a human being is to serve as a bridge between Earth and Heaven.

Gurdjieff spoke about "the right rhythms of the senses,"

saying that the reception of external impressions depends on it. Being connected to my own rhythms may lead me to become more "who I am" rather than the person I think others wish me to be. As far as I'm concerned, it's worth dedicating the rest of my life to finding my own right rhythms.

And finally, the master key to awareness of ourselves and of the world reaches us through breathing. I can connect with my breath merely by noticing it, without trying to change anything. As *The Secret of the Golden Flower* reminds us, "When the breathing is rhythmical the mistakes of laziness and distraction disappear of their own accord." If I follow its rhythm without judgment, as a moment-by-moment discovery, the mind quiets and feeling awakens.

◆

Only the Beggar Gets the Gold

Every effort adds a little gold to a treasure no power on earth can take away. — Simone Weil

Whenever we practice presence, we begin again. We come alive right where we are. It's in the present that we discover the meaning of our life and healing for our wounds. But, like the inward and outward flow of our breathing, our attention to this inner life comes and goes. We can't solve the riddle of presence once and for all and have done with it. We can't meditate ourselves into a permanent state of *satori*. Rather, our challenge in this life on earth is to practice consciously, again and again, the return to our "home base," to the whole of ourselves.

Such a daily commitment to contact "the spirit within the heart" will transform us from surface-dwellers to lovers of being-in-depth. When we meet life with all that we are, moment by moment, we no longer live an "ordinary" life, but the "extraordinary" life we were given. Remember yourself, as Gurdjieff said. Above all, don't let yourself be beaten down by the demands of life, no matter how tragic and inexorable they may be. In the end, we own nothing in this world. We are beggars on the golden bench of possibility, but our real treasure is only attainable when we are attached to nothing else. Like the secret recipes of the alchemists, the practice of presence can teach us how to transform the leaden quality of a life without meaning into gold.

The true name of eternity is today. — Philo

ACKNOWLEDGMENTS

M<small>Y</small> mother, Louise Welch, was both my progenitor and my first spiritual guide. When I think of her, two lines of a Thanksgiving hymn are called to mind, because it was she who introduced me to "the love that from our birth over and around us lies." I hope she and my stepfather, Dr. William J. Welch, would be pleased at this addition to the family list of published books. Always an enthusiastic supporter of my ventures into unknown territory, he, also, deserves special acknowledgment.

My children, Patricia Louise, Thalia Helena and Luis Fernando, have often inspired and renewed my sense of the joy of living and participated, with their encouragement, in the writing of this book.

My friend, Dawn Drzal, suggested that I put down on paper something about the several paths I've followed for so many years, and helped set the early stages of this project in motion.

What's a writer without editors? Grateful thanks to my brother, Dr. Richard Crampton, who brought a scientist's accuracy, a doctor's thoughtful evaluation and an editor's eye to bear on my flights of prose, with grounding effect; to Karen Speerstra, whose careful editorial suggestions focused me on communicating better with my reader and Luis Fernando Llosa, whose line-editing was both gentle and thorough; Barbara Davis (editor of *Taijiquan Journal*) provided input on Chinese language usage in the T'ai Chi section. Martha Heyneman and Shimon Malin generously offered suggestions and corrections on the early manuscript.

And what writer wouldn't be grateful for such a thoughtful publisher as Morning Light Press? Thanks to Darcy Sinclair and Steve Jadick for their attentive presence.

Many are the seekers of truth I met on my path, who nourished the growth and understanding that finally led me to write this book. Outstanding among them are G. I. Gurdjieff, Jeanne de Salzmann, Pauline de Dampierre and many essence friends and companions among the Gurdjieffians with whom I have shared the inner journey for more than fifty years.

T. T. Liang, Da Liu and Ed Young are among the T'ai Chi teachers I am grateful to have known.

Thanks to Joseph Wagenseller, Marion Woodman and the many Jungians who lit that way for me with the fire of their own exploration, as they forged their individual paths through the mysterious, exhilarating world of the psyche.

I owe much to Daniel Singer, Judy Stern, Jessica Wolf, and the many teachers and students at the American Center for the Alexander Technique who so generously shared their own search with me. Also to Michael Frederick and John Nicholls;

and to Walter Carrington for his warm welcome on my visit to his teacher-training school in London.

Some readers may want to know the exact source (page and volume) of the quotes sprinkled throughout the text. Almost all are identified by author, many of them from earlier editions of the works listed in the Selected Readings section that follows. All through my life I've collected quotes from what I've read, but I never wrote down the page numbers, book or publisher. What seemed important at the time, in the midst of my busy life, was the call of the message itself and the name of its author. Many of these quotes were posted weekly on my refrigerator in Peru or New York while my children were growing up (as much for my sake as for theirs). Since those slips of paper are sometimes my only reference, I apologize to any readers who would like more specifics, and assure them that I have mended my ways. While my refrigerator door continues to be blanketed by quotes, nowadays I always write down the page number.

Finally, it's important to acknowledge the words and practices of many seekers on many paths over thousands of years that have fed me, and others, widely and deeply in our search. All of us who have profited from their revelations owe them more than can ever be paid. We can only strive to join them in the current of the Great Tradition.

PERMISSIONS

✿

Rumi was quoted in Chapter One, with the kind permission of Mr. Barks, from *The Essential Rumi*, Coleman Barks (translator), with John Moyne, A. J. Arberry and Reynold Nicholson, Castle Books, Edison, NJ, 1997.

Roger Lipsey's poem was quoted in Chapter Three, with the kind permission of the author.

David Wagoner's poem about trees was quoted in Chapter Six with the kind permission of the author, from his book, *Traveling Light*, University of Illinois Press, 1999.

SELECTED READINGS

✺

Chapter 1 — Remembering Oneself: G. I. Gurdjieff

De Hartmann, Thomas and Olga, *Our Life with Mr. Gurdjieff*, Penguin Arkana, New York, 1992.

DeRopp, Robert, *Warrior's Way*, Delacorte Press, New York, 1979.

Gurdjieff, G. I., *Beelzebub's Tales to His Grandson*, Viking Arkana, New York, 1992. Audiotape available in MP3 format from Traditional Studies Press, 1930 Yonge St., Toronto, Canada M45 1Z4 and at www.TraditionalStudiesPress.com.

_____. *Life is Real Only Then When "I Am,"* E. P. Dutton, New York, 1982.

_____. *Meetings with Remarkable Men*, E. P. Dutton, New York, 1974.

_____. *Views from the Real World: Early Talks of Gurdjieff*, Viking Press, New York, 1991.

"Gurdjieff Movements," *Gurdjieff International Review*, Vol. V, No. 1 (Spring 2002) Gurdjieff Electronic Publishing, Los Altos, CA. Order at: www.gurdjieff.org.

Gurdjieff: Essays and Reflections on the Man and His Teaching, Jacob Needleman and George Baker (editors,) Continuum Press, New York, 1996.

Hulme, Kathryn, *Undiscovered Country*, Little, Brown, Boston/Toronto, 1966.

Moore, James, *Gurdjieff: Anatomy of a Myth*, Element Books, Shaftesbury, UK, 1991.

Nicoll, Maurice, *Living Time and the Integration of the Life*, Watkins, London, 1976.

_____. *The Mark*, Vincent Stuart, London, 1970.

_____. *The New Man: An Interpretation of Some Parables and Miracles of Christ*, Watkins, London, 1981.

Nott, C. S., *Teachings of Gurdjieff: The Journal of a Young Pupil*, Arkana, New York, 1990.

Orage, A. R., *The Active Mind: Psychological Exercises and Essays*, Weiser, New York, 1965.

_____. *On Love: With Some Aphorisms and Other Essays*, Weiser, New York, 1966.

*Ouspensky, P. D., *In Search of the Miraculous*, Harcourt, New York, 2001.

_____. *The Psychology of Man's Possible Evolution*, Knopf, New York, 1974.

Peters, Fritz, *Boyhood with Gurdjieff*, E. P. Dutton, New York, 1964.

Segal, William, *Opening*, Continuum Press, New York, 1998.

Tracol, Henri, *The Taste for Things That Are True*, Element Books, Shaftesbury, UK, 1994.

*Vaysse, Jean, *Toward Awakening*, Far West Undertakings, San Francisco, 1978.

Walker, Kenneth, *A Study of Gurdjieff's Teaching*, Jonathan Cape, London, 1957.

_____. *Venture With Ideas*, Luzak Oriental, 1995.

Welch, Louise, *Orage with Gurdjieff in America*, Routledge & Kegan Paul, Boston, 1982.

Welch, William J., *What Happened In Between: A Doctor's Story*, Braziller, New York, 1972.

Zuber, René, *Who Are You Monsieur Gurdjieff?* (Foreword by P. L. Travers) Arkana, London, 1980.

*Good general introduction

Chapter Two: Investing in Loss: The Tao of T'ai Chi Ch'uan
The Practice of T'ai Chi Ch'uan

Cheng, Man-ch'ing, and Robert Smith, *T'ai-Chi: The "Supreme Ultimate" Exercise for Health, Sport, and Self-Defense*, Tuttle Publishing, Boston, 1967.

*Cheng Man-ch'ing, *T'ai Chi Ch'uan: A Simplified Method*, North Atlantic Books, Berkeley, CA, 1981.

Da Liu, *T'ai Chi Ch'uan and I Ching: A Choreography of Body and Mind*, Harper & Row, New York, 1972.

_____. *T'ai Chi Ch'uan & Meditation*, Schocken Books, New York, 1986.

Davis, Barbara, *The Taijiquan Classics*, North Atlantic Books, Berkeley, California, 2004.

Huang, Al Chung-liang, *Embrace Tiger, Return to Mountain – The Essence of T'ai Chi*, Celestial Arts, Berkeley, CA, 1988.

Jou, Tsung Hwa, *The Tao of T'ai Chi Ch'uan: Way to Rejuvenation*, T'ai Chi Foundation, Piscataway, NJ, 1980.

Lehrhaupt, Linda Myoki, *T'ai Chi as a Path of Wisdom*, Shambhala Publications, Boston, 2001.

*Liang, T. T., *T'ai Chi Ch'uan For Health and Self-Defense: Philosophy and Practice*, Vintage Books, New York, 1977.

Lo, Benjamin P., *The Essence of T'ai Chi Ch'uan: The Literary Tradition*, North Atlantic Books, Berkeley, CA, 1979.

Lowenthal, Wolfe, *There Are No Secrets: Professor Cheng Man Ch'ing and His T'ai Chi Ch'uan*, North Atlantic Books, Berkeley, CA, 1991.

Taoism and Chinese Thought

Chuang-Tzu: The Inner Chapters, A. C. Graham (translator), Hackett Publishing, Indianapolis, IN, 2001.

Lao Tsu, *Tao Te Ching*, Gia Fu Feng and Jane English (translators), Vintage Books, New York, 1997.

Waley, Arthur, *The Way and Its Power: Lao Tzu's Tao Te Ching and Its Place in Chinese Thought*, Grove/Atlantic, New York, 1972.

Chopra, Deepak, *Quantum Healing: Exploring the Frontiers of Mind/Body Medicine*, Bantam Books, New York, 1990.

The I Ching: or Book of Changes, translated by Richard Wilhelm, English translation by Cary F. Baynes, Princeton University Press, NJ, 1970.

Huang, Alfred, *The Complete I Ching*, Inner Traditions, Rochester, VT, 1998.

The Book of Changes: Zhouyi, Richard Rutt (translator), Durham East Asia Series, Durham, UK, 2002.

The Secret of the Golden Flower: A Chinese Book of Life, translated by Richard Wilhelm, English translation by Cary F. Baynes, Harvest/HBJ Books, New York, 1970.

Sun Tzu, *The Art of War*, Denma Translation Group, Shambhala Publications, Boston, 2002.

*Good general introduction

Chapter Three: The Way of Individuation: C. G. Jung

Adler, Gerhardt, *The Living Symbol: A Case Study in the Process of Individuation*, Pantheon, New York, 1961.

Baynes, H. G., *Mythology of the Soul: A Research into the Unconscious from Schizophrenic Dreams and Drawings*, Rider, London, 1969.

Campbell, Joseph, *The Hero with a Thousand Faces*, Princeton University Press, NJ, 1990.

Chodorow, Joan, *Jung on Active Imagination*, Princeton University Press, NJ, 1997.

Conforti, Michael, *Field, Form and Fate: Patterns in Mind, Nature, and Psyche*, Spring Journal, Putnam, CT, 2003.

*Edinger, Edward, *The Creation of Consciousness: Jung's Myth for Modern Man*, Inner City Books, 1984.

_____. *Ego and Archetype: Individuation and the Religious Function of the Psyche*, Shambhala Publications, Boston, 1992

Fordham, Michael, *New Developments in Analytical Psychology*, Routledge & Kegan Paul, London,1957.

Harding, Esther, *The Way of All Women*, Shambhala Publications, Boston, 1970.

Hillman, James, *The Myth of Analysis*, Northwestern University Press, Evanston, IL, 1998.

_____. *The Soul's Code: In Search of Character and Calling*, Warner Books, New York, 1997.

Horney, Karen, *The Neurotic Personality of Our Time*, W. W. Norton, New York, 1994.

Johnson, Robert, *Inner Work: Using Dreams and Creative Imagination for Personal Growth and Integration*, HarperCollins, New York, 1986.

_____. *Owning Your Own Shadow*, HarperCollins, New York, 1991.

Jung, C. G., *The Collected Works of C. G. Jung*, H. Read, M. Fordham, G. Adler, and W. McGuire (editors,) 20 Volumes. Bollingen Series XX, Princeton University Press, NJ, 1992.

_____. *Memories, Dreams, Reflections*, Vintage Books, New York, 1989.

_____. **Modern Man in Search of a Soul*, Harcourt Trade Publications, New York, 1995.

Keyes, Margaret, *The Inward Journey: Art as Therapy*, Open Court Press, Peru, IL, 1983.

Leonard, Linda Schierse, *Witness to the Fire: Creativity and the Veil of Addiction*, Shambhala Publications, Boston, 1989.

_____. *The Wounded Woman: Healing the Father-Daughter Relationship*, Shambhala Publications, Boston, 1983.

May, Rollo, *The Courage to Create*, W. W. Norton, New York, 1994.

_____. *The Discovery of Being: Writings in Existential Philosophy*, W. W. Norton, New York, 1994.

_____. *Love and Will*, W. W. Norton, New York, 1969.

_____. *Power and Innocence: A Search for the Sources of Violence*, W. W. Norton, New York, 1998.

_____. *Psychology and the Human Dilemma*, W. W. Norton, New York, 1996.

Mundy, Talbot, *Om: The Secret of Ahbor Valley*, Kessinger Publishing, Whitefish, MT, 2004.

Neumann, Erich, *The Origins and History of Consciousness*, R. F. C. Hull (translator), Princeton University Press, NJ, 1995.

Singer, June, *Boundaries of the Soul*, Anchor Books, New York, 1994.

Stein, Murray, *Jung's Map of the Soul*, Open Court Press, Peru, IL, 2003.

Stevens, Anthony, *Archetype Revisited: An Updated Natural History of the Self*, Inner City Books, Toronto, 2003.

Storr, Anthony, *Solitude*, HarperCollins, New York, 1997.

Ulanov, Ann Belford, *The Functioning Transcendent: A Study in Analytical Psychology*, Chiron Publications, Wilmette, IL, 1996.

*Whitmont, Edward C., *The Symbolic Quest*, Princeton University Press, NJ, 1991.

Woodman, Marion, *Addiction to Perfection: The Still Unravished Bride*, Inner City Books, Toronto, 1982.

_____. *Bone: Dying into Life*, Viking Penguin, New York, 2000.

_____. *Leaving My Father's House: A Journey to Conscious Femininity*, with Kate Danson, Mary Hamilton and Rita Greer Allen, Shambhala Publications, Boston, 1993.

_____. *The Pregnant Virgin, A Process of Psychological Transformation*, Inner City Books, Toronto, 1985.

_____. and Robert Bly, *The Maiden King: The Reunion of Masculine and Feminine*, Owl Publishing, New York, 1999.

Zweig, Connie and Jeremiah Abrams, editors, *Meeting the Shadow: The Hidden Power of the Dark Side of Human Nature*, Jeremy P. Tarcher, Los Angeles, 1991.

*Good general introduction

Chapter Four: School for Presence: The Alexander Technique

All books listed below can be ordered from The American Society for the Alexander Technique (AmSAT), at AmSAT Books, P.O. Box 60008, Florence, MA, 01062, or at: www.alexandertech.org .

Alexander, F. Matthias, *Constructive Conscious Control of the Individual*, STAT Books, UK, 1997.

_____. *Man's Supreme Inheritance*, Centerline Press, Long Beach, CA, 1988.

_____. *The Universal Constant in Living*, Mouritz, UK, 2000.

_____. *The Use of the Self*, Orion Publishing Group, UK, 2002.

Caplan, Deborah, *Back Trouble: A New Approach to Prevention and Recovery Based on the Alexander Technique*, Triad Communications, Gainesville, FL, 1987.

Carrington, Walter and Sean Carey, *The Act of Living*, Mornum Time Press, Berkeley, CA, 1999.

_____. *Personally Speaking*, Mouritz, UK, May 2001.

_____. *Thinking Aloud: Talks on Teaching the Alexander Technique*, Mornum Time Press, Berkeley, CA, 1994.

De Alcantara, Pedro, *Indirect Procedures: A Musician's Guide to the Alexander Technique*, Oxford University Press, 1997.

Dimon, Theodore, *The Elements of Skill: A Conscious Approach to Learning*, North Atlantic Books, Berkeley, CA, 2003.

Garlick, David, *The Lost Sixth Sense: A Medical Scientist Looks at the Alexander Technique*, David Garlick Publications, New South Wales, 1990.

*Gelb, Michael, *Body Learning: An Introduction to the Alexander Technique*, Henry Holt, New York, 1994.

Gray, John, *Your Guide to the Alexander Technique*, St. Martin's Press, New York, 1991.

Herrigel, Eugene, *Zen in the Art of Archery*, Vintage Books, New York, 1999.

Jones, Frank Pierce, *Freedom to Change: The Development and Science of the Alexander Technique*, Mouritz, UK, 1997.

Langford, Elizabeth, *Mind and Muscle: An Owner's Handbook*, Garant, Belgium, 1999.

*Liebowitz, Judy and Bill Connington, *The Alexander Technique*, Harper-Collins, New York, 1990.

Macdonald, Patrick, *The Alexander Technique As I See It*, International Specialized Book Service, Portland, OR, 1989.

Maisel, Edward, *The Alexander Technique – The Essential Writings of F. Matthias Alexander*, Citadel Trade, New York, 1989.

McCallion, Michael, *The Voice Book*, Faber and Faber, UK, 1998.

Nicholls, John, *The Alexander Technique in Conversation with Sean Carey*, Brighton Alexander Training Centre, UK, 1991.

Sontag, Jerry, *Curiosity Recaptured: Exploring Ways We Think and Move*, Mornum Time Press, Berkeley, CA, 1996.

Westfeldt, Lulie, *F. Matthias Alexander: The Man and His Work*, STAT Books, UK, 1998.

*Good general introduction

Chapter Five: The Path of Prayer and Meditation
Buddhism

Armstrong, Karen, *Buddha*, Viking Penguin, New York, 2001.

Dhammapada: The Sayings of the Buddha, Thomas Byrom (translator), Harmony/Bell Tower, New York, 2001

The Doctrine of Awakening: The Attainment of Self-Mastery According to the Earliest Buddhist Texts, Julius Evola and H. E. Musson (translators), Inner Traditions, Rochester, VT, 1996.

Batchelor, Stephen, *Buddhism Without Beliefs: A Contemporary Guide to Awakening*, Riverhead Books, New York, 1998.

Govinda, Lama Anagarika Brahmacari, *Foundations of Tibetan Mysticism*, Wheel/Weiser, York Beach, ME, 1969.

Suzuki, Shunryu, *Zen Mind, Beginner's Mind: Informal Talks on Zen Meditation and Practice*, Weatherhill Publishing, New York, 1998.

Thurman, Robert A. F., *Essential Tibetan Buddhism*, Castle Books, New York, 1997.

The Tibetan Book of the Dead, W. Y. Evans-Wentz (translator), Oxford University Press, 1974.

Christianity

St. Augustine of Hippo, *Confessions*, edited by John E. Rotelle, R. S. Pine-Coffin (translator), Penguin Classics, New York, 1972.

The Cloud of Unknowing: The Classic of Medieval Mysticism, (foreword by Evelyn Underhill), Kessinger Publishing, Whitefish, MT, 1998.

Douglas-Klotz, Neil, and Matthew Fox, *Prayers of the Cosmos: Meditations on the Aramaic Words of Jesus*, HarperCollins, New York, 1990.

Hildegard of Bingen's Book of Divine Works, Saint Hildegard, Bear & Co., Santa Fe, NM, 1987.

The Holy Bible, Containing the Old and New Testaments, Authorized (King James Version,) Gideons International, Nashville, TN, 1971.

Keating, Thomas, *Open Mind, Open Heart: The Contemplative Dimension of the Gospel*, Continuum Press, New York, 2004.

Kierkegaard, Soren, *Purity of Heart*, Harper & Row, New York, 1956.

Klein, Jean, *The Ease of Being*, Acorn Press, Durham, NC, 1986.

Brother Lawrence, *The Practice of the Presence of God*, Hendrickson Publications, Peabody, MA, 2004.

Lewis, C. S., *Surprised by Joy*, Harcourt Brace, New York, 1995.

Meister Eckhart: A Modern Translation, Raymond Bernard Blakney (translator), Harper & Brothers, New York, 1976.

Merton, Thomas, *Contemplative Prayer*, Doubleday, New York, 1991.

_____. *No Man is an Island*, Harvest Books, New York, 2002.

_____. *The Seven Storey Mountain*, Harcourt Trade Publications, New York, 1999.

Pagels, Elaine, *The Desert Fathers*, Vintage Books, New York, 1979.

Philokalia: The Complete Text: Compiled by St. Nikodimos of the Holy Mountain and St. Markarios of Corinth, Vol. 1, G. E. H. Palmer, Philip Sherrard and Kallistos Ware (translators), Faber and Faber, London, 1985.

Ravindra, Ravi, *The Yoga of the Christ: In the Gospel According to St. John*, Element Books, Shaftesbury, UK 1990.

Underhill, Evelyn, *Mysticism: A Study in the Nature and Development of Man's Spiritual Consciousness*, Dover Publications, New York, 2002

The Way of a Pilgrim and The Pilgrim Continues His Way, translated by R. M. French, HarperCollins, San Francisco, 1991.

Weil, Simone, *Waiting for God*, Perennial Classics, New York, 2001.

Egypt of the Pharaohs

Gnosis and Hermeticism from Antiquity to Modern Times, edited by Roelof van den Broek and Wouter Hanegraaff, State University of New York Press, 1997.

The Hermetica: The Lost Wisdom of the Pharaohs, translated by Timothy Freke and Peter Gandy, Jeremy P. Tarcher/Putnam, New York, 1999.

The Kybalion Hermetic Philosophy, by Three Initiates, Yoga Publication Society, Chicago, 1976.

Schwaller de Lubicz, Isha, *The Opening of the Way: A Practical Guide to the Wisdom of Ancient Egypt*, Inner Traditions International, Rochester, VT, 1981.

Schwaller de Lubicz, R. A., *The Temple in Man: The Secrets of Ancient Egypt*, Autumn Press, Brookline MA, 1977

Hinduism

The Bhagavad-Gita: The Song of God, translation and commentaries by Swami Prabhavananda and Christopher Isherwood, Signet Classics, New York, 2002.

The Book of Secrets: The Science of Meditation: A Contemporary Approach to 112 Meditations Described in the Vigyan Bhairav Tantra, edited by Osho and Ma Shivam Suvarna, St. Martin's Press, New York, 1998.

Danielou, Alain, *The Myths & Gods of India*, Inner Traditions International, Rochester, VT, 1991.

The Gospel of Sri Ramakrishna, Swami Nikhilananda (translator), Ramakrishna-Vivekananda Center of New York, 1985.

How to Know God: The Yoga Aphorisms of Patanjali, translation and commentaries by Swami Prabhavananda and Christopher Isherwood, Vedanta Press, Hollywood, CA, 1996.

Iyengar, B. K. S., *Light on the Yoga Sutras of Patanjali*, Thorsons Publishers, New York, 2003.

Klein, Jean, *The Ease of Being*, Acorn Press, Durham, NC, 1984.

Prem, Sri Krishna, *The Yoga of the Bhagavad Gita*, Element Books, London, 1993.

_____. *The Yoga of the Kathopanishad*, J. M. Watkins, London, 1955.

Maharshi, Ramana, *Ramana, Shankara and the Forty Verses: The Essential Teachings of Advaita*, edited by Alan Jacobs, Duncan Baird Publishers, London, 2002.

Reymond, Lizelle with Sri Anirvan, *To Live Within, A Woman's Spiritual Pilgrimage in a Himalayan Hermitage*, Rudra, Portland, OR, 1995.

Shankara's Crest Jewel of Discrimination: Timeless Teachings on Nonduality, Swami Prabhavananda and Christopher Isherwood (translators), Vedanta Press, Hollywood, CA, 1947.

Upanishads: The Ten Principal Upanishads, translated by Shree Purohit Swami and William Butler Yeats, Faber and Faber, London, 1975.

Swami Vivekananda, *Raja Yoga or Conquering the Internal Nature*, Laurier Press, Ontario, Canada, 2004.

Islam

Farid ud-Din Attar, *The Conference of the Birds*, Dick Davis and Afkham Darbandi (translators), Penguin Classics, New York, 1984.

Corbin, Henry, *Alone with the Alone: Creative Imagination in the Sufism of Ibn 'Arabi*, R. Manheim (translator), Princeton University Press, NJ, 1998.

_____. *Avicenna and the Visionary Recital*, (Mythos: the Princeton/Bollingen Series in World Mythology, Volume LXVI), Princeton University Press, NJ, 1990.

Ernst, Carl W., *The Shambhala Guide to Sufism*, Shambhala Publications, Boston, 1997.

The Koran, J. M. Rodwell and Alan Jones (translators), Tuttle Publishing, Boston, 2003.

Jalal al-Din Rumi, *The Masnavi*, Book One, Jawid Mojaddedi (translator), Oxford University Press, 2004.

_____. *The Essential Rumi*, Coleman Barks (translator), with John Moyne, A. J. Arberry and Reynold Nicholson, Castle Books, Edison, NJ, 1997.

Judaism

Besserman, Perle, *Teachings of the Jewish Mystics*, Shambhala Publications, Boston, 1998.

Buber, Martin, *I and Thou*, Ronald Gregor Smith (translator), Continuum International Publishing Group, London, 1984.

_____. *The Way of Man*, Citadel Press/Kensington, New York, 1995.

Hoffman, Edward (editor,) *Opening the Inner Gates*, Shambhala Publications, Boston, 1995.

Kaplan, Aryeh, *Meditation and Kabbalah*, Weiser, New York, 1982.

Maimonides, Moses, *The Guide for the Perplexed*, Barnes & Noble Books, New York, 2004.

Scholem, Gershom, *Kabbalah*, Dorset Press, New York, 1987.

_____. *Major Trends in Jewish Mysticism*, Schocken Books, New York, 1995. Steinsaltz, Adin, *The Essential Talmud*, Basic Books, New York, 1984.

_____. *The Thirteen Petalled Rose: A Discourse on the Essence of Jewish Existence and Belief*, Basic Books, New York, 1985.

Other

LeShan, Lawrence, *How to Meditate: A Guide to Self-Discovery*, HarperCollins, New York, 1995.

Rilke, Rainer Maria, *Letters to a Young Poet*, W. W. Norton, New York, 1993.

Viney, Michael, *Ireland*, Smithsonian Books, Washington, D.C., 2003.

Chapter Six: Finding Your Own Unique Path

Bender, Sue, *Plain and Simple*, HarperCollins, New York, 1991.

Borysenko, Joan, *Inner Peace for Busy People: 52 Simple Strategies for Transforming Your Life*, Hay House, Carlsbad, CA, 2001.

_____. *Minding the Body, Mending the Mind*, Bantam Books, New York, 1993.

Buber, Martin, *I and Thou*, Ronald Gregor Smith (translator), Continuum International Publishing Group, London, 1984.

_____. *The Way of Man*, Citadel Press/Kensington, New York, 1995.

Cameron, Julia, *The Artist's Way*, Jeremy P. Tarcher, New York, 2002.

Cappachione, Lucia, *Creative Journal: The Art of Finding Yourself*, Career Press, Franklin Lakes, NJ, 2001.

Carrington, Walter, *Thinking Aloud: Talks on Teaching the Alexander Technique*, Mornum Time Press, Berkeley, CA, 1994.

The Cloud of Unknowing: The Classic of Medieval Mysticism, edited by Evelyn Underhill, Kessinger Publishing, Whitefish, MT, 1998.

Daumal, René, *Mount Analogue: A Novel of Symbolically Authentic Non-Euclidean Adventures in Mountain Climbing*, Penguin Books, New York, 2004.

Von Durckheim, Karlfried, *Hara: The Vital Centre of Man, Inner Traditions*, Rochester, VT, 2004.

_____. *The Way of Transformation: Daily Life as Spiritual Exercise*, Allen & Unwin, London, 1971.

Epstein, Mark, *Thoughts without a Thinker: Psychotherapy from a Buddhist Perspective*, Basic Books, New York, 1995.

Feldenkrais, Moishe, *The Potent Self: A Guide to Spontaneity*, Harper & Row, New York, 1985.

Frankl, Viktor, *Man's Search for Meaning: An Introduction to Logotherapy*, Washington Square, New York, 1985.

Gibran, Khalil, *The Prophet*, Random House, New York, 1997.

Hillman, James, *The Force of Character: and the Lasting Life*, Random House, New York, 1999.

_____. *Insearch: Psychology & Religion*, Spring Publications, Woodstock, CT, 1994.

Kabat-Zinn, Jon, *Wherever You Go, There You Are*, Hyperion, New York, 1994.

Klein, Jean, *The Ease of Being*, Acorn Press, Durham, NC, 1984.

Krishnamurti, *Beyond Violence*, Gollancz, London, 1973.

_____. *The Flame of Attention*, Harper & Row, New York, 1984.

Lusseyran, Jacques, *And There Was Light: Autobiography of a Blind Hero of the French Resistance*, Elizabeth R. Cameron (translator), Morning Light Press, Sandpoint, ID, 2005.

Moore, Thomas, *The Soul's Religion: Cultivating a Profoundly Spiritual Way of Life*, Perennial Classics, New York, 2003.

Needleman, Jacob, *Time and the Soul*, Berrett-Koehler Publishers, San Francisco, 2003.

Pinkola-Estes, Clarissa, *Women Who Run with the Wolves: Myths and Stories of the Wild Woman Archetype*, Ballantine Books, New York, 1997.

Ralston, Aron, *Between a Rock and a Hard Place*, Atria Books, New York, 2005.

Ravindra, Ravi, *Pilgrim Without Boundaries*, Morning Light Press, Sandpoint, ID, 2003.

Rechtschaffen, Stephan, *Timeshifting: Creating More Time to Enjoy Your Life*, Doubleday, New York, 1996.

Reymond, Lizelle, with Sri Anirvan: *To Live Within: A Woman's Spiritual Pilgrimage in a Himalayan Hermitage*, Rudra, Portland, OR, 1995.

Richards, Mary Caroline, *Centering in Pottery, Poetry, and the Person*, University Press of New England, Lebanon, NH, 1989.

Rumi, *The Essential Rumi*, Coleman Barks (translator), with John Moyne, A. J. Arberry and Reynold Nicholson, Castle Books, Edison, NJ, 1997.

Scott-Maxwell, Florida, *The Measure of My Days: One Woman's Vivid, Enduring Celebration of Life and Aging*, Penguin, New York, 1979.

Singer, Daniel, with Marcella Weiner, *The Sacred Portable Now: The Transforming Gift of Living in the Moment*, Prima Publishing, Rocklin, CA, 1996.

Steinsaltz, Adin, *The Thirteen Petalled Rose: A Discourse on the Essence of Jewish Existence and Belief*, Basic Books, New York, 1985.

Suzuki, Shunryu, *Zen Mind, Beginner's Mind: Informal Talks on Zen Meditation and Practice*, Weatherhill Publishing, New York, 1998.

Tolle, Eckhart, *The Power of Now*, New World Library, Novato, CA, 1999.

Wagoner, David, *Traveling Light*, University of Illinois Press, Urbana, 1999.

Weil, Simone, *Waiting for God*, Perennial Classics, New York, 2001.

Whispers from the Other Shore: A Spiritual Search – East and West, Theosophical Publishing, Wheaton, IL, 1984.

Woodman, Marion, *Bone: Dying into Life*, Penguin, New York, 2000.

ABOUT THE AUTHOR

✦❀✦

Patty de Llosa has led group classes, daylong workshops and week-long intensives in the Gurdjieff work, T'ai Chi and Taoist meditation and teaches the Alexander Technique both privately and in group classes. Among recent public venues are Northern Pines Health Resort, the Peruvian Association of Aikido, the Lake Conference Center, Columbia University Graduate Theater Program and the Society for Experimental Studies, Toronto.

After graduating from Swarthmore College (BA) and the Sorbonne (MA), Ms. de Llosa worked as a reporter for *Time* magazine for six years. She married a Peruvian and raised three children in Lima. When her husband became governor of Loreto province, she served as president of The Green Cross, bringing treatment and medicines to the needy in the Amazon jungle, and coordinating with the Peace Corps a summer visit of American doctors and young people to help build roads and schools there. Returning to, Lima she founded and ran a school for eight years—the first foreign chapter of the United Nations' preschool, International Playgroup.

De Llosa returned to New York in 1979, where she worked for six years as managing editor of *American Fabrics & Fashions*, then as associate editor of *Leisure Magazine*, a Time Inc. startup, moving on to *Fortune* magazine for thirteen years, where she became deputy chief of reporters. She retired in 1999 to take the full-time three year teacher-training program at the American Center for the Alexander Technique, while working half-time as communications director of Internet startup *e-academy, inc.* and writing this book.

Recently published articles appear in the winter 2004 issues of the *Taijiquan Journal* ("Are You a Leader or a Follower?") and *Parabola: the Magazine of Myth and Meaning* (a book review of T'ai Chi as a Path of Wisdom), and in the *Fall 2004 Parabola* ("Befriending the Body").